To Jane

with all good
& thank you for all
your friendship

best wishes

Dough.

Holding bankers to account

MANCHESTER
1824

Manchester University Press

Holding bankers to account

A decade of market manipulation,
regulatory failures and regulatory reforms

Oonagh McDonald

Manchester University Press

The right of Oonagh McDonald to be identified as the author of this work has been asserted by her in accordance with the Copyright, Designs and Patents Act 1988.

Published by Manchester University Press
Altrincham Street, Manchester M1 7JA

www.manchesteruniversitypress.co.uk

British Library Cataloguing-in-Publication Data
A catalogue record for this book is available from the British Library

ISBN 978 1 5261 1943 8   hardback

First published 2019

The publisher has no responsibility for the persistence or accuracy of URLs for any external or third-party internet websites referred to in this book, and does not guarantee that any content on such websites is, or will remain, accurate or appropriate.

Typeset in Sabon by R. J. Footring Ltd, Derby, UK
Printed in Great Britain
by CPI Group (UK) Ltd, Croydon, CR0 4YY

Contents

Preface

The purpose of this book is first of all to provide a clear and documented account of the manipulation of LIBOR (the London Interbank Offered Rate), the foreign exchange (FX) market and the London Gold and Silver Fixes. Existing books and articles too often focus on the role of traders, especially Tom Hayes and his associates, which is understandable given his colourful role as 'ringmaster' in a network of brokers and traders conspiring to rig LIBOR. My aim is to show that it was possible for such price fixing to take place over so many years only because the major banks operating in the UK, the USA, Germany, Japan and Switzerland had such weak systems and controls or, worse, no systems and controls at all. Potential conflicts of interest went unrecognised for years. Compliance officers were at best ineffective and at worst collusive.

In the first chapter, I trace the history of financial regulation in the UK. That has too often been dismissed as a period of deregulation, beginning in the 1980s. In fact, from the 1970s onwards, there was increasing regulation up until the mid-2000s, when the government began to espouse a 'light touch' approach. A combination of factors meant that banks were ill-prepared to meet the financial crisis. In its aftermath, as the banks embarked on the slow path to recovery, making profits was essential. The traders seized that opportunity, and it may well be the case that banks were simply relieved that some areas of their business were profitable.

In Parts I, II and III of the book, I describe in detail what actually happened. The excerpts from traders' emails and internet chatrooms show the ways in which traders from the leading banks colluded to fix the benchmarks so that they could make money out of derivatives contracts. I describe the methods used and the context in which such manipulation occurred. Once discovered, the banks faced huge fines from the regulators – the costs to the banks are listed in full in the appendix.

In Part IV, I set out the reforms which have taken place to ensure that the benchmarks are reliable indicators for the vast array of contracts which are based on them. The nature and scope of the reforms are not yet widely appreciated and their implications not yet fully understood. The argument of the book is that the final steps must now be taken. The banks must also reform themselves. These steps must include mandatory changes both in corporate governance and in the structure of systems and controls as set out in the UK's Senior Managers Regime. These should be applied to all major global banks. It is only when senior managers are individually responsible that the reforms outlined here will take full effect. The banks themselves should not regard these reforms as external impositions but internalise them, thus becoming well managed banks capable of restoring public trust.

A note on sources

The majority of sources cited are publicly available documents, some of which have been recently released into the National Archives under the 30-year rule. These documents include internal memos and notes referring to the Financial Services Act 1986 from the Department of Trade and Industry and the Treasury, speeches by government ministers (including the Prime Minister of the day), evidence submitted by the Bank of England to the Committee to Review the Functioning of Financial Institutions (the Wilson committee) and the Gower report. All other documents, including final notices, orders, dockets, enforcement notices, consultations, responses to consultations, rules, regulations and guidance are available on the websites of the Financial Conduct Authority, the Prudential Regulatory Authority, the US Commodity Futures Trading Commission, the New York Department of Financial Services, the US Department of Justice, the European Commission, the Bank of England (including its archives), the UK Parliament for the House of Commons Treasury Select Committee, the board of governors of the US Federal Reserve, IBA Benchmark, the Financial Stability Board, the London Bullion Market Association and others. These are detailed in the notes to each chapter. Unfortunately, all the documents produced by the British Bankers' Association (BBA) covering the period from 1987 onwards are also covered by the 30-year rule, which the BBA had imposed and, as it was a private organisation (which was merged into UK Finance in 2017), these are not available under the Freedom of Information Act. I did request access to documents from 1986, but these had been placed in a 1987 folder by the London Metropolitan Library, which holds the BBA papers, and I was thus denied access both by the Library and by the then chief executive of the BBA.

All that remains is for me to thank those who gave freely of their time for the background and private information they provided. They wish to remain anonymous.

Glossary of abbreviations and financial terms

Algorithm　An algorithm is a set of rules or procedures to be followed by a computer. Algorithmic trading involves the construction of a model to initiate a trade based on certain key inputs, such as momentum, correlations within or across markets and systemic responses to key economic data or news. Once a trade decision has been made, the algorithm carries out the trade.

BBA　British Bankers' Association.

BIS　Bank for International Settlements.

Brady bonds　So-called after US Treasury Secretary Nicholas Brady, who helped international monetary organisations institute a programme of debt reduction by converting defaulting loans into US bonds with zero-coupon Treasury bonds as collateral.

CDS　Credit default swap.

CEA　Commodities and Exchange Act (US).

Certificate of deposit　A certificate issued by a bank to an individual depositing money for a specific length of time at a specific rate of interest.

CFTC　Commodity Futures Trading Commission. An independent agency of the US government which regulates the futures and options markets.

Commercial paper　An unsecured form of promissory note which pays a fixed rate of interest.

EBF　European Banking Federation.

EBS　Electronic Broking Services.

ECB   European Central Bank.

Eurobond   An international bond that is denominated in a currency other than that of the country or market in which it is issued.

Eurodollar   A US dollar deposit, typically a 30–90-day or 180-day deposit, which is placed with a bank outside the United States. Neither the nationality of the bank nor the location of the supplier of funds is relevant, only the location of the bank accepting deposits.

FCA   Financial Conduct Authority.

Floating-rate note   A debt instrument with a variable rate of interest, which may be tied to a benchmark such as LIBOR, the prime rate or a US Treasury bill rate.

FRA   Forward rate agreement.

FRN   Floating-rate note (q.v.).

FSA   Financial Services Authority, which became the Financial Conduct Authority (FCA) in 2013, having succeeded the Securities Investments Board in 2001.

FSB   Financial Stability Board.

FX   Foreign exchange.

HFT   High-frequency trading (q.v.).

High-frequency trading   A subset of automated trading used by large investment banks, hedge funds and institutional investors to transact large numbers of orders at extremely high speeds.

IBA   Ice Benchmark Administration.

IBOR   Interbank offered rate.

ICMA   International Capital Market Association.

IMM dates   International money market quarterly settlement dates.

Interest rate swap   An agreement between two counterparties in which one stream of future interest rate payments is exchanged for another based on a specified principal amount. It usually involves the exchange of a fixed interest rate for a floating interest rate.

IOSCO   International Organization of Securities Commissions.

ISRO   International Securities Regulatory Organisation.

Last look   This originated in the early years of electronic trading in the foreign exchange market, where it was intended to ensure the market maker's price was not based on stale market data for the purposes of price information and that they had credit available to trade with the client. Some argue that it is not a risk management tool but is used to generate profits. Buy-side customers may be uncertain as to why they are receiving rejection rates on their foreign currency trades.

Latency   Any delay or lapse of time between a request and a response, or the delay between the transmission of information from one source and its receipt by another.

LBMA   London Bullion Markets Association.

LIBOR   London Interbank Offered Rate.

Lowballing   An offer that is significantly below the fair value of an asset or group of assets; in the context of LIBOR, it is a deliberately low estimate of the cost of borrowing.

Mark-to-market   Valuing assets by the most recent market price.

Momentum trading   Trading with regard to the overall rate of change in the price of an asset. If prices are changing rapidly in a market (the momentum is high), then a large number of traders are buying or selling to push the price change in a direction which suits them so that they can make a profit.

Netting off   A trader can offset a position on one security or currency either in the same security or in another. Similarly, an amount owed to another trader can be offset against any debt the second trader owes the first.

Off-balance-sheet   Trades, assets or financing activities that are not shown on a bank's balance sheet.

OFT   Office of Fair Trading (non-ministerial government department, 1973–2014).

OIS   Overnight index swap.

OTC   Over the counter (q.v.).

Over the counter   Off-exchange trading, conducted directly between two parties without the supervision of an exchange.

Pips   Measures the amount of change in the exchange rate for a currency pair. It is calculated by using the last decimal point. Currency pairs are usually given to four decimal places. One pip=0.0001.

PRA   Prudential Regulation Authority.

RBS   Royal Bank of Scotland.

SIB   Securities and Investments Board. Regulatory body established 1985 and which became the FSA (Financial Services Authority) in 1997.

SMR   Senior Managers Regime.

Spot exchange rate   The price for exchanging one currency for another for immediate delivery. It represents the price buyers pay in one currency to purchase a second currency. Although the spot exchange rate is for delivery on the earliest value date, the standard settlement date for most transactions is two business days after the transaction date. Usually, spot transactions in the interbank market involve large transactions which take place two days later.

SRO   Self-regulating organisation.

Stop loss order   A contingent order that triggers a buy or sell order for a specific notional amount when the reference price is reached or passes a pre-defined trigger level. There are a number of variants on a stop loss order, so it is important to provide the client with a clear definition, including the reference price, order amount, time period and trigger.

Swaption   The option to enter into an interest rate swap or another type of swap. The buyer pays a premium to gain the right but not the obligation to enter into a specified swap agreement with the issuer on a specified future date.

TIBOR   Tokyo Interbank Offered Rate.

Troy ounces   A system of measurement used for precious metals and gem stones, originally used in Troyes in France in the Middle Ages. One troy ounce is equivalent to 31.1 grams.

Walrasian market   A market in which orders are collected in batches of buys and sells and then analysed to determine a clearing price that will decide the market price.

Wash trade   A trade where the trader buys and sells the same securities simultaneously. These trades benefit brokers, who earn commission from the trades, and can be used to create a false impression that there is investor interest in the security.

Chapter 1

A decade of deregulation?

Much has been written about the rigging of LIBOR (the London Interbank Offered Rate), the foreign exchange markets and the gold and silver price fixes. However, it is widely assumed that these scandals began with the British government's orgy of deregulation in the 1980s. In this chapter, I shall argue that this was not in fact the case, but rather that these changes in regulation were the first steps in the development of a regulatory system which could have been more effective in preventing the misuse of such benchmarks. To see why, it is important to set out the way in which the banking system and its regulation developed in the UK and then to see what lay behind the 'Big Bang', although that was a separate development concerning the stock market.

The Banking Act 1979

Curiously, given a long-established and stable banking system, overseen by the Bank of England, the Banking Act 1979 was the first attempt to provide a legal framework for the regulation and supervision of banking. This was perhaps because the Bank of England and the government only slowly recognised that changes in the UK banking system meant that it would require more extensive regulation. At the end of the 1950s about 100 banks gave information to the Radcliffe committee, which was established to review the workings of the UK monetary system. Of these, the 16 London and Scottish clearing banks held £8.3 billion in assets, amounting to 85% of total UK banking assets. The banks were narrowly focused on customer deposits. The building societies (mortgage lenders) held a further £2.6 billion of mainly mortgage assets (about one-third of the value of clearing bank assets) in 1960.[1]

It is not quite correct to say that there was no banking supervision before the 1979 Act, but during the 1950s and 1960s the banking sector was relatively small and had a very limited range of activities – lending and deposit-taking – and little competition. It was possible for the Governor of the Bank of England to know the senior staff very well, in an environment in which staff stayed with the same bank and worked their way up to senior positions. The Bank did exercise a very wide authority. It depended on an analysis of a bank's accounts and discussions with senior management about the nature and the quality of the business. Bank of England staff would continue to inform themselves about the reputation and the quality of the management, and could intervene when dissatisfied: hence the importance of the 'Governor's eyebrow'.[2] Informal monitoring of the banks was conducted by the Discount Office, the key element of which was the interview, a type of regulation which the Bank regarded as 'non-statutory' rather than self-regulation.[3] It was all part of a tradition in which the Bank's role was to secure orderly markets and prudent banking.

Prior to the 1970s, 'a static market for credit dominated by a handful of major banks' meant that there was little need for a developed system of external supervisory regulation. 'Self-regulation by the banks, supported by the customary authority of the Bank of England, was enough to maintain adequate standards of liquidity and capital adequacy and to preserve the quality of banking business.'[4] By 1969, mergers and acquisitions meant that the 16 major retail banks had become just six. Of the 16 clearing banks in existence in 1960, 15 were owned by the four large banking groups by 2018: RBS, Barclays, HSBC and Lloyds Banking Group. Thus these four now account for the lion's share of the stock of UK customer lending and deposits. Meanwhile, what happened without comment, seven American banks had already located in London, including the First National Bank of Chicago (1959), Chemical Bank (1960) and Continental Illinois (1962), and between 1968 and 1970 another six large US banks followed. They did not use the Bank of England's discount window, designed to provide banks with short-term liquidity. They did not need the discount window at that time. Since London was the largest depository of US dollars outside the USA, banks in London recycled dollars back into the interbank market. Interbank lending was very significant until the late 1990s, a time which saw the introduction of the euro and the emergence of a trend towards lending to non-bank borrowers in the USA.

Banks grew steadily during the 1970s in terms of sterling assets but especially in terms of foreign assets, some £172 billion, mainly Eurodollars. Between 1962 and 1979, foreign-owned banks began to increase their presence in London, and were primarily engaged in wholesale activity, in part due to the rise of the Eurocurrency market. But they had an impact on the operations of UK monetary and financial institutions, which held over half of their total assets in foreign currencies. By 1980, the share of deposits held by foreign-owned banks rose to 70%, while their holdings of sterling deposits rose to 25%. British banks, on the other hand, held only 30% of total deposits. Japanese banks had begun to make their appearance as well, holding 16% of total deposits and 23% of non-sterling deposits. By 1990, foreign-owned banks had been in the majority in the UK for over two decades. For the US banks, servicing their corporate customers in the UK, together with the Voluntary Foreign Credit Restraint Program (1951), encouraged them to raise dollar loans abroad. For other foreign-owned banks, such as Moscow Narodny Bank (but also non-Russian banks), fears that dollars held in banks in the USA might be expropriated or frozen meant that they chose to keep their dollars in bank branches in London.

Another important factor in bringing about significant changes in the banking industry was the publication of the Bank of England's 'consultative document' *Competition and Credit Control*, on 14 May 1971, with aim of opening up competition between the clearing banks and the non-bank financial sector. The Bank sought to create a system whereby 'the allocation of credit is primarily determined by its cost'. The Governor of the Bank of England in a speech on 28 May 1971 made it clear that the aim was to end the long-standing cartel between clearing banks and the Scottish banks (all major deposit-taking banks) whereby they agreed between themselves what the deposit rate, linked to the Bank rate, should be, and also what their lending rates to the Bank should be. The Bank would seek to influence the general structure of interest rates through its control of the liquidity of the whole banking system. This would consist of a minimum reserve assets ratio, a fixed percentage of sterling deposit liabilities, applying uniformly to all banks. These would be held in certain specified reserve accounts. At the same time, the Bank's right to call for special reserve deposits to be held at the Bank of England would apply in the same way to all banks. However, the Bank of England realised that other financial institutions had sprung up outside the banking sector owing to the tight restrictions on the amount that banks could lend to individual private sector borrowers, but the Bank did not bring them into the banking sector and hence under its supervision. These were the so-called 'fringe' banks, comprising the 'secondary' banking sector.

Economic expansion and relaxation of controls on property development helped to fuel the rapid pace of lending, until the oil crisis of 1973. The associated contraction in liquidity stopped the property boom in its tracks in the autumn of 1973. London money market rates (interest rates) soared in February 1974, from less than 0.5% to almost 2.5% and then to 6% in the following June. The fringe banks had invested in property development using short-term money market funds, whereas major banks had been reluctant to lend to property developers owing to the length of time such projects require. The fringe banks found it easy to obtain wholesale deposits, usually from the money markets, which then included industrial and commercial companies and major institutional investors. The oil crisis led to sharp increases in the minimum lending rate, which had risen to 11.5% by July 1974. One fringe bank, London and County Securities, found itself in liquidity difficulties because it was unable to renew or extend the time frame of the deposit, taken through the money markets. Fringe banks could attract wholesale deposits, enabling them to lend for property development or mortgages, but when the renewal of deposits became difficult as economic conditions deteriorated, liquidity problems quickly arose for them. The Bank of England was faced with the collapse of several such deposit-taking institutions – the so-called 'secondary banking crisis', which threatened the banking system as a whole. The 'lifeboat' operation was established to rescue these failing banks, with senior representatives of the English and Scottish clearing banks and the Deputy Governor of the Bank of England as chairman. The 'lifeboat' consisted of recycling deposits, followed by a commitment of some £1,200 million on the part of the large commercial banks (about 40% of their estimated aggregate total capital reserves), but they would not continue with their joint lifeboat operation beyond that. The lifeboat was established to provide liquidity for the failing banks and to restore confidence in the banking system, and in that it succeeded. The lessons learnt were part of the reason for the 1979 Banking Act.

Under the Act, supervision of banks and other deposit-taking institutions was still carried out on a non-statutory basis, although, as we have seen, the Bank of England did exercise its wide powers, as a matter of custom and practice. Its powers were used in a somewhat haphazard way, such that some institutions were not really supervised at all. The Act continued the distinction between recognised banks and licensed deposit-takers, with the former being subject to the same kind of supervision as before. It became a criminal offence to accept deposits unless the deposit-taker was either a recognised bank or licensed to accept deposits. Both had to meet the criteria set out in the Act for their legal form, prudence and management. The Bank of England had the power to revoke licences. It could also require a recognised bank or a licensed deposit-taker (in fact, the directors or managers of the institution) to provide information to the Bank about the nature and conduct of its business and its plans for future development, or an independent report by an accountant on the bank's affairs, as well as any other 'books and papers' required by the Bank for supervisory purposes. The Act also set up (for the first time) a Deposit Protection Scheme to be funded by the banks and deposit-takers.

Quite apart from the secondary banking crisis of 1973/4, the European Economic Community's First Banking Directive anyway required the UK to pass legislation like the Banking Act 1979 because Article 3 (1) required member states to ensure that 'credit institutions subject to the Directive' obtained 'authorization before commencing their activities'. The Act therefore extended the requirement for authorisation beyond credit institutions (i.e. institutions that both take deposits and make loans) to cover all deposit-taking institutions (i.e. to include those that to any meaningful extent finance their business by taking loans). The Directive in Articles 3(2) and (4) set out the minimum conditions for authorisation, but the ones contained in the Act were more stringent.

In the background, the governors of the central banks of the Group of Ten countries set up the Committee on Banking Regulations and Supervisory Practices (later called the Basel Committee). This was established in 1974 in the aftermath of serious fluctuations in the international currency and banking markets (including the significant failure of a small bank, Bankhaus Herstatt, in West Germany).[5] One of its important aims was to close gaps in international supervisory coverage so that: (1) no banking establishment would escape supervision; and (2) supervision would be adequate and consistent across member jurisdictions. That meant that the days of the informal approach to supervision on the part of the Bank of England were numbered, although vestiges were to remain in the years to come, as the subsequent chapters will demonstrate. Change was inevitable, though, as London became an international banking centre with a far larger number of banks and the nature of banking business changed radically.

The Big Bang

The Conservative government in the UK deregulated the City of London in 1986 in a series of measures dubbed 'Big Bang'.[6]

The UK Banking industry ... was transformed by Prime Minister Thatcher's 'Big Bang' financial deregulation program of 1986.[7]

It is often assumed that the failures associated with LIBOR and the foreign exchange markets were all due to the decision to 'deregulate' financial institutions during the 1980s, and in particular the 'Big Bang' of 1986. This, though, is a complete misrepresentation of the Big Bang: rather than deregulation, it is better understood as a replacement of one form of regulation by another, applying solely to the London Stock Exchange. The story is a little convoluted but it is worth setting out in some detail so that the reasons for the changes become clear.

The Restrictive Trade Practices Act 1976 extended the 1968 Act of the same name to cover both goods and services, including stock broking. The 1976 Act required all restrictive trading agreements to be registered with the Office of Fair Trading (OFT). The Director General of the OFT, then Sir Gordon Borrie, was required to produce a report on the Stock Exchange's rule book prior to a referral to the Restrictive Practices Court.[8] The book included rules governing fixed commissions and the 'single capacity' system, under which 'brokers' acted as investors' agents and 'jobbers' were the market makers, and neither could encroach on the other's territory. In 1979, the Director General referred the Stock Exchange to the Court. After the failure of an appeal to the Secretary of State for Prices and Consumer Protection (Roy Hattersley, now Lord Hattersley), the challenge was allowed to proceed, with the OFT as plaintiff and the Stock Exchange as defendant.[9] Preparations for the court case, which cost millions of pounds, drifted on for five years, with the Stock Exchange's argument being that ending fixed commissions would result in the ending of the single-capacity market, since brokers' margins would be squeezed and, in order to maintain profits, brokers would become dealers, especially in large block deals.[10] If the fixed commissions ended, brokers would also be able to make 'matched bargains' between buyers and sellers among their own clients, but this role of brokers as principals would mean greater risks and therefore more capital. Brokers, who all operated in the City of London as unlimited partnerships, would certainly be unable to acquire sufficient capital to manage the risks involved in acting as broker-dealers. Once jobbers began losing their profits, they would seek to trade directly with the public.[11]

However, in 1976, during the course of preparation of the Stock Exchange's case, Nicholas Goodison (later Sir Nicholas) became its new chairman. He recognised that the single-capacity structure put the Stock Exchange at a disadvantage in the face of increasing foreign competition, especially from the USA. In a much later interview, Goodison stated:

> [the] key requisite was to establish London as an international centre for equities and the Big Bang worked unquestionably. If we had not done it London would have lost ground ... we decided to go for a market-making system because it was more conducive to the old jobbing system.[12]

In fact, on the eve of Big Bang in 1986, there were only five jobbing firms left in existence.

The Restrictive Trades Practices (Stock Exchange) Bill was debated in Parliament in December 1983 and became law in March 1984. Although the Stock Exchange rule book was registered in 1977 and referred to the Restrictive Practices Court in 1979, almost five years had passed without the case being heard. It was due to be heard by Mr Justice Lincoln early in 1984, but the legislation prevented that. Its purpose was to exempt the Stock Exchange from the Restrictive Trade Practices Act.

This was not a matter of a Conservative government favouring the Stock Exchange, but an attempt to find a practical solution. The Stock Exchange Council had already recognised that the practices were restrictive, but had argued that the fixed commission was part of a whole structure that would have to be revamped if the fixed commission went. In effect, the Stock Exchange had already pleaded guilty. The problem was that the Court might well strike down individual rules, which could lead to piecemeal but unworkable reforms. The Secretary of State for Trade and Industry, Norman Tebbit, said 'There was no obligation on the court or the Office of Fair Trading to construct a new rule book to ensure the continued effective working of the stock exchange'.[13] The government undertook this action only because, on 27 July 1983, an agreement had been reached (between the Secretary of State for Trade and Industry, then Cecil Parkinson, and the chairman of the Stock Exchange, Goodison) that the Council of the Stock Exchange would abandon the minimum commission rules before the end of 1986.

In fact, the agreement went further than that. A Department of Trade and Industry internal briefing note, dated 9 July 1984, set out the full terms of that agreement:

- action to dismantle, by stages, minimum scales of stockbroking commissions, completing this by 31 December 1986;
- continuation of rules prescribing the separation of capacity of brokers and jobbers;
- permission for non-members of the Stock Exchange to become non-executive directors of corporate member firms;
- introduction of lay members to the Council of the Stock Exchange;
- establishment of a new independent membership appeals committee;
- introduction of lay members onto the disciplinary committee.

Towards the end of 1983 the Stock Exchange had already implemented the last four items and in April 1984 it abolished minimum commissions for overseas securities. It had circulated a discussion paper on a new dealing system, the abolition of commission scales and new membership rules.

The briefing note clearly set out the government's objectives in its negotiations and agreements with the Stock Exchange. It stated:

> Our main policy objectives are a securities market able to provide services to UK industry and commerce, private investors and the Government in the most efficient and cheapest way and which is internationally competitive [as the Stock Exchange was not]; and secondly an acceptable system of investor protection.

This was hardly a deregulation agenda, but rather an attempt to transform an outdated, costly and enclosed market.

The Department of Trade and Industry's briefing note added 'It is now generally recognised that dealers in securities need to be well capitalised in order to take the necessary risks in market-making' but that the Stock Exchange's rules of corporate membership had made it more difficult for jobbers and brokers to obtain the necessary capital. However, since July 1983, the briefing note stated, the Stock Exchange's approach had changed so that the plan was to introduce a new dealing system together with freely negotiated commissions. The Department agreed that the single capacity 'cannot survive the advent of negotiated commissions', so 'a different form of investor protection is needed'.

The prospect of the end of single capacity was seen as a stimulus for regroupings of firms. The Stock Exchange proposal to allow 100% outside ownership was welcomed for the additional capital it would bring to the UK securities market. The report noted that officials should make known to the Stock Exchange that 'investor protection would best be met by disclosure, including a best execution rule, the existence of an audit trail and immediate publication of the price and volume of transactions as they are carried out'. Such an approach to investor protection may seem incomplete now, but it was a move in the direction of acceptable regulation. On the issue of disclosure, the Stock Exchange was apparently somewhat hesitant, but as time went on and before the introduction of the Financial Services Bill in 1986, that issue was settled.

Discussions in the summer of 1986 between the Treasury, the Department of Trade and Industry, the Bank of England and the Stock Exchange covered a range of practical issues. They led to the introduction of dual-capacity broker-dealers, dealing directly with the public as well as making markets.

> This in turn has led to the main British participants needing massive injections of capital. Even the largest Stock Exchange firms were tiny by international standards; and the Exchange itself has needed to invest heavily in technology to underpin the new trading system.[14]

The whole long-drawn-out process was overseen by the Bank of England and also by Securities and Investments Board.

The Big Bang reforms were completed on 27 October 1986 and led, as expected, to a complete restructuring of the Stock Exchange, partly through its accession to the International Securities Regulatory Organisation (ISRO). The transformation of its membership brought in well-capitalised firms, such as British and foreign banks and securities houses, and the new UK financial conglomerates took shape. Of the outside entities with stakes in the original 200 member firms, over half were commercial or investment banks from the USA, the UK and the rest of Europe. As hoped, transaction costs fell sharply after Big Bang, especially for institutional investors, partly because of a cut in stamp duty and partly because there was a much larger number of equity market-makers (previously there had been only 13 jobbers, most of which were very small firms). Since broker-dealers were prepared to take positions in more active equities, the market was much more competitive and much more liquid than expected. However, the combination of considerably improved information on the new Stock Exchange Automated Quotation (SEAQ) system and market-makers prepared to deal in high volumes lowered both the costs and the risks for investors. What was perhaps not anticipated was the speed with which the trading floor would disappear, as traders retreated to their own dealing rooms. The jobbers (market-makers, often described in a somewhat derogatory fashion as the 'white socks brigade', in reference to their working-class origins), already much reduced in number, disappeared from the Stock Exchange once the reforms were under way.

The accession to the ISRO was partly for commercial reasons and partly to provide the 'regulatory cover' for the large number of banks and securities firms engaged in the international bond and equities markets. This arrangement meant that the Stock Exchange became the basis for a single investment exchange covering trading in gild-edged and other fixed-interest securities, domestic and foreign equities and options. The ISRO was to seek recognition under the Financial Services Act 1986 as a self-regulating organisation, the Securities Association, to fulfil all the regulatory requirements under the new system.

The Financial Services Act 1986 established an entirely new regulatory framework, with the Securities and Investments Board (SIB) as the regulatory authority with oversight of the self-regulating organisations (SROs) responsible for each sector of the financial services industry (which had to report to the SIB). This legislation was introduced by the Conservative government in response to the Gower report. In 1981 the government had asked Professor Laurence Gower to review investor protection; his report was submitted in 1984. One of the most significant scandals at the time which lay behind the Gower report was the Barlow Clowes affair. Two companies were involved: Barlow Clowes Gilt Managers, which had 7,400 clients who had invested £52 million; and Barlow Clowes International, a Gibraltar company, with 11,500 clients who had invested over £138 million. Apparently, £62 million had been lent to companies associated with Peter Clowes, one of the company's founders, including £13 million to James Ferguson Holdings, the parent company for Barlow Clowes, a further £2 million to a Geneva accountant and £1 million to a Dr Peter Naylor, another director of James Ferguson Holdings. About £40 million went missing (80% of the loans authorised by Peter Clowes). A large number of MPs, mainly Conservatives, received letters of complaint from their constituents, many of whom were retired and could ill afford to lose their savings, which they thought Barlow Clowes had invested in safe government gilt-edged securities. The government's response to these scandals was to accept many of the proposals in Gower's report in a white paper published in 1985, followed by the Financial Services Act 1986.

The Act itself was the most comprehensive overhaul of the regulation of investment business for over 40 years. One of its main provisions was that anyone conducting investment business had to be authorised.

It covered the marketing activities of life insurance companies (such as the selling of policies) and the authorisation of the managers and independent trustees of unit trusts and other collective investment schemes. It also provided an industry-wide compensation scheme and established the concept of a 'Recognised Investment Exchange', which gained that status only if it had sufficient financial resources and provided a fair and efficient market. The Council of the Stock Exchange continued to be responsible for admitting securities to listing and listing rules as well as for the rules concerning prospectuses. Other groups were excluded from the full scope of the legislation, including the Bank of England, Lloyd's of London and various official organisations. The Act came into force in 1987 and extended the scope of formal regulation into areas such as financial and commodity futures and options, and the international securities markets in London, where supervision had previously been non-statutory or remote. It consolidated legislation on insider dealing and on the offering and listing of securities, and was part of a process of updating financial regulation that had included the Banking Act 1979 and the Building Societies Act 1986.

The regulatory and rule-making powers which were previously in the hands of the Secretary of State for Trade and Industry and the powers to initiate proceedings against individuals or companies for offences under the Act were transferred to the SIB, which was not a government agency or department. The SIB had the oversight of the SROs, which were based on trade associations, but which had the power to set rules and enforce them. In other words, this was not self-regulation as that might be easily understood but 'self-regulation in a statutory framework'.[15] Although the SIB had the power to alter the rules set by the SROs, it was decided that this should be held in reserve and rule changes settled through consultation and discussions. The SIB had the power to prosecute a new criminal offence of carrying out investment business without authorisation, a process which required firms to meet a series of stringent requirements. Senior staff of investment businesses were required to be 'fit and proper', 'honest and competent'. Staff of all of the SROs and the SIB were given legal immunity from suits arising from carrying out their statutory functions, provided they acted in good faith.

After being granted 'delegated powers' in 1987, the SIB had to recognise the SROs and ensure that their rules were equivalent to its own and that they had adequate resources for monitoring and enforcement. There were five in all: the Securities Association (TSA); the Financial Intermediaries, Managers and Brokers Regulatory Association (FIMBRA);

the Investment Management Regulatory Organisation (IMRO); the Association of Futures Brokers and Dealers (AFBD), covering firms dealing and broking in futures and options; and the Life Assurance and Unit Trust Regulatory Organisation (LAUTRO), covering the agents or sales staff of life assurance companies, friendly societies and unit trusts. These had originally been trade associations and initially some tended to act as such. Most of the SROs slowly evolved into regulatory bodies. The AFBD merged with the TSA to become the Securities and Futures Association in 1990, and LAUTRO and FIMBRA merged to become the Personal Investment Authority in 1994. FIMBRA, in particular, and LAUTRO were seen to have failed as regulatory and enforcement authorities, the former being too close to its membership (consisting of independent financial advisers).

The regulatory system faced a series of failures, some of which were very costly in terms of compensation to investors by the companies involved. These included the mis-selling of personal pensions, whereby many of the 5 million personal pensions sold between 1988 and 1994 would disadvantage their purchasers. Other failures included the Maxwell pension fund scandal (discovered after his death in 1991), in which Robert Maxwell removed £350 million from Mirror Group Newspapers, and the collapse of Barings Bank in 1995 owing to the risks taken by a derivatives trader, Nick Leeson. I recall the attempts to hold the senior management of Barings to account, as I was both a board member of the SIB and a member of its enforcement committee at the time, but we lacked the powers to do so.[16] Sir Andrew Large then introduced the concept of senior management responsibility but it was insufficiently developed until recently to provide the necessary framework or supervision and enforcement.

A decade of deregulation or self-regulation?

It was not a decade of deregulation or even self-regulation in any straightforward sense. The so-called move to principles-based regulation by Sir David Walker, when he was chairman of the SIB, was designed only to provide over-arching principles, not to displace rules.[17] It was a period in which the SROs developed into regulatory authorities but with the problem that they were part of a regulatory system based on separate functions for each financial institution, a system which no longer corresponded with reality. Financial institutions, especially banks and insurance companies, provided a much wider range of financial services to their clients. The result was that, all too often, they were dealing with more than one regulator, having to meet the requirements of each. The SIB's lack of powers over the SROs made the system unworkable at times.

The Banking Act 1987

Yet another scandal in the banking sector led to the strengthening of another aspect of regulation. Johnson Matthey Bankers Ltd (JMB), a member of the London Gold Fix, was the subsidiary of a long-established company, specialising in a wide range of operations, including chemicals, emission control technologies, precious metal products and banking. In 1980, JMB had made the mistake of moving into the US jewellery trade, a new venture into unfamiliar territory, resulting in losses of over £60 million. Although JMB had benefited from the increase in bullion sales after the Soviet invasion of Afghanistan in 1980, the subsidiary was encouraged to move into high-risk lending. Its loan book grew rapidly, from £50 million at the end of 1981 to some £500 million by March 1984, its contribution to group profits going from about 25% in 1981 to over 60% in 1983. The Bank of England began to doubt the quality of some of its loans and later the practices of Arthur Young, JMB's auditors. When the full extent of the bad loans taken on by JMB became clear, the Bank of England organised a bail-out by the bank's creditors, shareholders and UK clearing banks. The Bank of England bought JMB for a token £1.

The case was much debated in Parliament, with accusations from some Labour MPs which proved to be unsubstantiated when all inquiries were completed. The investigations into allegations of fraud were 'put in perspective' by the chairman's statement, released on 11 December 1985:

> [Although] it does indeed seem that some acts of fraud may have been committed against the bank ... the losses sustained on the loan book ... are principally attributable to the very poor quality of the lending in the past.[18]

The losses amounted to £217 million, of which £152 million was borne by Johnson Matthey plc, other banks £26.65 million and the Bank of England, under indemnity as shareholder, £39.15 million.

However, as a result of the Johnson Matthey debacle, the Chancellor of the Exchequer, Nigel Lawson, set up a committee to review banking supervision under the chairmanship of the Governor of the Bank of England. On 20 June 1985, Lawson announced in the House of Commons that he agreed with the committee's findings that the Johnson Matthey debacle had exposed 'major shortcomings in the present legislative and supervisory arrangements' as set out in the Banking Act 1979.[19] That Act drew a distinction between 'licensed deposit-takers' and 'recognised banks', with most of its provisions focused on the former. It had led to a dual supervisory system: more rigorous for the former but heavily reliant on the integrity and co-operation of the management of recognised banks, of which Johnson Matthey was one. This two-tier system was abolished and the powers given to the Bank applied to all authorised institutions, with tougher criteria, including the minimum net assets required.

The committee proposed removing constraints on dialogue between the auditors and supervisors, since the former are uniquely placed to monitor a bank's control systems and assess its financial prudence. The Chancellor emphasised that it is a bank's senior directors and senior managers who are responsible and that responsibility 'cannot be shuffled off to auditors or supervisors'. Lawson pointed out that because the Johnson Matthey failure stemmed from a number of large and related exposures, the legislation would not allow an exposure to a borrower, or closely related borrowers, in excess of 25% of the lender's capital base.[20] Finally, the committee made a number of recommendations on increasing and training the supervisory staff of the Bank of England. By then, the Bank was supervising over 290 recognised banks and just over 300 licensed deposit-takers, a far cry from the 1950s and 1960s.

The Economic Secretary to the Treasury introduced the Banking Bill on 28 November 1986 and correctly argued that it contained few surprises, since it closely followed the white paper. It was the third element in the new regulatory structure, which already covered investment, securities and the building societies. The Bank of England retained supervision and regulation of the banks, but under a new Board of Banking Supervision, with a majority of outside members.[21] The two-tier system was ended. All organisations wishing to be recognised as banks had to go through the same procedures for authorisation and meet the same regulatory requirements.

One curious feature of the Bill was the change in the 'large exposure' guidelines from 10% to 25% of a bank's capital, especially in view of the fact that JMB's failure was due to the high concentration of loans to a very few connected borrowers.[22] The Bill, however, did require exposures above 10% of an institution's capital base to be reported to the supervisors *post hoc*, and supervisors had to be notified in advance of an exposure of over 25% of the capital base. The Economic Secretary added that 'Criminal sanctions will attach to any deliberate non-compliance with these provisions, in addition to the new criminal offence of knowingly or recklessly providing any information to the supervisors which is false or misleading'.[23] The provisions of the Bill did become law, but the background changed as 'Basel I' recommendations on banking regulations came into force in 1988.[24]

The single regulator: the Financial Services Authority

The system of financial regulation derived from the Financial Services Act 1986 was subject to much criticism, including from its chairman, Sir Andrew Large, whose 1993 report, *Making the Two-Tier System Work*, had stated that significant improvements to the system should be made. The Treasury Select Committee in its 1995 report concluded:

> It is clear that the current tensions within the regulatory structure – particularly the role of SIB – need to be resolved. The solution depends on the view taken as to the depth of the cause of the problems. In any event it is clear that in-fighting amongst the regulators and jostling for position in any potential new structure is not helping to enhance the regulatory system nor adding anything to the achievement of investor protection.... it will be necessary, in the context of a review of the Financial Services Act ... also to review whether there is a need to perpetuate the two 'tiers' represented by the SIB and the SROs.[25]

As Sir Andrew Large had pointed out to the Committee, 'Yes, the SROs have become stronger frontline regulators and I think we should regard that as a success'.[26]

The tensions which did exist were due primarily to the SIB's lack of powers over the SROs, powers which were requested but refused by the Secretary of State, on the grounds that they might lead to squabbling on the part of the chief executives of the SROs and the chairman of the SIB. Other serious problems concerned the confusing 'alphabet soup' of the wider range of organisations concerned with financial regulation beyond the SIB and its three SROs. For financial services companies, each category – banks, insurance and securities firms – had taken on a much wider range of activities than had traditionally been the case. So banks engaged in insurance and securities, for example. Each had to comply with the rules and supervision of at least two and perhaps all three of the SROs, where the approach might be somewhat different in each case. That was obviously time-consuming, so the possibility of a one-stop shop was appealing.

This was the approach which the new Labour administration took up on coming into office in 1997. The Chancellor of the Exchequer, Gordon Brown, announced to the Commons on 20 May 1997 the establishment of a single regulator, based on the SIB:

> It is clear that the distinctions between different types of financial institutions … are becoming increasingly blurred. Many of today's financial institutions are regulated by a plethora of different supervisors. This increases the cost and reduces the effectiveness of the supervision.[27]

Sir Andrew Large later welcomed the single regulator:

> In my experience the two-tier system was very inefficient. There was significant duplication and overlap and it was extremely hard to produce a really focussed response to some of the consumer issues of the day.

He saw the single regulator as 'the most efficient and at the same time the fairest and least complex system'.[28]

These were not the only reasons for changing the system of regulation. Another was pensions mis-selling. The option to purchase a personal pension and opt out of a defined-benefit pension company scheme had been introduced by the Conservative government in the mid-1980s to encourage greater personal provision for retirement. About 8 million personal pensions were sold between 1988 and 1995, often by sales staff on commission. It turned out that many had been sold to public sector employees (who tended to be Labour Party supporters) in good occupational schemes. The SIB not only conducted a review to determine the extent of the damage but also required insurance companies to compensate the 1.5 million people who had been mis-sold a pension, at a cost of some £4 billion for the companies concerned. This provided useful support for the claim that a system of City self-regulation had let pensioners and others down and should be replaced with a single statutory regulatory agency for securities and investments. The incoming Labour government was unfamiliar with the system of regulation and was unaware of the remit of the US Securities and Exchange Commission, which had been seen as a model.

However, even if for inadequate reasons, the single regulator, the Financial Services Authority (FSA), was established under the Financial Services and Markets Act 2000, and responsibility for banking supervision was removed from the Bank of England. This was also because the government planned to establish the Bank of England's independence in respect of monetary policy and presumably considered that if it was responsible for banking supervision as well, then too much power would be concentrated in the central bank.

The Financial Services and Markets Act 2000 set out in detail the FSA's constitution and governance, as well as its objectives, principles and functions. The FSA was given the status of a company limited by guarantee,[29] making it an independent agency (i.e. it was not a government body). The FSA was set up quickly, simply by making the SIB the core of the new authority and renaming it by special resolution, although it also absorbed at least seven other regulatory bodies as well as large numbers of staff from the Bank of England. Its staff were not civil servants, so they were not subject to their pay restraints, enabling the FSA to attract staff with experience in the financial services industry. Perhaps the most important consideration from the government's point of view was that its funding was not part of public expenditure. It was funded by fees in the form of a levy on each financial services company. The advantages for the FSA were much greater control over its own finances and not having to deal with politicians (who might demand more regulation, supervision or enforcement and then cut the budget).

The FSA was, though, accountable to government, in that the chairman and the board were appointed (or could be dismissed) by the Treasury. There were no formal criteria set out for appointment or dismissal, but the principles of public appointments did apply, including 'fit and proper' requirements, and the skills, knowledge and experience required for the role. The Chancellor, Gordon Brown, announced the appointment of Howard Davies, then Deputy Governor of the Bank of England, as the new body's first chairman. Its accountability to consumers and practitioners was met by the establishment of the Consumer Panel and the Practitioner Panel. The former arose out of my report on involving consumers in regulation, commissioned by Colette Bowe (now Dame Colette Bowe), when she was Director of Retail Regulation at the SIB. The FSA was also obliged to produce an annual report to the Treasury that set out how it had fulfilled its functions and any other matters the Treasury required. In addition, the Treasury could appoint an individual to report on the way in which the FSA was carrying out its obligations, supposedly confined to the economy, efficiency and effectiveness of its use of resources.

The legislation set four objectives for the FSA: market confidence; public awareness; the protection of consumers; and reduction of financial crime. The last was introduced because financial services regulators considered that they had insufficient powers to deal with financial crime, in particular market manipulation and insider dealing. This was partly because regulators had no powers over market abuse by those who were not 'authorised persons'. It was also because, as Sir Andrew Large frequently argued, the evidence could often be interpreted only with specialist knowledge, so that the resulting criminal cases led to few convictions. As a result, market abuse became a civil offence and a new Code of Market Conduct was introduced.

The first objective was defined as 'maintaining confidence in the financial system', which included 'fair, efficient and transparent markets' and the FSA's responsibilities in terms of the oversight of individual firms, markets and clearing and settlement. The Bank of England was responsible for the 'overall stability of the financial system as a whole', including the infrastructure, such as the payments system. This is the extent of the description of the division of responsibilities as set out in the Memorandum of Understanding between the FSA, the Bank of England and the Treasury.[30]

The FSA's responsibilities under the Act were as follows:

- the authorisation and supervision of banks, building societies, investment firms, insurance companies and brokers, credit unions and friendly societies;
- the supervision of financial markets, securities listings and clearing and settlement systems;
- regulatory policies in these areas.

The FSA's role included advising on the implications for authorised firms of developments in domestic and international markets and initiatives. The FSA's policy-making and rule-making activities were increasingly dominated by European Union Directives and regulations.

The Treasury's responsibilities were as follows:

- the overall institutional structure and the legislation which governs it, including the often long negotiations over EU Directives;
- informing and accounting to Parliament for the management of any serious problems in the financial system and any measures taken to resolve them.

Much of the rest of the 1997 memorandum is concerned with sharing information between the three bodies. This was supposed to be achieved through standing committees, and by reciprocal membership of each other's boards. The chairman of the FSA was a member of the Court of the Bank, and the Bank's Deputy Governor for Financial Stability was a member of the FSA's board. That was a requirement from the start and when I was on the board, David Clementi was also a member, by virtue of his position as Deputy Governor of the Bank of England.

Vaughan and Finch, in their book *The Fix*, imply that there was something suspicious about Paul Tucker's position on the board of the FSA, but it was merely a statutory requirement:

> It didn't help that the Bank of England's Paul Tucker was on the board of directors of the FSA, and Margaret Cole (then head of enforcement) would already have known that and presumably have anticipated any views he may have expressed.[31]

Paul Tucker became Deputy Governor of the Bank of England for Financial Stability, following the departure of Sir John Gieve in 2009, and then joined the board of the FSA.

In March 2006, the Memorandum was updated to reflect developments in financial markets and institutional roles. It set out the role of the Treasury, the FSA and the Bank of England in operational crisis management. The Treasury was to ensure that ministers were kept up to date on developments in order to allow them to make key decisions quickly; the Bank of England was to ensure the orderly functioning of the financial markets and especially adequate liquidity; and the FSA was to ensure the health of its regulated institutions. Cross-membership of the FSA makes for close understanding of each other's agenda. The chairman and the chief executive of the FSA had regular meetings with the Governor and senior Treasury officials.

Despite all the arrangements for maintaining constant communication and awareness of what the other knew or did not know at the relevant times, the system did not work in the severe international financial crisis of 2007–8. The so-called tripartite system was deemed a failure and after the financial crisis it was replaced. Communication problems were also a factor in the failure to recognise warning signs in relation to LIBOR, as we shall see later.

From the beginning, the workload of the FSA was extremely heavy, starting with the logistics of bringing so many organisations together. In 2000 it set out its goals and approach to regulation in its publication *A*

New Regulator for the New Millennium. The principles were summarised in the FSA's Memorandum for the Treasury Select Committee:[32]

> Over time we envisage moving to a regulatory regime which:
> - is built on a clear statement of the realistic aims and the limits of regulation;
> - recognises the proper responsibilities of consumers themselves and of firms' own management, and the impossibility and undesirability of removing all risk and failure from the financial system;
> - is founded on a risk-based approach to the regulation of financial businesses which integrates and simplifies the different approaches adopted by the current regulators;
> - operates a transparent new framework for identifying and addressing the most important risks facing firms, markets and consumers.

These were the key principles governing the FSA's approach to regulation. Even if they may now be considered incomplete or requiring greater emphasis on supervision, they cannot be considered a 'light touch' approach to regulation.

However, having set up a regulatory body designed to be independent of the government, as it should be, the Chancellor found it difficult to remain at a distance and commissioned a series of reviews of the FSA. The first, *Competition in UK Banking: A Report to the Chancellor of the Exchequer*, commissioned in November 1998, was conducted by Don Cruickshank. Then the Sandler report, *Medium and Long-Term Retail Savings in the UK*, was commissioned in June 2001, to identify the competitive forces driving the retail financial services industry. It was published in July 2002. It proposed a suite of simple savings products (stakeholder products), easy to understand, which would shift the focus of the FSA from the sales process to the products themselves. This, however, failed to recognise the problem that no matter how simple a financial product might be, the people who buy it may not realise that they do not actually need it.

Despite these time-consuming diversions from its main tasks, the FSA sought to carry out its proper roles as regulator. This was soon to change, as, apparently, Chancellor Gordon Brown learnt to appreciate banks. In his speech at the opening of Lehman Brothers European headquarters in April 2004, one which he must surely regret, he praised Lehman Brothers:

> always ... an innovator, financing new ideas and inventions before many others began to realise their potential ... as the world economy has

opened up, you have succeeded not by sheltering your share of a small national protected market but always by striving for a greater and greater share of the growing global market.[33]

The FSA board, in a 2011 report on the failure of the Royal Bank of Scotland, referred to a 'sustained political emphasis on the need for the FSA to be "light touch" in its approach'.[34] Indeed, according to the Treasury in 2005:

> The new model we propose is quite different. In a risk-based approach there is no inspection without justification, no form filling without justification, and no information requirements without justification. Not just a light touch but a limited touch. Instead of routine regulation attempting to cover all, we adopt a risk-based approach which targets only the necessary few.[35]

This was at the launch of the Better Regulation Action Plan in May 2005. A year later, in his Mansion House speech, the Chancellor of the Exchequer, Gordon Brown, stated:

> In 2003, just at the time of a previous Mansion House speech, the WorldCom accounting scandal broke. And I will be honest with you, many who advised me including not a few newspapers favoured a regulatory crackdown. I believe that we were right not to go down that road which in the United States led to Sarbanes-Oxley, and we were right to build upon our light touch system through the leadership of Sir Callum McCarthy [chairman of the FSA] – fair, proportionate, predictable and increasingly risk-based.[36]

The FSA's senior leaders were conscious of the need to reassure political leaders that they were not being 'heavy-handed'. So when Prime Minister Tony Blair, in a speech in 2005, expressed concerns that a heavy-handed approach by the FSA was limiting innovation, the then chairman of the FSA, Sir Callum McArthy, wrote to the Prime Minister saying that the FSA was efficient and proportionate and that, for example, only six supervisory staff were responsible for HSBC![37]

Ed Balls, when he was Economic Secretary to the Treasury, in a speech entitled 'The City as the global finance centre: risks and opportunities', 14 June 2006, referred proudly to the government's achievements:

> According to the City of London Corporation our regulatory system is ranked as the best in the world, ahead of both New York and Frankfurt. We have a single unified regulator. And it is clearly independent of day-to-day political control.... It is important that the FSA continues to deliver a light-touch and risk-based regulatory approach.

Even after Enron and WorldCom, together with the introduction of the Sarbanes-Oxley Act in the USA) Balls stated that he believed 'we are right to avoid prescriptive, heavy-handed regulation in Britain'.[38]

Gordon Brown continued to stress the importance of 'light-touch' regulation very shortly before he became Prime Minister (on 27 June 2007, when Tony Blair formally resigned), when he addressed the City in ever more glowing terms.

> So let me say as I begin my new job, I want to continue working with you in helping you do yours, listening to what you say, always recognising your international success is critical to that of Britain's overall [success] and considering together the things that we must do – and, just as important, things we should not do, to maintain our competitiveness: enhancing a risk-based regulatory approach, as we did in resisting pressure for a British Sarbanes-Oxley after Enron and WorldCom.[39]

It is important to remember the context in which Brown called for lighter-touch regulation. When he was Chancellor, he announced the end of business cycles and shared the belief that periods of recession belonged to history. The whole political and economic atmosphere was hostile to any notion of counter-cyclical buffers. This was also a time when bank regulators were spending much of their intellectual effort on preparation for the complexities of Basel II. What that work consistently 'showed' was that for whole areas of lending, especially residential mortgages, loss rates were well below what regulators had assumed in calculating capital requirements. Banks had also been able to 'demonstrate' how well their models were forecasting losses, which meant that no one examined the limitations of the models.

Regulation with a lighter touch coincided with the adoption of risk-based supervision not only in the UK but also in many other countries. The reasons were similar, such as the need to prioritise resources. It is arguable that the FSA always had too few staff. In 2004, the FSA regulated a wide range of financial institutions of varying kinds with a staff of 2,165. But in that year, the government required the FSA to supervise mortgage lending and then, in 2005, it was obliged to take on general insurance. By the end of March 2009, after the financial crisis, its staff had increased only to 2,643. Other reasons for the introduction of risk-based supervision included the need to bring supervisory practices in line with developments in financial institutions' operational and risk management practices, although, as regulators were soon to discover, these often existed on paper rather than in practice. But the focus of risk-based supervision could all too readily be on assessing the risk of a particular financial institution rather than on ensuring that the problems identified were actually sorted out. It is easy to follow procedures, to miss unanticipated risks and fail to meet with senior managers and assess the risks such personalities might pose to their own organisations. I always remember a senior regulator saying at a conference, 'You know how to run your business', because it was believed that the prime responsibility for managing risks lay with the senior management and boards of individual firms, who were felt to be better placed to assess business-model risks than bank regulators. Then the fact that so many did not make such assessments, or chose to ignore the risks, was fully exposed by the financial crisis and subsequent failures. I was sceptical of the remark at the time. The question was then and still is: but how are you running your business?

Nevertheless, whatever the limitations of risk-based supervision, the widely reported commitment to it of the Chancellor and the Economic Secretary to the Treasury would undoubtedly have undermined any regulators who took their work seriously in terms of protecting the public and ensuring a safe and fair financial system. Having set up a regulatory authority which could have worked well – and indeed did in its early days – the Chancellor then wrecked any chance it had of being effective with the 'light touch' approach to regulation. That demotivated the staff. Much has been written about how to prevent another financial crisis and some of that will no doubt be followed in the UK by its new regulators. Politicians, however, in their desire to be seen to be 'doing something' in the aftermath, have taken the usual course of changing the structures, a visible response, and one which increases the risk of lack of communication between regulatory authorities. Communication failures, as we shall see in the following chapters, was one reason, but not the only reason, for the length of time it took to deal with LIBOR and other attempts to manipulate benchmarks.

Notes

1 R. Davies, P. Richardson, V. Katinaite and M. Manning, 'Evolution of the UK banking system', *Bank of England Quarterly Bulletin*, December 2010, pp. 321–32, available at https://www.bankofengland.co.uk/-/media/boe/files/quarterly-bulletin/2010/quarterly-bulletin-2010-q4.pdf (accessed 17 April 2018).

2 Bank of England, 'The secondary banking crisis and the Bank of England's support operations', *Bank of England Quarterly Bulletin*, April 1978, p. 230, available at https://www.bankofengland.co.uk/-/media/boe/files/

quarterly-bulletin/1978/the-second-banking-crisis-and-the-boes-support-operations.pdf (accessed 17 April 2018).

3 Evidence submitted by the Bank of England, Committee to Review the Functioning of Financial Institutions, *Second Stage Evidence* (HMSO, 1979), vol. 4, p. 96.

4 J. S. Fforde, 'Competition, innovation and regulation in British banking', *Bank of England Quarterly Bulletin*, September 1983, p. 367, available at https://www.bankofengland.co.uk/archive/Documents/historicpubs/qb/1983/qb83q3363376.pdf (accessed 1 May 2018).

5 The Group of Ten countries at that time consisted (despite its name) of 11 industrial countries: Belgium, Canada, France, Germany, Italy, Japan, the Netherlands, Sweden, Switzerland, the UK and the USA. Bankhaus Herstatt was closed by the German regulators at 16:30 German time, because it was insolvent. It had made the wrong bet on the dollar, which was experiencing extreme volatility during the oil crisis. Partly owing to the time difference, it left the dollars it owed on its foreign exchange deals unpaid. Banks rushed to freeze their outgoing payments and the market ground to a halt.

6 Kevin Rodgers, *Why Aren't They Shouting? A Banker's Tale of Change, Computers and Perpetual Crisis* (Random House Business Books, 2016), p. 201.

7 Liam Vaughan and Gavin Finch, *The Fix: How Bankers Lied, Cheated and Colluded to Rig the World's Most Important Number* (John Wiley & Sons, 2017), p. 16.

8 Gordon Borrie, 'Legal and administrative regulation in the United Kingdom of competition and consumer policies', *University of New South Wales Law Journal*, 5 (1982), p. 82.

9 The Department of Prices and Consumer Protection was short-lived, set up in 1974 and abolished in 1979. The Office of Fair Trading, a non-ministerial government department, was abolished in 2014.

10 There were in fact tapering tariffs of minimum commission rates, which meant that brokers could compete to provide cheaper dealing but still could not trade on their own account.

11 The argument for linking fixed commissions with the single-capacity system was put forward by David LeRoy Lewis, Director of the London Stock Exchange 1970–6, who chaired the committee developing the Exchange's case. Interview with David LeRoy Lewis on the website 'The jobbing system of the London Stock Exchange: an oral history', http://www.history.ac.uk/projects/research/jobbing (accessed May 2018).

12 Nicholas Goodison in interview with Richard Northedge, 'The men who lit the fuse for the Exchange', *The Telegraph*, 8 October 2006.

13 Restrictive Trades Practices (Stock Exchange) Bill, *Hansard*, 22 November 1983, vol. 49, cc. 184–261.

14 Note for the Prime Minister from the Department of Trade and Industry, 7 May 1986, National Archives.

15 L. C. B. Gower, *The Gower Report: A Review of Investor Protection*, command no. 9125 (HMSO, 1984); L. C. B. Gower '"Big Bang" and City regulation', *Modern Law Review*, 51: (1988), pp. 1–22.

16 I was an independent director of the SIB, subsequently the Financial Services Authority, from 1993 to 1998.

17 He was chairman from 1988 to 1992.

18 Bank of England, 'Johnson Matthey Bankers Limited', press release, 11 December 1985.

19 Banking supervision (review committee's report), *Hansard*, 20 June 1985, vol. 81, cc. 452–63.

20 Statement by Chancellor Lawson as reported by the Earl of Gowrie, *House of Lords Debates*, 20 June 1985, vol. 465, cc 384–93, 384, § 4.28 p.m. (Johnson Matthey Bankers).

21 Though consideration was given in the white paper to setting up a separate supervisory body, that was considered too disruptive, and instead the Bank of England set up its Board of Banking Supervision, with three ex-officio members (the Governor, the Deputy Governor and the Executive Director for Banking Supervision) and six independent members. Numbers were increased, changes were made to shorten and clarify lines of responsibility and communication, and more frequent supervisory visits were introduced.

22 As I was an MP and Opposition Treasury spokesman, I led for the Opposition on this Bill as it went through the House of Commons, and large exposures were certainly one of my concerns.

23 Banking Bill, *Hansard*, 28 November 1986, vol. 106, cc. 542–90.

24 The Basel I Accord was where the Basel Committee on Bank Supervision set out, for the first time, the minimum capital requirements for banks, with the aim of reducing credit risk. The Committee itself is a committee of banking supervisory authorities, established by the central bank governors of the G10 countries in 1974. Its aim is to improve the understanding of key supervisory issues and to improve the quality of banking supervision on a global basis.

25 Treasury Select Committee, *Sixth Report: The Regulation of Financial Services in the UK*, 1994–5, HC 322-I, para. 93.

26 Ibid., para. 92.

27 Bank of England and financial regulation, *Hansard*, 20 May 1997, vol. 294, c. 510.

28 Treasury Select Committee, *Minutes of Evidence*, Examination of witnesses, Questions 120–4, 7 December 1998.

29 This kind of company has no share capital or shareholders, and is often used for non-profit organisations requiring a legal personality.

30 Memorandum of Understanding between HM Treasury, the Bank of England and the Financial Services Authority, now available in the National Archives (http://webarchive.nationalarchives.gov.uk/+/http://www.hm-treasury.gov.uk/documents/financial_services/regulating_financial_services/fin_rfs_mou.cfm). This memorandum is dated 22 March 2006, but it was simply an updating of the original Memorandum in the Banking Act Report, 1997–8, pp. 37–9.

31 Vaughan and Finch, *The Fix*, p. 106.

32 Treasury Select Committee, *Minutes of Evidence*, Memorandum by the Financial Services Authority, 8 March 2000.

33 Quoted in Hannah Furness, 'Regulating the banks: what politicians used to say about the City', *Daily Telegraph*, 4 July 2012.

34 Financial Services Authority, *The Failure of the Royal Bank of Scotland: Financial Services Authority Board Report* (FSA, December 2011), p. 261, available at https://www.fca.org.uk/publication/corporate/fsa-rbs.pdf (accessed 1 May 2018).

35 HM Treasury, press release, 24 May 2005. This was part of the government's 'Better Regulation Agenda', based on reforms proposed in the Hampton review and reports from the Better Regulation Task Force.

36 Chancellor Gordon Brown, Mansion House speech, 21 June 2006, available at http://webarchive.nationalarchives.gov.uk/20100407173744/http://www. hm-treasury.gov.uk/speech_chex_210606.htm (accessed 1 May 2018).

37 See Financial Services Authority, *The Failure of the Royal Bank of Scotland*, p. 262. The speech by Tony Blair was on the compensation culture and delivered to the Institute of Public Policy Research on 26 May 2005.

38 The full speech is on his website, https://www.edballs.co.uk/blog/speeches-articles/the-city-as-the-global-finance-centre-risks-opportunities-my-speech-at-bloomberg-14th-june-2006 (accessed 1 May 2018).

39 Chancellor Gordon Brown, Mansion House speech, 20 June 2007, available at http://webarchive.nationalarchives.gov.uk/+/http://www.hm-treasury.gov. uk/2014.htm (accessed 1 May 2018).

Part I: LIBOR, a chequered history, 1968–2018

Chapter 2

The evolution of LIBOR

What is LIBOR?

LIBOR is the London Interbank Offered Rate, that is, the interest rate at which banks offer to lend funds to each other in the international interbank market. It is an indication of the costs of unsecured borrowing for the banks. It is a benchmark that reflects the interest rate, credit premium and liquidity premium that a leading bank would expect to be offered by a similar bank. It is set at 11 a.m. UK time in 10 currencies and for several maturities. Until 1 February 2014, LIBOR was owned by the British Bankers' Association (BBA), the trade body. From 1984 onwards, the data compilation and calculation were undertaken by Reuters for the BBA and the process was overseen by an independent committee of market participants, the Foreign Exchange and Money Market Committee. The membership of the Committee included corporate treasurers and representatives from banks, the money market and exchanges.

It is important to understand the way in which LIBOR was calculated in order to see how it was manipulated in later years. LIBOR was calculated as a 'trimmed' average of statistics submitted by the contributory banks. The calculation was repeated for all borrowing periods and all currencies to which LIBOR relates. There were in fact 150 different LIBORs in total, calculated for 15 different maturities and 10 different currencies. Maturities ranged from one day (overnight) to 12 months (three months was standard) and currencies include sterling, US dollars, euros, yen and Swiss francs, as well as less important currencies such as the Australian dollar and New Zealand dollar.

Contributory banks had to make daily submissions to Reuters between 11.00 and 11.10 a.m. Greenwich meantime. The rates submitted were required to be of reasonable market size, simple and unsecured, and given to at least two but no more than five decimal places. The trimmed average was determined by discarding the rates submitted which were in the top and bottom quartiles of all submissions and calculating the mean average of the remaining middle two quartiles. This average was the LIBOR 'fixing'. After checking for errors, Reuters published the LIBOR fixings as well as the individual rates submitted by the contributor banks. Even before the controversy over market manipulation, LIBOR was often called a 'convenient fiction' because the actual interbank borrowing was frequently for a week or even less, rather than the three-month period which most transactions referenced when using LIBOR.[1]

LIBOR has a longer history than might appear from the recent attempts to 'fix' the rates of interest to the advantage of some of its users. Several market participants claim to have been the first to introduce its use as an informal benchmark. No doubt they each contributed, but it would not have had that status without the developments in the markets that began in the 1960s and accelerated in the 1970s.

This chapter will trace both market developments and the macro-economic and regulatory environment in which the transition from the informal to the formal use of LIBOR as a universal benchmark took place. Its purpose is to explain why both the establishment of LIBOR and its oversight by the BBA seemed entirely logical at the time, when its informal use was so well established, owing in part to the dominant and colourful market participants who incorporated it into the new types of lending and financial instruments they developed or promoted. Introducing a different benchmark would undoubtedly have been difficult.

The early days

David Clark, chairman of the Wholesale Markets Brokers Association, connected LIBOR to the advent of the Eurodollar:[2]

> geopolitical forces, especially the Vietnam war, the emergence of global trade imbalances and restrictive legislation in the U.S., ... resulted in the unexpected and sudden creation of the Eurodollar market in London in the 1960s. It was from this start that syndicated lending and capital markets recycled offshore dollars using floating interest rates based on LIBOR.[3]

The legislative constraints of the 1960s included Regulation Q, which limited the amount of interest US banks paid on deposits, and

Regulation M, which prescribed the reserves to be held against deposits, which was more than required of banks outside the USA. In 1963, the Interest Equalization Tax was levied on US investors' purchases of foreign borrowing in the US market, at 1%. This led to a sharp reduction of the issuance in the Yankee bond market; with access to other markets subject to restrictions, issuance was diverted to the emerging Eurodollar bond market. Then in 1965, the Voluntary Foreign Credit Restraint Progam established voluntary limits on foreign direct investment outside the USA. In 1968, these limits were replaced by mandatory restrictions. US multinationals had no alternative but to fund their foreign subsidiaries through the Euromarkets. The Eurobond market grew rapidly in the 1960s, and that continued throughout the 1970s, even though some of the restrictions were removed, such as the Interest Equalization Tax in 1974. The *Bank of England Quarterly Bulletin* records that:

> The Eurobond market consolidated its position as a channel of intermediation for international capital flows, largely because an infrastructure for economical primary distribution and secondary trading had become well-established, and because many domestic markets were subject to strict issuing requirements.[4]

According to Minos Zombanakis, the story began when he organised one of the first syndicated loans, linked to what he called a 'London interbank offered rate' (LIBOR), in 1969. This was an $80 million loan for the Shah of Iran, and it signalled the way in which the cross-border financial markets opened up then. Minos (as he became generally known), by then Senior Vice President of the London branch of the bank Manufacturer's Hanover Ltd, claims, with considerable justification, to have been the first to use LIBOR in this way. He had seen a gap in the Euromarkets which he wanted to exploit. He saw that it was difficult to obtain a medium-sized loan for three to seven years from an individual bank, although the demand for such loans was growing. This was because US banks had to 'match' their loans with deposits of equal size and maturity, and restrictions on dollar lending and borrowing in New York in the 1960s and 1970s, together with the Interest Equalization Tax and the Voluntary Foreign Credit Restraint Program, placed limits on loans available to foreigners and US companies investing abroad. The Federal Reserve's Regulation Q limited the interest paid on domestic deposits and hampered the growth of deposits, but these did not apply in the Eurodollar market. A $1 million loan in the USA required a $1 million one-year deposit, but borrowers wanted loans of five years or more and five-year deposits were not available. Minos is quoted as saying, 'No commercial bank would even consider making longer-term loans to finance a project'.[5] Even the Eurobond market was restricted in the amount of money it could lend, whereas borrowers wanted larger loans than that. Once his branch of the bank was opened on 6 January 1969, he put advertisements in the *Financial Times* and the *Herald Tribune* announcing the arrival of a 'new concept in international finance'. He was fortunate in that through his wide network of contacts, Atta Salmanpour, one of the Vice Governors of the Bank of Iran, came knocking at the door for a loan of $80 million to enable him to make a contribution to the country's five-year plan in 1969. He began discussing his idea with bankers in London of advancing a term loan at which the rate repayable by the borrower would be reset every three to six months. The rate would be based on the cost of funds available to banks, which Minos called the London interbank offered rate.

The syndicated loan involved the division of the loan between a number of banks in different countries with different histories, cultures and customs. Minos dealt with this problem by identifying one bank as the lead, to run the syndicate, and another as the agent, to look after all the detailed management issues, according to a 'memorandum of presentation', a loan agreement which all the participating banks had to sign. He introduced the idea that a select group of 'reference banks' within the syndicate would report their cost of funds to the agent bank shortly before the rollover date. The loan agreement set out the basis of the syndication and pricing formula, and it protected the interests of borrowers and lenders.

Minos had contacted all the large US banks in London with interests in Iran, and soon put together more than the $80 million required. All that helped to make the loan an instant success. Other major loans soon followed, such as the $200 million loan to the Istituto Mobiliare Italiano (IMI), the Italian state-owned industrial funding agency. It was a more complex loan, since it required upgrading management and documentation. The loan was in the context of money flying out of Italy, often in suitcases smuggled into Switzerland. Minos, however, took the view that the country could be helped by raising the loan for a reliable state agency, thus bringing capital into the country and also strengthening its creditworthiness in the international markets. This time, the syndicate consisted of 22 banks from nine countries and helped to standardise the required documentation. The market took off after that, first with large European and America corporations, then with loans to South

America, Africa and the Asian Pacific; loans were also made to sovereign borrowers, who then came to dominate the market.

From 1969 onwards, that syndicated lending and capital markets recycled offshore dollars using floating interest rates based on LIBOR. How did LIBOR work for the syndicated loans? LIBOR changes continuously, but the rate on any particular loan is readjusted every three or six months, on a roll-over basis. The borrower is usually given the choice between a three-month or a six-month readjustment period. The new base rate is calculated two days prior to the rollover date as the average of the offer rates of several reference banks in the syndicate. The reference banks are carefully specified in the agreement. The spread above LIBOR paid by the borrower may understate the bank's actual return on a loan, generally 0.125% to 0.25% above the rate at which banks purchase funds from large depositors.

Some dispute the claim that Minos invented LIBOR, pointing out both that Minos was an excellent self-publicist, but, more important, that it was inevitably a collaborative process, involving other people at other banks. During the same period, the volatility in interest rates led to another financial innovation. Credit for this is given to Evan Galbraith, then a director of Bankers Trust International, who reportedly was taking a bath at his home when he experienced a Eureka moment and came up with the idea of a floating-rate note, whereby the interest rate on a loan might vary at regular intervals in line with the general movement in interest rates. Galbraith explained:

> Eurodollar syndicated bank loans were taking off, and it was familiarity with the bank market that inspired the idea to take the banking concept (changing the interest rate every six months) and apply it to a negotiable bond, marketing it to both banks and bond dealers.[6]

He was, in fact the first to link a bond with LIBOR.

The first floating-rate note was launched in 1970 for ENEL, the Italian electricity authority. Galbraith discussed the idea with Siegmund Warburg, a banker who recognised the value of the idea at once, since with high interest rates borrowers were reluctant to use fixed-rate debt obligations, whereas a floating rate would give them maximum flexibility. Warburg contacted Guido Carli, Governor of the Banca d'Italia, who suggested ENEL. The loan was for $125 million with a maturity of seven years, with the interest rate being fixed every six months at 0.75% over LIBOR. Minos was apparently very worried when he heard about this and took the next flight to Rome to talk to Carli: 'The next thing he

[Carli] calls me up and says "I have cancelled the mandate. You are to do the loan",' to which Minos replied, 'I am not going to do the loan, the other guys will do it on my terms'.

In addition to the issuance of the floating-rate note, Warburg placed a $300 million loan on a private basis mainly with the London branches of US banks.[7] David Clark, then a money market dealer at Bankers Trust International, points out that the prospectus for the ENEL deal was the first time the term 'LIBOR' was used in a bond prospectus. Bankers Trust International became the leading market-maker in the sector until a poorly received floating-rate note for Argentina in late 1970 put paid to any further issues for the next few years.

LIBOR becomes a formal benchmark

LIBOR evolved from syndicated loans and from the ways in which an agreed interest rate for the loan was established by means of an agent, the lead bank, contacting other banks (usually three or four) to ask what their rate would be for a six-month loan, and the latter became reference banks. As the use of LIBOR developed through syndicated loans and floating-rate notes, the members of the BBA looked for a more transparent way to fix the rate. In response to requests from UK banks to develop a calculation which could be used as an impartial basis for calculating interest on syndicated loans, a working party was established in 1984 to set out the procedures, culminating in the publication of LIBOR for the first time on 1 January 1986. The Bank of England was an observer at the meetings of the working party but apparently did not participate or receive minutes. The BBA took the opportunity to oversee the process in part no doubt because LIBOR did not form part of the Financial Services Act 1986 or of the Banking Act 1987, and its members would have known that, having participated in the consultation process and responded to the white papers preceding the Bills.

The key concept was that BBA LIBOR was based on the offered rate, not the bid rate. At first, every contributor bank was asked to base its LIBOR submissions on its replies to the following question:

> At what rate could you borrow funds, were you to do so by asking for and then accepting inter-bank offers in a reasonable market size just prior to 11 a.m.?

Therefore submissions were based on the lowest perceived rate at which a bank on a certain currency panel could go into the interbank money market to obtain sizeable funding, for a given maturity. The BBA argued that it would not be possible to base LIBOR on actual transactions, since not all banks would require funds in a marketable size each day in each of the currencies they quoted for, but this did not mean that the rates were inaccurate, since 'a bank will know what its credit and liquidity risk profile is from the rates with which it has dealt, and can construct a curve to predict accurately the correct rate for currencies or maturities in which it has not been active'.[8] 'Reasonable market size' was intentionally left undefined, since defining it would create too many problems, including a need for constant monitoring.

In 1998, following a review by the BBA, the submissions from each reference bank had to be in response to the following question:

> At what rate do you think interbank term deposits will be offered by one prime bank to another prime bank in a reasonable market size today at 11 a.m.?

The new definition was thought to encourage accountability for the rates. It is easy to see the BBA LIBOR as a step forward in the context of syndicated loans and floating-rate notes, since banks were familiar with the use some kind of agreed interest rates. London was an international banking centre in the mid-1980s, where business between banks 'dominated the total international banking business' conducted in London:

> At the end of 1985, interbank loans accounted for over three-quarters of outstanding international claims, and interbank liabilities for a similar proportion of outstanding liabilities.... Analysis of the 'pure' international interbank market in London (that is business between unrelated banks) on an individual bank basis shows that, at end-1985, there were almost identical numbers of net lenders and net borrowers.... Twelve banks of various nationalities, out of a total of 472 reporting international business, accounted for half of all net international interbank lending, and 37 for three-quarters.[9]

So, not only was the setting of rates in some collective way familiar, but the context of banking in London was one in which the emergence of LIBOR as an interest rate benchmark seemed appropriate, given the size the market for interbank lending and the instruments to which it applied. There seemed to be no reason to question its validity. But during the decades leading up to the financial crisis, the wide range of commonly used financial instruments was to change banking out of all recognition. Financial innovation abounded. Neither governments nor the Bank of England thought to include LIBOR in financial regulation. It apparently worked well.

Further changes in banking

From the late 1970s to the early 1980s, the financial market was dominated by sovereign debt. Between 1971 and 1982, medium-term syndicated loans were widely used to promote development in non-oil-producing developing countries in Asia, Africa and especially Latin America. The loans also went to assist newly industrialised countries. New credit facilities of about $83 billion were announced in 1980 and a further $133 billion the following year, of which the lion's share, 67%, went to developing countries. This lending ground to a halt when Mexico decided to suspend interest payments on its loans to creditors in August 1982. It was quickly followed by other countries, including Brazil, Argentina, Venezuela and the Philippines.[10] In 1985, the value of new international syndicated loans fell to $19 billion. The banks turned to the Eurobond market. Gross Eurobond issues increased from $74 billion in 1982 to $163 billion in 1985. The syndicated market grew rapidly over the second part of the decade, but borrowing by central governments represented only 5% of the market after 1982 and the less developed countries were excluded altogether. Industrial borrowers represented over 45% of all syndicated loans in every year after 1982 and reached 88% of all announcements in 1988 and 81% in 1989, with loans denominated in US dollars accounting for over 60% of all international syndicated loans.[11]

Thus, after a dramatic fall in syndicated loans in 1986, the market recovered and lending increased but to a different set of borrowers, such as corporate institutions in developed countries. They aimed to restructure their existing lines of credit into more flexible arrangements, for example multiple-option facilities, that a number of credit and money market fund-raising mechanisms, which are documented in a single agreement and are administered by a single agent on behalf of a number of banks. Other factors leading to the growth included the increase in debt-financed takeovers and competitive lending rates for corporate borrowers.

By the beginning of the 1990s, banks had experienced extensive losses as a result of the sovereign debt crisis. Consequently,

[they] started applying more sophisticated risk pricing to syndicated lending ... [making] wider use of covenants, triggers which linked pricing explicitly to corporate events such as changes in ratings and debt servicing.... Eventually, guarantees and unfunded risk transfer techniques, such as synthetic securitisation, helped banks to buy protection against credit risk whilst keeping the loans on the balance sheet. Companies also saw such loans as useful, flexible sources of funds that could be organised quickly.[12]

Because of these developments, the market grew strongly until 2003, when the arrangements for new loans reached $1.6 trillion. The gross amount of syndicated loans to developing economies rose from about $400 billion per quarter in 2002 to almost $1.3 trillion in the second quarter of 2007.

However, all that was to change with the financial crisis of 2007–8. After the collapse of Lehman Brothers, the funding markets froze for a time. Together with rapidly growing credit losses towards the end of 2008, bank balance sheets were under enormous strain. At the same time, the value of global exports of goods and services fell by 18% in the last quarter of 2008. So syndicated lending declined by 67% in developed economies and to the same extent in emerging markets in Asia and the Middle East. Syndicated lending recovered only very slowly after the recovery in the global financial markets in the second half of 2009, but by 2011 the market had recovered, with global syndicated lending reaching US$3.9 trillion in 2011, the best full year since 2007, when it had reached $4.8 trillion.[13]

Floating-rate notes

The use of syndicated loans was superseded to a large extent by the funds raised through floating-rate notes. These rose from $5 billion in 1980 to $15 billion in 1983 and in the first half of 1984 alone, at $13 billion, exceeded the announcements of the syndicated credits for the first time. Floating-rate notes (FRNs) were introduced in 1970, another innovation, this time designed to fill the gap between the demand for and the supply of medium- and long-term funds by paying investors an interest rate linked to a short-term money market reference rate, such as LIBOR. Fixed-rate bond markets are inevitably unresponsive to volatile interest rates, which leave the lenders bearing the interest rate risk alone. As noted above, the first FRN was issued to ENEL in 1970, during a period of rising interest rates and investor disillusionment with fixed-rate bonds. Borrowers could not raise more than $25 million in one issue. Despite the fact that FRNs allowed borrowers easier access to the bond market, they were less flexible than syndicated loans and did not make any progress during the 1970s. Before 1982, banks provided half the funds raised by FRNs.

However, after the collapse of Bankhaus Herstatt and the price increases in the interbank bank market, the importance of long-term funding for banks without easy recourse to dollars became clear. Banks in France and Japan, for example, were obliged by their regulators to match a proportion of their lending with long-term liabilities, but Japanese banks were able to take advantage of FRNs, and fund their purchases at very short notice. In a number of other countries, such as the USA and the UK, FRNs in a subordinated form counted as capital. Given this background, it is not surprising that banks bought a large proportion of FRNs, possibly 80% or more.

After the sovereign debt crisis of 1982, bank syndicated lending and bank deposits were regarded as more risky, leading to a real opportunity for FRNs, especially as it appeared that large issues were possible and that secondary market liquidity was more certain. An FRN of $1.2 billion was issued by Sweden in 1983, and although FRNs of $1 billion or more were unusual, the average amounts increased, with a large number being of the order of $300–$500 billion. The Swedish FRN was a 10-year issue, priced at LIBOR plus 25 basis points.

> At one stroke the issue succeeded in establishing a credible alternative to the syndicated loan market, the collapse of which was starving banks of suitable assets and through its sheer size changed the conditions in which FRNS were traded in the market.[14]

Lower fees and spreads of only 0.125% over LIBOR were charged, and some banks issued FRNs with a coupon of LIBOR only, which were obviously attractive. It was these lower costs that led to borrowers moving to the FRN market rather than syndicated loans.

In 1984 and 1985, FRNs were the fastest-growing area of the Eurobond market, with the FRN sector accounting for 23% of all the borrowing in that market in 1985. As banks left the FRN market as issuers, they were replaced by sovereign issuers. The rapid growth of the FRN market led to a rapid decline in the spreads paid by borrowers, from 45 basis points over LIBOR in 1982 to 15 basis points over LIBOR by early 1984, and fees for new issues were also falling, to such an extent that the decline in front-end fees meant that often only the lead manager made a profit. Even so, in 1985, new issues of FRNs also gained in comparison with fixed-rate bonds, and FRNs accounted for 38% of the total volume of fixed-rate and floating-rate bonds; by 1986, FRNs had reached $50 billion, while the volume of international syndicated loans had fallen to $58 billion.

In April 1984, the first perpetual FRN was issued by County Bank for National Westminster Bank. For the issuer, if structured correctly, the regulator could treat the FRN as capital on the bank's balance sheet. After 1985, the floating-rate market introduced a number of innovations, such as an upper limit on the 'coupon' (the interest payment to the investor), a 'cap' and, perhaps more important, a 'floor', that is, a guarantee of a minimum level of interest, if the index dropped below a certain level. But it was the large-scale issue of perpetual FRNs by commercial banks, especially by the UK banks, which attracted attention. In 1986, there were about 60 issues of these notes, which in the UK, USA, Canada, Australia and France were regarded as part of a bank's primary capital. But by December of that year, the market collapsed, partly because excessive competition drove yields down to unattractive levels, partly because of the concerns of central bankers that the FRNs did not spread risk outside the banking sector, and partly because of fears in the industry that impending changes in international banking regulations issued by the Basel Committee would require banks to deduct holdings of 'perpetuals' issued by other banks from the calculation of their capital for regulatory purposes. The Bank of England had already taken that approach and had warned of the risks of perpetuals in 1984. The secondary market in perpetual floating-rate notes had virtually disappeared by 1987.

The 1980s were probably the heyday of FRNs, but they have continued to be a means of raising funds for banks, companies and even sovereign states at times, especially when interest rates make other forms of borrowing unattractive; for example, the Bank of England's review of international markets observed that in 1994 fixed-rate borrowing remained subdued, but that was offset partly by increased issues of FRNs, 35% higher than the previous year, to the tune of $93 billion. In 2001, the first FRN was issued priced against the sterling overnight interest rate, rather than six-month LIBOR (the typical arrangement). This was probably a matter of following the practice in the euro area, where the euro overnight rate was often used as a funding benchmark.

By 2012, after the financial crisis, issuance of short-dated FRNs by EU and UK banks had picked up, no doubt reflecting a demand from money market funds and bank treasurers for improved returns.

The growth of the Eurobond market

Eurobonds are simply bonds denominated in a currency other than that of the country in which they are issued.[15] They are generally issued in more than one country and traded across international financial centres. The 50th anniversary of the Eurobond was celebrated in June 2013 at a dinner organised by the International Capital Markets Association.[16] The first issued was a $15 million bond for Italy's Autostrade. SG Warburg arranged the bond because it saw that the huge amount of Eurodollars outside the USA (for tax reasons) was clearly available for recycling. The opportunity had been created by US President Kennedy's Interest Equalization Tax, just 17 days after the Autostrade deal was completed. The only surviving member of the Warburg team recalled that the loan was supposed to be for Finsider, the Italian steel company, as Warburg's friend, the then governor of Banca d'Italia, Guido Carli, suggested, but it could not work as the firm was not allowed to pay gross interest, so it went to the Autostrade project. The $5 million, 5.5% bond was guaranteed by IRI, the principal industrial financial holding company owned by the Italian state. The originators, of course, did not know that by 2012 the market would produce $14 trillion of issuance. Because Eurobonds are 'bearer bonds', which means they can be held anonymously, many investors purchased them in order to avoid tax, and they became the target market. Conventional Eurobonds have a fixed coupon, usually paid annually, and a maturity date when all the principal is repaid; zero-coupon bonds do not pay interest but there may be tax reasons for purchasing them.

One of the others celebrating the 50th anniversary, Eugene Rotberg, Treasurer at the World Bank throughout the 1970s and much of the 1980s, pointed out that mistakes had been made in the largely un-regulated or self-regulated market, which market participants tried to hide by techniques such as off-balance-sheet trades or avoiding mark-to-market. Nevertheless, Rotberg is quoted as saying, worryingly:

> We respond to peer pressure. We want to patent that magic zero coupon bond with a perpetual maturity so we need pay neither interest nor principal. We deny blame or responsibility … we rely on sympathetic

accounting conventions. We design performance measures to cover up error.[17]

The Eurobond market began to develop in the 1960s as an offshore market in dollar bonds (as already indicated) in response to the US Interest Equalization Act 1963, as well as the appearance of a substantial current account deficit in the 1960s, and the impact of Regulation Q, limiting the amount of interest paid on deposits. The tax was levied on US investors' purchases of foreign securities and in turn raised the cost of borrowing in the US market by 1%. In 1968, mandatory restrictions on foreign direct investment out of the USA were introduced, which left US multinational companies with little alternative but to fund their foreign subsidiaries through the euromarkets. Eurobond issuance grew rapidly in the 1960s, reaching $3 billion in 1970, and markets in other currencies such as the Deutsche Mark and Canadian dollar became well established. It continued to grow even though some of the factors which led to its early growth disappeared, such as the abolition of the Interest Equalization Tax Act in 1974. However, the Eurobond market retained its position because it provided a well-established infrastructure for economic primary distribution and secondary trading. London was (and indeed remains) the centre for the Eurobond market, partly because of the entrepreneurial spirit of its merchant banks, and partly because it had well-developed skills and experience to launch the Eurobond. London accounts for 70% of the secondary market turnover in international bonds, including those issued by sovereign states, government agencies, supranational banks and industrial corporations. The creation of the Euro-clear system in 1968 provided the means of dealing with all the problems of settlement. London also had the legal firms able to provide the merchant banks with all the expertise required.

Eurobond issuance grew very rapidly, from $26 billion in 1980 to $185 billion in 1986, but then dropped $142 billion in 1987 before rising again to $224 billion in 1989, partly due to a fall in issuing FRNs and the extremely high volume of dollar equity warrant bonds issued by Japanese borrowers in 1989. It rose again in 1991 as confidence returned to the markets following the Gulf War and investors switched into longer maturities as yields were falling. Fixed-interest Eurobonds were the dominant instrument in the euromarket, although their relative importance fell from 72% of the Eurobond issuance in 1980 to 61% in 1990.

Most Eurobond issuers were highly rated borrowers from member states of the Organisation for Economic Co-operation and Development

(OECD) with issuers from non-OECD countries averaging about 3.7% of total bond issuance between 1985 and 1990. The number of issuers in the US private sector, the largest national group of issuers, dropped sharply from 1987 onwards, due to the abolition of a withholding tax and the introduction of 'shelf registration', which speeded up issuing domestic bonds, when speed was one of the advantages of the Eurobond market. US corporate debt had begun to increase, which led to investor awareness of credit risk. Up until the early 1990s, Eurobonds were the dominant means of raising finance. Syndicated loans, which had fallen out of favour, due to the international debt crisis in the early 1980s, reached a record level of $165 billion in 1990 because the numbers of mergers and acquisitions suddenly increased. Both Eurobonds and syndicated loans provide long-term finance. Syndicated loans provide loans for borrowers with a lower credit rating, but both can raise vast loans for those with high credit ratings, to finance takeover bids for example.

The market for various kinds of short-term borrowing such as euro-commercial paper, note-issuance facilities and euro-medium-term notes also grew. They can be distinguished from Eurobonds in that they are continuously offered and because they usually have shorter-term maturities, varying between four years for the medium-term maturities and between 90 and 180 days for euro-commercial paper. Eurobond maturities began to be reduced to under six years on average, compared with over eight years in the early 1980s, in order to offer some protection from volatile interest rates and exchange rates.

The Eurobond market was a leading channel for financial innovation. It allowed financial products to be developed to suit the needs of issuers and investors. The market for Eurobonds began to change as dealers started to make more use of brokers, and of domestic instruments, including futures, swaps and options. The development of the repurchase market provided a means for traders to offer bonds for sale which they did not own. The size of individual issues increased from $62 million in 1980 to $155 million in 1990 on average, although some issues were over $500 million. Meanwhile, the status of the Eurobond market continued to change as it ceased to be purely domestic in character. An increasingly international bond market emerged and the instruments traded in the different markets became more homogeneous. Yield differentials narrowed between the domestic and Eurobond markets, but they remained. All of this contributed to the growth of London as an international bond market, with about 65% of Eurobond issues being syndicated in London (including Eurodollar and Euroyen bonds) in spite of the deregulation of the domestic bond markets in many countries, which seemed to threaten London's position.

The free-wheeling days of the 1960s and 1970s gradually disappeared. The Association of International Bond Dealers, founded in 1969 and which ultimately became the International Capital Market Association (ICMA) in 2005, produced its first handbook for the primary market in 1985. The handbook was then just a few pages, setting out basic standards, but is now a comprehensive work covering the procedures and conduct involved in issuing a broad range of international securities, in what ICMA claims is a highly competitive market. Ten major global banks are the lead managers, but ICMA stresses the extent of competition over fees and that bond issuers do frequently change lead managers. Its handbook is not enforceable but does provide standards which market participants are expected to follow. Following the financial crisis, however, the Eurobond market is now subject to the EU's Market Abuse Directive, which was implemented in June 2016. It imposes significant new obligations on Eurobond issuers.

This excursion through the development of the Eurobond market is designed to show both how the market changed and how it grew through the years into a market worth trillions, but, despite its size, it is still frequently dependent on LIBOR as an essential benchmark. Bond issuers confident enough to use the Eurobond market include, for example, the Bank of England, which launched another $2 billion Eurobond to finance its foreign currency position in March 2016 as part of its normal procedures. Apple issued €2.8 billion in Eurobonds in 2014 and Ericsson issued two €500 million bonds in 2017. These major issuances show that it is still a large and thriving market.

The swap market

It is generally considered that the swap market formally came into existence in 1981, when IBM and the World Bank entered into a swap agreement, because the World Bank needed to borrow German marks and Swiss francs to finance its operations, but the governments of those countries prohibited it from borrowing. IBM had already borrowed large amounts of these currencies, but needed US dollars when the rates were high for corporate borrowers. Salomon Brothers suggested the idea that the two institutions should swap their debts, enabling IBM also to manage its currency exposure.

The focus in this section is on the interest rate swap market, which initially developed as a means of exploiting the differentials between the bond market and the short-term credit market arising from differing views of credit between bond investors and banks. In the 1980s, swaps were arranged between a bank and a company because banks found that it was possible to raise fixed-rate finance, and corporations found it cheaper to borrow floating-rate funds. It was not very efficient, since these swaps were matched deals, which meant that the intermediary bank had to find two counterparties with matching requirements.[18] The reason for the development of the swap market in the very early 1980s was volatility, the causes of which emanated from the USA, in particular the suspension of the gold standard in 1971, which led, world-wide, to exchange rates being determined by the market. In addition, Paul Volcker, chairman of the Federal Reserve 1979–87, changed the Reserve's operating target from short-term interest rates to bank reserve growth targets. Companies had, of course, always been affected by changes in exchange and interest rates, but it was worth developing the financial instruments to hedge those risks only when they would be profitable, that is, when volatility was high. This happened first with exchange rates after the breakdown of Bretton Woods Agreement in 1971 and later with interest rates.

Another reason for the introduction of swaps, curiously enough, was the difference between the way in which financial institutions developed in the USA and Europe during the 1980s. In the early 1980s, the USA funded long-term, fixed-rate loans such as the typical 30-year mortgage with short-term deposits such as certificates of deposit, whose interest rates fluctuated with Treasury-bill rates, with the risk that the costs of borrowing could increase due to the mismatch between assets and liabilities. At that time, banks in Europe typically funded themselves through long-term, fixed-rate Eurobonds, but offered variable-rate loans. Therefore, the two sets of financial institutions could manage interest rate risks through interest rate swaps.

A variety of reasons emerged for the use of interest rate swaps. These included a corporate treasurer seeking to keep the floating-rate debt issue from becoming too high and an insurance company executive seeking to align the interest rate sensitivities of the firm's assets and liabilities. They did not involve the use of financial arbitrage. One of the key elements in their success was the flexibility of the contract because each individual swap was negotiated 'over the counter' (OTC), but the essential elements included the level of the fixed rate, the way in which the variable rate was to be determined, the size of the transaction, the notional principal, the dates of settlement payments and the events that define default. Commercial banks emerged as both market-makers and end-users of swaps to manage their own balance sheet exposures, as well as acting as intermediaries.

Swaps have become increasingly complex. The basic interest rate swap is a contract between two counterparties to exchange fixed interest payments for floating interest payments. The Bank of England noted in 1987 that the floating rate used was LIBOR in the vast majority of cases, although other rates, such as those on US commercial paper, Treasury bills, prime rate and Federal funds, could be used.[19] Floating/floating basis swaps can be regarded as a subset of interest rate swaps, where the interest rate payments calculated on one basis are swapped for floating-rate payments in the same currency calculated on another basis; for example, three-month LIBOR over six-month LIBOR. The Bank of England carefully distinguishes between currency swaps in the foreign exchange markets (a spot sale and forward purchase of a currency) and capital markets swaps, which are usually the exchange of interest payments in one currency for payments in another. These can be either a fixed interest payment in one currency for a fixed interest payment in another, or a swap in which either or both interest payments are on a floating-rate basis.

The banks developed techniques in the dollar interest rate swap market to enter into an agreement with one counterparty while taking out a temporary hedge in the bond or futures market until an offsetting swap was found. This is called 'warehousing', introduced in 1984. At that time, the classic swap transactions had ceased to produce a floating rate for US dollar funds at significant margins under LIBOR, and so experiments with new structures took place, designed to meet investor and borrower preferences and to take advantage of the inefficiencies between one market and another. Banks began to develop ever more innovative structures in interest rate swaps, including amortising swaps, forward swaps, zero-coupon swaps, options on swaps ('swaptions'), callable swaps, multi-legged swaps and index swaps – a bewildering array indeed.[20] Despite the variety, most of these swaps referenced LIBOR.

The purposes of swaps began to change as they became a way of managing existing liabilities rather than just reducing the cost of borrowing. Such developments were facilitated by the emergence of a large number of intermediaries acting as market-makers in the swaps market. This part of the market grew rapidly because of the ease with which hedging swaps in the US Treasury bond repo or futures markets could be carried out. Liquidity in this market was helped first by the moves towards product standardisation, facilitated by the International Swap Dealers Association (ISDA), which published standardised dealing terms and documentation in 1985, soon after its founding. The Association is essentially a trade body for OTC derivatives dealers and other market participants. It has become more than that, though. But what turned out to be more important than the 1985 initiative was the development of 'master agreements' in 1987, revised in 1992 and in 2002. Before their introduction, each agreement would have to be negotiated separately; standardisation facilitated cross-transaction and close-out netting, applicable only in cases of default or bankruptcies by one of the parties. Each master agreement contains certain fundamental standard terms, which are not specific to any specific transactions, yet it is able to handle all the transactions between the parties over a long period, because it establishes all of the terms (representations and warranties, obligations, definitions, events of default and so on) two companies have to agree between themselves.

Once a master agreement is signed, any future arrangements between the two companies are relatively straightforward. A 'confirmation' needs to be exchanged, listing only what is being exchanged, at what price, in what currency and on what date, along with any deviations for that particular transaction from the standard terms set out in the master agreement. This confirmation becomes part of the master agreement, and is only a small part of that large single contract. Obviously, this simplified the whole process of entering into individual contracts and the standard terms clarified the nature of the commitments. The Enron crisis and the collapse of Lehman Brothers put master agreements to the test, leading to several major court cases. The agreements were successfully interpreted and applied, even though some weaknesses were exposed.

The ISDA's most important contribution to the development of the swap and derivative markets was a reduction in transaction costs, updating definitions in the light of continuing innovations, and economic and perhaps legal certainty in what could have become chaotic markets.

The further development of the swap market

Writing in the *Bank of England Quarterly* in 1987, G. M. S. Hammond doubted that the rapid growth of the swap market over the previous few years would continue or whether the market imperfections would be arbitraged away, resulting in a stabilisation of the market. 'Empirically it is certainly true that the profit margins which could be achieved in the early days of the swap market have been whittled away, yet the market doubled in size last year.'[21] She argued that opportunities for arbitrage would continue to decline and that the real engines of growth depended crucially on developments in risk and credit assessment, including a general re-evaluation of the risks and profitability of swaps. This could perhaps be due to the increasing sophistication of investors, who had become less willing to accept credit and currency risks at below 'market' rates. Hammond believed that arbitrage would become less important, but that the use of swaps for asset and liability management was most important and that their use as hedging instruments would increase, depending on the volatility of markets in the future (and there certainly have been periods of volatility in the past). At that time, interest rate swaps, for example, extended the markets in interest rate futures beyond the then 18-month limit, into the medium term. They could also be a substitute for markets in long-term debt. These were seen as advantages by Hammond. She saw two possible outcomes as a result of the decline in profit margins:

> First, there may be a tendency towards increasingly complex swaps related to more exotic underlying instruments, and the spread of swap techniques into new markets. More complex hedging techniques are likely to emerge. Moves to increase the tradability of swaps might include a swap futures contract....[22]

These remarks are interesting and perspicacious.

The swaps contract formed the basis for the master agreements. The use of swaps in hedging and extending the markets continued, but above all the market grew far beyond those expectations. First of all, the Bank for International Settlements (BIS), wary of the growth of the market in swaps, had worked on developing techniques for its measurement. The BIS announced in 1998 that it would produce semi-annual statistics on open positions in the global OTC derivatives market, especially given the financial events of 1998, when the Russian financial crisis, the collapse of Long-Term Capital Management and the Asian financial crisis all combined to create extreme market uncertainty. The statistics included the notional amounts, a term which refers to the cash flows in each individual contract, and so they give some idea of the transfer of risk, as well as the gross market value. At the end of June 1998, interest rate contracts in terms of gross market value totalled $48.1 trillion, with swaps predominating in that market, at 68% of the contracts.[23] Then, of course, the financial crisis hit the OTC derivatives market, especially credit default swaps. The market for interest rate derivatives faced its first significant downturn, after recording an above average rate of growth in the first half of the year. In spite of that decrease, declining interest rates resulted in a 98.9% increase in the gross market value of interest rate derivatives, to $18.4 trillion. The picture looked rather different in the BIS's statistics at the end of June 2013. Single-currency interest rate derivatives, the largest part of the OTC derivatives market, dominated the global aggregates because of the importance of these derivatives in managing interest rate risks on private and public debt in the countries taking part in the semi-annual survey. The gross market value of all interest rate derivative contracts reached $2 trillion between end-2012 and mid-2013, a decline which was only partly due to the changes in exchange rates which lowered the dollar value of yen-denominated contracts.

The risks of swaps

The main risks involved with interest rate swaps are the interest rate risk and the counterparty risk. As defined, an interest rate swap is an agreement between two parties to exchange cash flows at a future agreed time. One makes payments based on a fixed interest rate and the other makes payments on a variable interest rate, usually determined by LIBOR. The risk is that the interest rates may not change in the way either party hopes. The one with the fixed interest rate risks the floating interest rate going higher, in which case that party loses interest payments which they would otherwise have received. The one with the variable interest rate risks interest rates going lower, which leaves them losing out on the cash flow, since the holder of the fixed-interest part of the swap (the fixed leg) still has to make the stream of payments to the counterparty.

The other main risk with swaps is the counterparty risk, that is, the risk that counterparty to a swap will default and be unable to meet the terms of the agreement. For instance, if the holder of the floating-rate leg cannot make the payments under the terms of the swap agreement, the holder of the fixed-rate leg is exposed to credit risk (i.e. to changes in the interest rate), which is precisely the risk the swap was drawn up to avoid.

LIBOR as a widely used reference rate

The development of interest rate derivatives shows how the application of LIBOR changed over the years, from its straightforward use in syndicated loans, to its use in floating-rate notes to interest rate derivatives and swaps in particular. Up to and during the financial crisis, LIBOR was extensively used as a reference rate, as a means of making the terms of contracts clear, so that funding risk could be managed. Even after the financial crisis and after the extent of attempts to manipulate LIBOR were revealed, it is still used as a benchmark for contracts running into trillions of dollars. Its use after the revelations of such corruption is due to a raft of reforms carried out since then. These reforms will be described in the next chapter.

Before examining the nature and extent of the manipulation of LIBOR, it is worth asking the question: are reference rates essential for the range of contracts described here? That they are useful is clear enough, but what are they for? Loans and derivatives are vast asset classes, and LIBOR is the dominant reference rate.

In the context of bank lending, the role of the reference rate is to enable banks to hedge their funding risks, which is why LIBOR is especially useful, since it reflects banks' funding costs. LIBOR is an estimate of a bank's current short-term funding costs. The risk in funding arises from the uncertainty surrounding short-term financing, but LIBOR as a reference rate is standardised, publicly available and contractible, that is, capable of being incorporated into a contract such as a swap. Hedging strategies are considered to be essential for banks to operate. The bank as lender can choose to offer only fixed-rate loans and to back these loans with certificates of deposit. Floating interest rates move the risk to the borrower, but an interest rate swap is designed to share this risk, though it does, of course, introduce further risks, such as unexpected changes in interest rates and the counterparty risk described above. Even then, the swap does provide more flexibility for the bank, which need not transfer the whole loan to the swap but only part of it. This might be the choice a bank makes if the transfer of the whole risk costs too much. These considerations explain why LIBOR continued to be used as a reference rate, well beyond its traditional use in syndicated loans, forward-rate agreements and floating-rate notes, and then its use continued when the surge in interest rate derivatives took place in the 1990s. It contained the necessary reference to bank funding. LIBOR was familiar and respected. The next two chapters will show why many saw that it was worth seeking to manipulate LIBOR, how they went about it and who was responsible.

Notes

1 Created in 1999, the Euro Interbank Offered Rate (EURIBOR) was the rate at which leading European banks were willing to lend to each other. The EURIBOR panel consisted of the 43 banks with the highest volume of business in the euro zone money markets, overseen by the European Banking Federation. The contributory banks all came from the euro zone but large international banks based in non-EU countries were also allowed to join the panel. It was the same structure as the BBA LIBOR. After the discovery of the manipulation of LIBOR, the European Benchmarks Regulation (2016/1011) changed all that and it is now overseen by a college of supervisors, chaired by the Belgian Financial Services Markets Authority. It is now a transaction-based system, calculated by the Global Rate Set System.

2 The term 'Eurodollar' is misleading. The Eurodollar was not a new currency but at first merely referred to US dollar-denominated deposits at foreign banks or foreign branches of American banks, which, since they were located outside the USA, escaped regulation by the Federal Reserve, including reserve requirements. By the 1970s, the currency base of the market broadened, as Deutschemarks, the yen and Canadian dollars became well established. More formally, a Eurodollar is a US dollar deposit, typically a 30–90-day or 180-day time deposit, which is placed in a bank outside the USA (often called a Eurobank). Neither the nationality of the bank nor the location of the supplier of funds is relevant, only the location of the bank accepting deposits.

3 Quoted in 'Insight: a Greek banker, the Shah and the birth of Libor', *Chicago Tribune*, 7 August 2012.

4 A. C. Chester, 'The international bond market', *Bank of England Quarterly Bulletin*, November 1991, p. 521.

5 D. Lascelles, *The Story of Minos Zombanakis: Banking Without Borders* (Economia Publishing, 2011), p. 85.

6 Quoted in Ian M. Kerr, *A History of the Eurobond Market: The First 21 Years* (Prentice Hall, 1984), p. 38.

7 P. Spira, *Ladders and Snakes: A Twist in the Spiral Staircase* (privately printed, 1997), pp. 164–5; Chris O'Malley, *Bonds Without Borders* (John Wiley & Sons, 2015), pp. 48–9.

8 Supplementary memorandum from the British Bankers' Association provided as written evidence to the Treasury Select Committee, session 2007–8, available at https://publications.parliament.uk/pa/cm200708/cm select/cmtreasy/536/536we05.htm (accessed October 1028).

9 Andrew Lamb, 'International banking in London, 1975–85', *Bank of England Quarterly Bulletin,* September 1986, p. 369, available at https://www.bankofengland.co.uk/-/media/boe/files/quarterly-bulletin/1986/international-banking-in-london-1975-85 (accessed 4 May 2018).

10 Brady bonds (so called after the Treasury Secretary, Nicholas Brady) were used to help international monetary organisations institute a programme of debt reduction by converting defaulting loans into US bonds with zero-coupon Treasury bonds as collateral. A decade later, Mexico, Argentina, Venezuela, Brazil and the Philippines were speeding up programmes to buy back high-interest Brady bonds and replace them with cheaper debt raised in the Eurobond or global bond market.

11 T. J. Allen, 'Developments in the international syndicated loan market in the 1980s', *Bank of England Quarterly Bulletin,* February 1990, pp. 71–2, available at https://www.bankofengland.co.uk/-/media/boe/files/quarterly-bulletin/1990/developments-in-the-international-syndicated-loan-market-in-the-1980s (accessed 4 May 2018).

12 B. Gadanecz, 'The syndicated loan market: structure, development and implications', *BIS Quarterly Review*, December 2004, p. 76, available at https://www.bis.org/publ/qtrpdf/r_qt0412g.htm (accessed 4 May 2018). Synthetic securitisation is defined as a transfer of risk from the bank by the use of credit derivatives or guarantees, but the exposure being securitised remains the exposure of the originator institution, that is, the bank or banks making the loan. Basically it is an insurance policy bought by banks to hedge against any risks in their loan as part of the lending syndicate.

13 Thomson Reuters, 'Syndicated loans review: full year 2011', available at http://dmi.thomsonreuters.com/content/files/4q11_global_loans_review.pdf (accessed 3 May 2018).

14 Quoted from *AIBD Gazette*, issue 13, May 1984, p. 20, by O'Malley, *Bonds Without Borders*, p. 82.

15 See note 2 above.

16 'The mighty Eurobond celebrates its 50th anniversary', *Euroweek,* 28 June 2013.

17 Ibid.

18 Swaps are an agreement between two parties, where each party agrees to exchange future cash flows, such as interest rate payments, but they do not derive their values from an underlying asset. The so-called 'plain vanilla' swap is one in which both parties agree to exchange interest rates, when, for example, one is based on a fixed interest rate, while the other is based on a floating interest rate. Apparently, they were called 'plain vanilla' because they were as bland as American vanilla ice cream. A derivative is also a contract between two parties, but its value is determined by the underlying asset's price, which could be derived from the performance of an asset, index, interest rate, commodity or currency.

19 G. M. S. Hammond, 'Recent developments in the swap market', *Bank of England Quarterly Bulletin*, February 1987, pp. 66–79, at p. 67, available at https://www.bankofengland.co.uk/-/media/boe/files/quarterly-bulletin/1987/recent-developments-in-the-swap-market (accessed 4 May 2018).

20 Amortising swaps are swaps with a decreasing principal amount set out in a predefined schedule and are usually used to hedge a stream of amortising payments, for example a floating-rate mortgage, or to an interest rate benchmark such as LIBOR. Forward swaps have all the characteristics of a

standard interest rate swap but start on a predetermined future date. They allow fixing of the interest rate today for interest rate obligations which will start at a certain time in the future. A zero-coupon swap is an exchange of income streams in which the stream of fixed-rate payments is made as one lump-sum payment when the swap reaches maturity. A swaption is the option, but not the obligation, to enter into a specified swap agreement with the issuer on a future date. An overnight index swap is an interest rate swap involving the overnight rate being exchanged for a fixed interest rate, using an overnight rate index. A callable swap is an interest rate swap where the fixed-rate payer has the right but not the obligation to end the swap at one or more predetermined dates during the life of the swap. A multi-legged swap usually involves a series of bilateral contracts between each party and an intermediary bank, which are transacted at the same time.

21   Hammond, 'Recent developments in the swap market', p. 73. Her name is given only in a footnote at the bottom of the first page, where she is described as a member of the Bank's International Division.

22   Ibid., p. 74.

23   The BIS defined 'gross market value' as 'the sum (in absolute terms) of the positive market value of all reporters' contracts and the negative market value of reporters' contracts with non-reporters'. It is a measure of 'the replacement costs of all outstanding contracts' and it also indicates the reporters' aggregate gross credit exposure. 'Reporters' are the banks surveyed. Bank for International Settlements, 'The global OTC derivatives market at the end-June 1998', press release, 23 December 1998, at https://www.bis.org/press/p981223.htm (accessed May 2018).

Chapter 3

Manipulation abounds

In the previous chapter, market developments leading up to LIBOR being established as a formal benchmark were set out. Once that was achieved in 1986 and refined in 1998, LIBOR became the most widely used benchmark in the world with its 150 specific rates every weekday, 15 for each of the currencies listed below, of which the listings in the four leading currencies – US dollar, the euro, the British pound and the Swiss franc – were most frequently used. Among the most important derivatives depending on LIBOR were interest rate swaps, swaptions, swap futures and options, as well as most floating-rate mortgages, many commercial loans, money market deposit accounts, structured products, such as mortgages and other asset-backed securities, credit products, accounting, tax and capital and risk valuation methods. It was a far cry from its modest beginnings as an informal benchmark for syndicated loans. The present chapter will cover why and when uncertainties about the reliability of LIBOR arose during 2008, in the midst of the financial crisis.

Doubts set in

It was during the financial crisis that reliance on LIBOR was undermined, probably sparked by two articles in 2008 in the *Wall Street Journal* which suggested that a number of banks may have reported flawed interest data for LIBOR.[1] One article concerned a study commissioned by Carrick Mollenkamp and Mark Whitehouse which suggested that Citigroup, West LB, HBOS, JP Morgan Chase and UBS were among the banks that reported significantly lower borrowing costs for LIBOR than another market measure indicated that they should be. The *Journal* compared the numbers from the default insurance market, which provides an insight into the financial strength of banks. The cost of insuring banks against defaulting on their debts and the borrowing rates indicated by LIBOR increased when the markets thought that certain banks were in difficulties. From late January 2008 onwards, the gap between the two rates began to widen. It was wider for five of the banks than for another 11 banks, with one possible explanation being that some banks understated their borrowing costs. The article indicated that there could be a number of reasons for that, including the fact that banks had virtually stopped lending to each other for three months or more, so their estimates of the costs of borrowing could be largely guesswork. US banks such as Citigroup had large customer deposits and the ability to borrow from the Federal Reserve, which meant that they could borrow at a reduced rate (although banks were wary of borrowing from the Federal Reserve as, if detected, that would be interpreted by depositors, analysts and creditors as a sign of financial weakness). The *Wall Street Journal*, however, argued that the analysis was sound, had been thoroughly reviewed and enabled a reconstruction of what the borrowing rate should have been, based on the default-insurance figures, which showed that the LIBOR was lower for Citigroup by 0.87%, 0.7% for WestLB, 0.57% for HBOS and 0.42% for UBS between late January and 16 April, the date of the first report of doubts.

Early warnings

When the regulators finally released the results of their investigations, it became clear that early warnings from a variety of sources had been overlooked. Evidence given at the trial of Tom Hayes (a trader standing accused of dishonestly manipulating LIBOR) in June 2015 indicated that the BBA had been warned that some banks were deliberately distorting their LIBOR submissions for profit as long ago as 2005.[2] In an article on the trial for Reuters, Anjuli Davies reported that BBA notes made at the time following 'relationship visits' stated that banks such as Credit Suisse were concerned about the quoted rates. Representatives at Credit Suisse had told the BBA that they had accepted 'that different banks have different costs of capital but suspect that certain banks may be quoting high or low depending on the shape of their book or loan portfolio at any given point in time'. Representatives of JP Morgan stated that 'GBP and the USD LIBOR are higher than the true position but everyone in the market knows this and prices accordingly. Do not want the BBA to attempt to "correct" this.' In June 2005, both the Bank of Japan and the Japanese Ministry of Finance had 'made it clear' that '"they don't want to see negative BBA YEN LIBOR rates being set even if this would be reflective of reality", Citigroup representatives told the BBA'.[3]

The very early warnings seem to have been ignored. What is perhaps more serious is that apart from the FSA's own assessments of the market, reports from external sources, such as the reference banks, were not taken on board between 2007 and 2009. The FSA's internal audit report (of March 2013) covering that period lists at least 30 occasions out of a total of 74 on which various members of its staff received inside information from the banks. The report notes that Barclays disclosed to the Treasury Committee 13 contacts it had with the FSA where LIBOR fixings were mentioned, of which three were itemised in the 'final notice'[4] issued to Barclays on 27 June 2012. Some examples of the communications between the FSA and individual banks have been selected from the FSA's internal audit report:

> Note for the record of a liquidity visit to a LIBOR Panel Bank [by staff at the FSA, 6 December 2007]. '[The LIBOR Panel Bank] have questions over the quality of certain LIBOR fixes across the currencies – with the feeling that many may be too low.'

This was a note of a liquidity visit to a LIBOR panel bank, at which the FSA was represented by staff from the Wholesale Firms Division, Prudential Policy Division and the Wholesale Management Services Unit.[5]

An email summarising certain financial institutions' views of wholesale funding conditions noted the following comment from a LIBOR panel bank:

> There is very little interbank lending past 0/N, liquidity conditions past 1 month are still poor. Where cash is available, it is expensive this is not really spinning over into Libors, or at least only marginally.

This was circulated to the chief executive and directors of the FSA.

A compliance officer at a non-LIBOR panel bank contacted its FSA supervisor on 1 April 2008 claiming that:

> The issue is that the LIBOR rate is daily being set at least 25bp to 30 bp below what can be obtained in the market. This has the impact of distorting the market as a number of products are based on LIBOR. If the contributor banks are quoting below market rates, then surely they should be made to lend at least a certain amount at these rates.[6]

On 7 April 2008, during a conference call with a non-LIBOR bank on its funding position, a supervisor noted that:

> US LIBOR appears to be low compared to US cash. European investors can make use of FX arbitrage to swap US LIBOR ... back to £ sub-LIBOR.

On 9 April, one of the supervisors present at the conference call followed up in an email, stating that the supervisors would pass on 'their concerns that US LIBOR might be manipulated'.[7] In October 2008, a non-LIBOR panel bank commented:

> current GBP LIBOR fixings do not reflect the true price of offers in the interbank market, if and when they do materialise. All LIBOR fixings have also registered large reductions but where they are fixing and where they are trading is a wholly different story.[8]

Of the LIBOR panel banks, Barclays was the only one to have reported its views on the LIBOR fixings to the FSA. One example is its comment in a routine liquidity call with the FSA:

> We did stick our heads above the parapet last year, got it shot off, and put it back down again. So to the extent that ... the LIBORs have been understated, are we guilty of being part of the pack? You could say we are. We've always been at the top end and therefore one of the four banks that's been eliminated.... So I would, I would sort of express us maybe as not clean clean, but clean in principle.[9]

Ironically, Barclays was the first bank to be investigated by the FSA.

Surely, with so many warnings, the FSA should have investigated LIBOR more thoroughly and promptly. However, as the internal audit report recognises, between 2007 and 2009 the FSA's focus was inevitably on 'deteriorating market conditions for individual firms' capital and liquidity conditions and in some cases their very viability'.[10] Even so, the report concluded that the likelihood that 'lowballing' was occurring should have been considered. In reply, the FSA's chairman, Adair Turner, argued:

> the FSA's bank supervisors were primarily focused on ensuring that they understood the prudential implications of severe market dislocation. And the FSA had no formal regulatory responsibility for the LIBOR submission process.[11]

Adair Turner did have a point with regard to the domination of the financial crisis. It is easy now to forget its severity – the global financial system teetered on the verge of collapse. Turner added:

all of the authorities, both UK and US and elsewhere only discovered trader manipulation as a by-product of enquiries launched into potential lowballing.[12]

There are one or two hints of manipulation of LIBOR in the examples quoted but they are very indirect. Since it was later discovered that that manipulation apparently went back to 2005 on the part of some banks, the banks should have developed the tools to be aware of what was happening. Developing the management tools for dealing with so much information is, as Turner readily agrees, essential. The internal audit team reviewed 97,000 documents in detail and only 26 were judged as providing a direct reference to lowballing or a reference that could have been interpreted as such.

Investigating banks

In response to pressures from the media and from regulators, the FSA began its investigation into Barclays first in 2010, two years after the US Commodity Futures Trading Commission (CFTC) began its own investigations. The necessity for such investigations was not acknowledged by other authorities, such as the Bank for International Settlements, whose *Quarterly Review* in March 2008 stated that the 'available data does not support the hypothesis that contributor banks manipulated their quotes to profit from positions based on the fixings'.[13] In October 2008, the International Monetary Fund (IMF) stated in its *Global Financial Stability Report*:

> although the integrity of the U.S. dollar LIBOR fixing process has been questioned by some market participants and the financial press, it appears that the U.S. dollar LIBOR remains an accurate measure of a typical creditworthy bank's marginal costs of unsecured U.S. dollar term functioning.[14]

Since these documents appeared during the financial crisis and did not raise the most demanding issue facing regulators and central banks, namely fighting to restore stability to the global financial system, in most cases the investigations did not take place immediately and the outcomes were not revealed until 2012 and subsequent years. The FSA, having started later than the others, was in fact first to issue notices and impose fines, with the CFTC following with its first imposition of fines in 2014. These investigations took many months, since they involved interviewing witnesses and examining hundreds of emails and tapes of telephone calls. The final notices of the FSA and its successor from 2013, the Financial Conduct Authority (FCA), the CFTC's enforcement actions and to a lesser extent the European Commission's press releases regarding the various anti-trust fines imposed on banks for allegedly manipulating LIBOR provide the most information. The Commission's press releases provide little insight into the behaviour of the banks. The final notices issued by the FSA and the FCA clearly set out the reasons for the fines and the ways in which LIBOR manipulation took place, as does the CFTC (and the US Department of Justice). A selection of the emails, oral trader requests to submitters and trader-to-trader requests are presented in the remainder of this chapter, for two leading UK banks, Barclays and the Royal Bank of Scotland (RBS), so that the nature of the evidence is clear.

Barclays

The FSA's final notice to Barclays Bank, 27 June 2012

Barclays was a contributor to various benchmark rates, including LIBOR and EURIBOR, published by the European Banking Federation (EBF), making submissions for LIBOR in 10 currencies and at 15 maturities from overnight to one year in each currency and for EURIBOR also in 15 maturities on a daily basis. Responsibility for determining the LIBOR and EURIBOR submissions rested with the money market desks within the bank, as they managed Barclays' liquidity position and were therefore best placed to assess the rates at which cash would be available to Barclays within the money markets. They should have been weighing up a range of factors relating to the interbank market each day to determine the LIBOR and EURIBOR submissions. In making that determination, submitters may have consulted with (as opposed to colluded with) interdealer brokers, key conduits in the market of information. The interdealer brokers would have several screens of data on their desks as well as a constant stream of information coming in by telephone and internet chat rooms and instant messaging provided by Bloomberg or Reuters, with news, jokes, market sentiment and industry gossip. The submitters, however, who should have been giving an independent view, often took other factors into account and based their submissions on those. This is, of course, the nub of manipulation of LIBOR and EURIBOR.

Submissions at the request of derivatives traders

Barclays made frequent US dollar LIBOR and EURIBOR submissions between January 2005 and July 2008, which took into account requests made by its interest rate derivatives traders. These sometimes included requests made on behalf of derivatives traders at other banks. These, according the FSA, were 'motivated by profit and sought to benefit Barclays' trading positions'.[15]

At Barclays, many of the money market desks (responsible for determining its LIBOR and EURIBOR submissions) were close to the derivatives traders' desks, so that the submitters were aware of the latter's trading positions. At least one derivatives trader would, before making a request to the submitters, shout across the euro swaps desk to confirm that other traders had no conflicting requests. The requests were made verbally as well as by email and instant messaging. Requests were made routinely, by at least 14 traders, and involved trading desk managers as well as submitters. Some examples of the emails are given below.

On 16 March 2006, in response to trader C's request for a high one-month and a low three-month US dollar submission, a submitter replied:

> For you … anything. I am going to go to 78 and 92.5. It is difficult to go lower than threes, looking at where the cash is trading. In fact, if you did not want a low one I would have gone to 93 at least.[16]

The FSA's analysis concluded that on the majority of occasions when Barclays' submitters were contacted by Barclays' derivatives traders with requests, Barclays' submissions were consistent with those requests. Requests were made by external traders as well, often traders who had previously worked at Barclays but now worked at non-LIBOR panel banks. For example, on 26 October 2006, an external trader asked for a three-month US dollar LIBOR submission from trader G at Barclays, saying 'If it comes in unchanged, I'm a dead man'. Trader G promised to 'have a chat' and the submission came in half a basis point lower than it was the day before. The external trader thanked trader G for Barclays' LIBOR submission. He said, 'Dude. I owe you big time! Come over one day after work and I'm opening a bottle of Bollinger.'[17] The FSA notes that on at least 20 occasions, EURIBOR requests were made on behalf of external traders working at banks which were not panel banks for EURIBOR. For example, on 1 February 2007 the same external trader sent several messages to trader E requesting a low one-month submission. Trader E passed on the request to a submitter, who responded positively.[18]

Barclays' involvement did not stop there. The derivatives traders attempted to influence the EURIOBOR and, though to a much lesser extent, US dollar LIBOR by asking external traders at other banks to make submissions according to the needs of Barclays' traders. The FSA notes that one of the derivatives traders established a coordinated strategy to align Barclays' positions with those of traders at other banks and so influence EURIBOR. The methods used involved making internal requests to Barclays' submitters and external requests to traders at other contributing banks in advance of and on particular days on which the derivatives traders stood to benefit. Their efforts even went as far as encouraging cash traders to make bids or enter into transactions which might influence (albeit indirectly) the EURIBOR submissions of any contributing bank.

The FSA gives an example of trader E's activities when working towards an 'IMM' date (that is, an international money market quarterly settlement date for traded interest rate futures contracts) of 19 March 2007. He got in touch with traders at three panel banks in advance of that date. An instant message with a trader at one of the banks read:

> If you know how to keep a secret I'll bring you in on it … we're going to push the cash downwards on the imm day … if you breathe a word of this, I'm not telling you anything else … I know my treasury's firepower … which will push the cash downwards … please keep it to yourself otherwise it won't work.

Trader E continued to keep in contact with other traders until 16 March, the last working day before the IMM day, asking for a low three-month EURIBOR submission to traders at two of the panel banks, which he had already discussed with a trader at the third bank. He made further requests on 19 March 2007, including asking a trader at yet another panel bank to 'tell your cash to put the 3m fixing in the basement'. The traders concluded that these and other strategies had been successful.

Trader E commented to a trader at one of the panel banks:

> this is the way you pull off deals like this chicken, don't talk too much, 2 months of preparation … the trick is you must not do this alone … this is between you and me but really don't tell ANYBODY.

Others, without a vested interest, observed what was going on. A trader at a hedge fund commented to trader E, also on 19 March 2007:

It's becoming very dangerous to trade in 3m imms ... especially when Barclays sets the 3m very low ... it does draw attention to you guys. It doesn't look very professional.[19]

All of this made it quite clear, according to the FSA, that Barclays took the derivatives traders' positions into account, when the rules did not allow for this. This is based on the frequency and regularity of traders' requests, the positive responses from Barclays' submitters, the evidence provided by the submitters and the consistency of Barclays' submissions with its derivatives traders' requests.

The impact of negative media comment on Barclays' LIBOR submissions

The FSA concluded that between September 2007 and May 2009, Barclays submitted LIBOR positions 'which took into account concerns over the negative media perception of Barclays' LIBOR submissions'.[20] Liquidity issues were a major concern for Barclays and other banks at that time, especially after the collapse of Lehman Brothers in September 2008. Barclays had higher LIBOR submissions than other banks, which, in Barclays' view, were too low and did not reflect market conditions. For example, Bloomberg published an article entitled 'Barclays takes a money market beating' which noted that Barclays' LIBOR submissions in three-month sterling, euro and US dollars were the highest of all banks on the LIBOR panel. That gave rise to the question, 'What the hell is happening at Barclays and its Barclays Capital securities unit that is prompting its peers to charge it premium interest rates in the money market?'[21]

Barclays was at the centre of adverse publicity related to the lack of liquidity in the market. The FSA notes that towards the end of August 2007, it became known that Barclays had borrowed from the Bank of England's emergency standby facility twice in a fortnight. Its LIBOR submissions during 2007 and 2008 were often higher than those of other banks. A submitter expressed the view in an internal email that:

> Today's USD LIBORS have come out and they look too low to me.... Probably the lowest rate you could get in threes would be 5.5% and I am not too sure how much you would get at that level. For that reason I went to 5.58% perhaps a bit high but realistic.... It is true to say that, if a lender has room for your name, you can achieve very attractive funding levels at a rate well below LIBOR. It would, however, be imprudent to assume that it is always going to be the case that investors have credit for your name, especially in view of the general reluctance to place money

for longer than one month. Draw your own conclusions about why people are going for unrealistically low libors [often called 'lowballing'].

The FSA noted that 'the Submitter believed that Barclays was submitting US dollar LIBOR at an appropriate level at that time, but by the next day he indicated that Barclays (and in his view other banks) should be submitting LIBOR at a higher level'.[22]

Barclays' LIBOR submissions were usually at the higher end of the range, as the FSA pointed out. From 1 September 2007 to 31 December 2008, Barclays' three-month US dollar submissions were higher than the submissions of 12 of the other contributing banks on 66% of occasions. That was despite the best efforts of the senior managers. Although the latter did not directly seek to influence the submitters, lower-level managers received the impression that it might be appropriate for them to do just that. For example, by 28 November 2007, one submitter stated in an internal email:

> LIBORS are not reflecting the true cost of money. I am going to set 2 and 3 months, 5.13 and 5.12 probably at the top of the range of rates set by libor contributors, although brokers tell me that [Panel Bank 7] is going to set at 5.15 for both (up 8.5 and 10 from yesterday). The true cost of money is anything from 5–15 basis points higher. Not really sure why contributors are keeping them so low but it is not a good idea at the moment to be seen too far away from the pack, although reality seems to be setting in for a few libor contributors who are belatedly moving libors up in line with where the money is really trading.

Manager D replied, 'Fine on LIBOR settings – thanks for remaining pragmatic but at the upper end'.[23]

LIBOR submitters were required to continue to reduce Barclays' submissions throughout 2007 and into 2008. On 17 March 2008, Bear Stearns was acquired by JP Morgan to prevent the collapse of the former. The shock led to another period of extreme illiquidity in the market. The submitters were told by telephone to set their LIBORs where the rest of the market was setting them. For example, in response to a question from a submitter, 'I presume then that you want me now to set [Barclays] LIBORS ... exactly where the market is setting them?', manager E confirmed that he did. In a routine call to the FSA regarding liquidity, manager D referred to the lack of 'term money' and its effect on LIBOR:

> Some people consider LIBOR to be set too low, but then others reply, well, they are not being set too low because there aren't really any offers

there.... I think that people just generally recognise that in the absence of actual flows in those periods, where LIBORS are being posted, is perhaps as good an indication as anything.... So if transactions aren't really going on, or there are only odd transactions with certain names, then what is the right LIBOR?[24]

So, apart from lowering its LIBOR submissions in response to criticism from the financial press, Barclays claimed that the lack of transactions made it impossible to know what the LIBORs really were.

Royal Bank of Scotland

The FSA issued its final notice to the Royal Bank of Scotland (RBS) on 6 February 2013, after examining and assessing the process of setting LIBORs. On the same day, the US CFTC issued its own 'Order ... making findings and imposing remedial sanctions'.[25] The CFTC and the FCA worked together in gathering evidence on RBS's behaviour (as they did in relation to other banks). The attempts to manipulate yen and Swiss franc LIBOR continued despite questions in the media in 2007 and 2008 about the integrity of banks' LIBOR submissions, LIBOR guidance and reviews by the BBA in 2008 and 2009, and the CFTC's request in April 2010 that RBS conduct an internal investigation into its US dollar LIBOR practices. Its derivative and money market trading positions were indexed to (and hence value based on) yen and Swiss franc LIBORs. These products included interest rate swaps, forward rate agreements, foreign exchange forwards, cross-currency swaps, overnight index swaps and tenor basis swaps.

Before October 2006, RBS's money market desks and derivatives desks were separate business units with little interaction. In January 2006, managers at RBS began to consider the business benefits of combining the two desks to create a unified short-term markets (STM) desk. By mid-2006, the yen swaps market became much more active and trading volume increased. This allowed traders to share information about currencies and markets with the money market traders, so giving them the opportunity to learn how to manage risk more effectively. The idea was discussed throughout the organisation, including at senior management level. But, as the FSA pointed out, the issue of conflicts of interest (and hence compliance risks) was never discussed. Following the establishment of the STM desk in London, the money market traders (including the primary submitters) sat alongside the derivatives traders and the two groups were encouraged by managers to share information about currencies and markets, including what their trading positions were, with no limitations on what could be discussed.

LIBOR and LIBOR submissions could impact the profitability of RBS's money market books in a variety of ways. LIBOR determined the cost of large new cash transactions, and the primary submitters were sometimes advised in advance of the details, including the amount and tenor (the amount of time left for the repayment of the loan or until a financial contract expires) of large forthcoming cash transactions. Borrowing and lending facilities were reset or rolled over with reference to LIBOR and again the primary submitters had access to information which enabled them to predict in advance the details of these trans-actions. Naturally, the money market traders developed a range of strategies to profit from the differences in LIBORs and to use derivatives to hedge their money market risk.

Manipulation of submissions to benefit derivatives trading books

As noted above, the remodelling of the desk arrangements meant that it was easy for the traders to ask the primary submitters to put in the LIBOR submissions they wanted. There was no record of this, as all of these requests were made verbally and surprised no one in the room. This arrangement persisted until late 2008, when the money market desks and the derivatives trader desks became separate business units once again. The derivative traders were motivated by profit both for themselves and for RBS's trading positions and so they sought to affect the final LIBOR position by influencing RBS's LIBOR submissions. These requests took place over a number of years, in relation to at least 300 benchmarks, and involving 21 derivatives traders and submitters, not only in the London and Tokyo offices but also in the USA and Singa-pore. According to the FSA, between December 2008 and November 2010, there were 96 requests regarding yen LIBOR submissions, 53 regarding Swiss franc LIBOR and five regarding US dollar LIBOR. Derivatives traders' requests and their implications are itemised by the FSA in its final notice to RSB.

The primary submitters were supposed simply to consider market information in determining RBS's yen and Swiss franc LIBOR sub-missions, such as RBS's funding needs, money market transactions, futures and other derivative prices, 'market colour' communications with derivatives traders, information from interdealer brokers, arbitrage transactions and synthetic cash deposits in various currencies. But it seems that all that could be swept aside when submitters were asked to consider requests from the derivatives traders to benefit their positions or indeed their own positions.

The CFTC's report shows that RBS decided to increase its activity in the yen swaps market, so the bank recruited two experienced yen derivatives traders for its subsidiary in Tokyo, one to act as a manager responsible for RBS's yen trading globally and the other as a senior yen derivatives trader, and both were given significant discretion to assume great risks and to establish RBS as a major player in the yen interest rate derivatives market. That they did, starting from a small loss to a gain of over $20 million between 2006 and 2007. In 2008 revenues exceeded $90 million, and in 2009 to 2010 a further $90 million or more. RBS's yen derivatives were traded 24 hours a day from RBS trading desks in the USA, the UK and Asia under the direction of the yen manager and senior yen trader, with the latter focusing on short-term tenors, assisted by a yen derivatives trader in Connecticut and a yen trader in London, who was also the back-up yen LIBOR submitter. The yen manager usually managed the trading of longer-term tenors, assisted by another yen derivatives trader in London.

The requests, which were made openly on trading floors in Asia and London, were usually for the most frequently traded tenors: one month, three months and six months. To maximise profit, the traders either asked for specific rates to be submitted or asked for a directional move (higher or lower), either for a particular day or for several days and sometimes even weeks.

LIBOR *submitters acceded to traders' requests*

To a request made by derivatives trader A to submitter B, 'Can we pls get a very very very low 3m and 6m fix today, pls, we have rather large fixings!', the submitter replied 'Perfect, if that's what you want'. The trader then added, 'tks, and then from tomorrow, we need them thru the roof!!!' Primary submitter B agreed, and the three-month submissions were consistent with trader A's requests on those days.[26]

May 3, 2007
Senior Yen Trader: can you drop a note to [primary submitter] to set low 1m and low 3m JYP Libor today please? Thanks
Yen Trader 5: just gave him a shout, said already on it.[27]

As the CFTC points out, the senior yen trader and other yen traders knew that they could affect the fixing of the daily yen LIBOR and that their submissions could be called into question by the BBA. Here the senior yen trader boasts about how RBS succeeded in moving the six-month yen LIBOR and then discussed how they could justify a low submission to the BBA:

> April 2, 2008
> Senior Yen Trader: nice libor. Our 6m fixing move the entire fixing. Hahaha.
> Yen Trader 1: the BBA called me to ask me about that today.
> Senior Yen Trader: they complain?
> Yen Trader 1: no just to make sure I was happy with it....
> Senior Yen Trader: i think some banks must have complain
> Yen Trader 1: he called b4 any of the other banks saw out data, at about 11.15 to check it was ok.
> Senior Yen Trader: oh then its fine.

He then added:

> we will say we lower every tenor ... 1m 3m 6m ... we feel rbs name has very good credit ... no problem getting money in a good way to boost share price! Our 3m libor is at the top end ... 6m at bottom end ... just the ideal level![28]

Substitute submitters

The FSA also records the way in which substitute submitters took not only their own but also other derivatives traders' positions into account when making RBS's yen LIBOR submissions. For example, on 21 August 2007, manager A asked derivatives trader B via Bloomberg chat where he was calling LIBOR, to which the trader replied 'Where would you like it? LIBOR, that is ... same as yesterday's call'. The chat continued with multiple derivatives traders expressing their LIBOR preferences. Trader B then said he would go the 'same as yesterday' and 'maybe a touch higher tomorrow'.[29]

Collusion with panel banks and broker firms

Between February 2007 and June 2010, derivatives traders attempted to influence yen LIBOR submissions of panel banks either through broker firms or directly. Requests were also received from external traders and a broker who tried to influence RBS's yen and Swiss franc submissions but none of this was ever reported to compliance or the FSA. For example, the FSA reports that derivatives trader B phoned broker A at one of the broker firms on 26 June 2009:

> 'Has [external trader A] been asking you to put LIBOR's up today?' Broker A responded, 'He wants ... ones and threes a little bit lower and sixes probably about the same as they are now. He wants them to stay the same.' Derivatives Trader B replied, 'I want them lower...'. Broker A then stated, 'Alright, well, alright, alright, we'll work on it.'

Later that same day, broker A responded:

> just confirming it.... We've spoke to a couple of people so we'll see where they come in alright.... There's a couple of other people that the boys have spoke to but as a team we've basically said we want a bit lower so we'll see where they come in alright? [30]

They 'spoke to' four panel banks in all. The number of panel banks involved is significant – seven in all, showing that the attempt to obtain the right level for LIBOR could involve a number of people. The method the two RBS derivatives traders used was to influence the submissions through requests from external traders and a broker to alter RBS's yen and Swiss franc LIBOR submissions. At other times, a trader made requests directly to external traders and another derivatives trader made requests to brokers who then made requests to panel banks.

On 14 September 2009, trader B asked for a 'high 3 and 6s please'. This was followed the next day by a request for the fixings to be lowered, to which primary submitter B replied: 'Make your mind up, haha, yes no probs'. Trader B: 'im like a whores drawers'. [31]

These requests often changed very rapidly because their trading positions changed equally rapidly, again underlining the fact that the submissions often had nothing to do with activities in the interbank money market. [32] All of this continued until well into 2010, by which time the bank had been informed about potential misconduct in relation to LIBOR submissions. The FSA quotes the emails and other exchanges between traders and submitters, which show that the submitters were sufficiently aware of the issue, but only to the extent that they knew they had to be discreet: no more emails and no more conversations over Bloomberg. The conversations also show that the new guidelines issued by the BBA were not being taken very seriously.

The CFTC docket is more forthcoming about RBS's awareness that other banks were also manipulating yen LIBOR. RBS's senior yen trader, yen manager and other yen traders coordinated their requests for beneficial LIBOR submissions with the primary submitter; 'they discussed at times how the Yen LIBOR panel was a "cartel" in which rates were being "manipulated"', ironically![33] They talked about how the UBS yen trader was also manipulating the yen LIBOR by coordinating with others:

> Despite the recognition that manipulation was occurring, at least one RBS trader welcomed having the UBS Yen Trader in the market because his aggressive trading brought increased liquidity, allowing traders, such as the RBS traders, to take on larger positions and potentially obtain greater trading profits.[34]

Here is an example of such exchanges:

August 20, 2007
Yen Manager: it seems to be [UBS] is pushing for these libors partnering up with a number of cash guys as well.
Yen Trader 2: yeah [UBS Yen Trader] all over it.

August 20, 2007
Senior Yen Trader: this libor is getting nuts
Bank A Trader: im puzzled as to why 3m libor fixing not coming off after the FED action.
Bank B Trader: [UBS] is lending dolls through my currencies in 3 month do u see him doing the same in urs
Senior Yen Trader: yes, he always led usd in my mkt, the JPY libor is a cartel now
Senior Yen Trader: its jst amazing how libor fixing can make you that much money.[35]

What also happened was that RBS, through two traders, colluded with the UBS yen trader in coordinated attempts to manipulate the yen LIBOR. From early 2007 to at least late 2008, the UBS yen trader, who was a former employee of yen trader 2 at RBS, attempted to manipulate yen LIBOR to his advantage. The two traders often discussed how change in the yen LIBOR could benefit their respective trading positions. The UBS yen trader asked yen trader 2 at RBS to ask the primary submitter for certain submissions and yen 2 trader often did so. The primary submitter agreed to carry out some of these requests. For example:

February 9, 2007
UBS Yen Trader: thx help 1m/y/day appreciated

Yen Trader 2: no worries

UBS Yen Trader: can you ask for a low 1m again today pls if oK/ todays fix is 12m you need anything on 3m or 6m?

Yen Trader 2; no my book is still tiny i will go for a low libor again. It suits me too as i am short the spreads

UBS Yen Trader: ok thanks

Yen Trader 2: i told my cash guy i want low 1m and 3m fixes and high 6m that suits uu right??

UBS Yen Trader: yes absolutely, is that ok with you? We will be exactly the same ... I am going to talk to Bank E as well.

Yen Trader 2: perfect.

UBS Yen trader: cool ... you in Monday?

Yen Trader2: yeah a bit

UBS Yen Trader: ok get them to set the same fixes Monday as well if ok.

Yen Trader 2: sure.

February 15, 2007

Yen Trader 2: how many people can y get to put this 1m libor low

UBS Yen Trader: well us, [Bank E] and a few others i think.[36]

It is possible that this was more one-way traffic, with the UBS yen trader asking for help from yen trader 2 than the other way round.

A former colleague of the UBS yen trader, an RBS sterling cash trader in London, also assisted the UBS yen trader in his efforts to manipulate LIBOR. He was a friend of the primary submitter and readily agreed to help the UBS yen trader, asking the primary submitter to make submissions reflecting the rates specified by the UBS yen trader. The primary submitter readily agreed:

May 7, 208

UBS Yen Trader: Hi [Sterling Cash Trader] if this is you can you pls ask for a low 6m in jpy for the next few days. Hope you are ok, was good seeing you last week. Cheers.

Sterling Cash Trader: Hi mate, I mentioned it to our guy on Friday and he seemed to have no problem with it, so fingers crossed.[37]

RBS also attempted to manipulate Swiss franc LIBOR from at least late 2006 until mid-2009 through the activities of the principal Swiss franc trader and the primary submitter. From December 2006, they sat together, as part of the short-term markets arrangement. They were the only two senior traders in the Swiss franc at RBS. The requests typically related to the three- and six-month tenors of the Swiss franc. These were often considered by the primary submitter, who frequently based his submissions on the trader's requests, except when he needed to make submissions to benefit his own money market and derivatives trading positions. Occasionally the requests were made in writing:

> December 31, 2008
> Swiss Franc Trader: High 3m libor pls!!!
> Primary Submitter: ok if I must
> Swiss Franc Trader: Yes pls U the man.

> March 19, 2009
> Swiss Franc Trader: Hello Mr, can we go unch for libors again pls? 42 54? or any lower in 6m would make u the best guy ever.
> Primary Submitter: 40 52
> Swiss Franc Trader: can we make the 3 m higher pretty pretty please? How about 41 53?
> Primary Submitter: ok you win
> Swiss Franc Trader: u r the man.[38]

The Swiss franc trader at RBS colluded with a former RBS trader who was then working for another bank (bank E). They talked nearly every day on Bloomberg chats, discussing their respective trading positions linked to LIBOR, their preferred LIBOR and their potential benefit from such rates and the requests they made to their own submitters. For example:

> April 15, 200
> Bank E Swiss Franc Trader: you know what I hope, that libor 3m is not going up
> Swiss Franc Trader: Yes ... should not go up. Just hang here ok just weird that zurich put it at 2.77 today
> Swiss Franc Trader: So fx basis will be negative if 3m usd ever starts to go down.
> Bank E Swiss Franc Trader: you should tell [Primary Submitter] if you can the set it at 2.78
> Swiss Franc Trader: I ask him for a low today 3m and 6m.

> May 14, 2009
> [Related Bloomberg chats reflecting attempts to manipulate Swiss Franc LIBOR.] ...
> Swiss Franc Trader: we are good!
> Bank E Swiss Franc Trader: yes look at it now low libor and chf libor good too
> Swiss Franc Trader: [Primary Submitter] did me a big favour today he set 41 and 51
> Bank E Swiss Franc Trader: sweet.[39]

Wash trades

The FSA final notice identifies a yen derivatives trader at RBS who knowingly engaged in at least 30 'wash trades' to enable corrupt brokerage payments to broker firms between September 2008 and August 2009. Wash trades involve a trader buying and selling the same securities simultaneously. These may benefit the broker, who can earn commission from the trades. The RBS derivatives trader made two wash trades so that he could make corrupt brokerage payments of over £12,000 to a particular broker firm. This was designed to give him influence to press the broker firm to persuade panel banks to change their LIBOR submissions to benefit his trading positions.

The use of wash trades became ever more complicated and costly. Trader B entered into at least 23 wash trades with a panel bank and paid at least £199,000 to facilitate corrupt payments to two broker firms to increase his influence over them. At the same time, trader B also knowingly entered into five wash trades with a panel bank which did not receive any brokerage payments, but instead paid a broker firm as a reward to that firm for its efforts to influence the panel bank's yen LIBOR submissions. All of this took place between September 2008 and August 2009.

The FSA provides some examples of the complexity of the wash (or 'switch') trade agreements, such as a series of telephone calls between a broker and derivatives trader B:

> Broker A said to Derivatives Trader B, 'I need a massive, massive favour.... Can you flat switch me something? Won't cost you any money.... It's going to make our week mate ... I obviously won't bro [charge a brokerage fee] it on it ... but [External Trader A] is going to bro on both sides.[40]

On 3 December 2008, trader B executed the wash trades and RBS did not pay any brokerage.

According to the CFTC, yen trader 1 did engage in the attempts to manipulate the yen LIBOR through interdealer brokers and wash trades, while at the same time wondering how effective his attempts would be, given that the UBS yen trader 1 was so active. For example, in August 2007 he commented to the senior trader about the information he had acquired from interdealer broker B: 'i was out with [Interdealer Broker B] yesterday every day [UBS Yen Trader] comes down and asks the jpy desk to tell all the banks to set libor low'.[41] Such comments did not prevent him from agreeing to execute 'wash' or 'switch' trades with UBS to compensate interdealer brokers B and C for assisting the attempt of the UBS yen trader to alter the yen LIBOR. RBS even went so far as to pay brokerage commissions on some of these wash trades to keep good relationships with the interdealer brokers.[42]

Eventually, yen trader 1 asked interdealer broker B to try to influence other panel banks.

> June 26, 2009
> Interdealer Broker B [responding to yen trader 1's question about UBS's requests]: He wants ones, ones and threes a little bit lower and sixes probably about the same where they are now. He wants them to stay the same.
> Yen Trader 1: I want them lower.
> Interdealer Broker B: You want them lower? What the sixes?
> Yen Trader 1: Yeah

The broker agreed to 'work on it' and later confirmed:

> We've spoke, basically one second, basically we spoke to [Banks F, H and G] who else did I speak to? [Bank I]. There's a couple of other people that the boys have spoke to but as a team we've basically said we want a bit lower so we'll see where they come in alright?

Yen trader 1 then executed a wash trade with UBS to compensate interdealer broker B for its assistance, generating about $20,000 in commissions for that broker.[43]

Money market traders

The primary submitters were the money market traders, supposedly setting the LIBOR submission rate through their knowledge of the markets. However, as far as RBS was concerned, they also considered the effects of LIBOR or RBS's trading books when making or directing others to make LIBOR submissions. The performance of the money market books was a factor in the determination of the size of their own personal bonuses. The FSA provides two examples: one primary submitter acknowledged that this was what mattered when he said internally 'I set a rate to benefit my interest as a money market trader'; and another observed to a broker during the financial crisis when liquidity had virtually dried up that 'people are just setting LIBOR to suit their books'.[44]

Between 9 March and 18 March 2010, one of the primary submitters made US dollar submissions which took into account the pricing of large forthcoming floating-rate US dollar transactions. Money market trader B told another submitter that even though the money market trader wanted higher submissions, the primary submitter 'wanted to keep them [US dollar LIBORs] down because of some fixes'. In fact, RBS's US dollar LIBOR submissions stayed low during this period when there were five large US dollar floating-rate transactions (but they were unchanged from the rates submitted over the previous three weeks). RBS's US dollar LIBOR submissions increased after the last large transaction was fixed.[45]

Conclusion

Barclays Bank and RBS particularly attracted the attention of both the regulators and the Treasury Select Committee, partly because they were leading UK banks. Barclays was the first to admit to any problems with LIBOR and was the major subject of one of the first investigations into the financial crisis by the Treasury Select Committee. RBS, under the leadership of Sir Fred Goodwin, became notorious for other reasons besides LIBOR manipulation. Its disastrous and ill-timed takeover of ABN-AMRO in December 2007 led to pre-tax losses in August 2008 of £691 million, the group's first loss for 40 years. Its urgent need for capital led to the government taking a 58% stake in the bank in November 2008, to the tune of £15 billion. This was followed by a second bank rescue plan, in January 2009, with losses largely due to the write-down on the ABN-AMRO acquisition. It all came to an end when RBS announced losses of £24.1 billion for 2008, the largest loss in UK corporate history.

LIBOR manipulation was only a small part of the story in the case of RBS, but for both banks, LIBOR manipulation provides examples of the lack of responsibility on the part of senior management for the way in which the business of the bank was conducted. Of course, these were not the only banks involved in the manipulation of LIBOR. Others were deeply involved as well, and the ways in which others misused LIBOR are explored in the next chapter.

Notes

1 Carrick Mollenkamp, 'Bankers cast doubt on key rate amid crisis', *Wall Street Journal*, 16 April 2008, available at https://www.wsj.com/articles/SB120831164167818299 (accessed 4 May 2018); Carrick Mollenkamp and

Mark Whitehouse, 'Study casts doubt on key rate', *Wall Street Journal*, 29 May 2008, available at https://www.wsj.com/articles/SB1212007037620 27135 (accessed 4 May 2018).

2　Tom Hayes had been a trader at both UBS and Citigroup. He was sentenced to 14 years in prison for dishonestly manipulating LIBOR himself and also for establishing a network of traders who colluded with each other to manipulate LIBOR for their own benefit.

3　Anjuli Davies, 'British bank body was warned of distorted LIBOR as early as 2005, court told', Reuters, 8 June 2015, available at https://www.reuters. com/article/uk-trial-libor-bba-idUKKBN0OO25Q20150608 (accessed 4 May 2018).

4　The FSA (which became the FCA in 2013) issued a series 'final notices' of its imposition of a financial penalty to the banks. These documents detail the results of investigations and the reasons for penalty, and are widely are drawn upon in this and later chapters. Similarly, the US Commodity Futures Trading Commission (CFTC) issued a series of 'orders' instituting proceedings pursuant to the Commodity Exchange Act, 'making findings, and imposing remedial sanctions', and these are likewise drawn upon.

5　Financial Services Authority, *Internal Audit Report: A Review of the Extent of Awareness within the FSA of Inappropriate LIBOR Submissions* (FSA, March 2013), p. 24, available at https://www.fca.org.uk/publication/ corporate/fsa-ia-libor.pdf (accessed 3 May 2018).

6　Ibid., p. 32.

7　Ibid., p. 43.

8　Ibid., p. 79.

9　Ibid., p. 52.

10　Ibid., p. 90.

11　Financial Services Authority, 'FSA publishes its Internal Audit Report on: review of the extent of awareness within the FSA of inappropriate LIBOR submissions', press release, 5 March 2013, available at https://www.fca. org.uk/news/press-releases/fsa-publishes-its-internal-audit-report-review- extent-awareness-within-fsa (accessed October 2018).

12　Ibid.

13　Jacob Gyntelberg and Philip Wooldridge, 'Interbank rate fixings during the recent turmoil', *BIS Quarterly Review*, March 2008, p. 70, available at https:// www.bis.org/repofficepubl/arpresearch_dev_200803.02.htm (accessed 3 May 2018).

14　International Monetary Fund, *Global Financial Stability Report. Financial Stress and Deleveraging: Macro-Financial Implications and Policy* (IMF, 8 October 2008), p. 76, available at https://www.imf.org/en/Publications/ GFSR/Issues/2016/12/31/Global-Financial-Stability-Report-October-2008- Financial-Stress-and-Deleveraging-Macrofi-22027 (accessed 3 May 2018).

15　Financial Services Authority, 'Final notice, Barclays Bank plc', 27 June 2012, p. 2, available at https://www.fca.org.uk/publication/final-notices/barclays- jun12.pdf (accessed 3 May 2018).

16　Ibid., para. 64, p. 13.

17　Ibid., para. 83, p. 19.

18 Ibid., para. 86, p. 19.

19 Ibid., paras 96–8, pp. 21–2.

20 Ibid., p. 3.

21 Ibid., para. 111, p. 24, citing Mark Gilbert, 'Barclays takes a money market beating', Bloomberg, 3 September 2007.

22 Financial Services Authority, 'Final notice, Barclays Bank', para. 109, p. 24.

23 Ibid., para. 117, pp. 25–6.

24 Ibid., para. 128, p. 28.

25 Commodity Futures Trading Commission, 'In the matter of the Royal Bank of Scotland plc and RBS Securities Japan Limited', CFTC Docket No. 13–14, 6 February 2013, 'Order instituting proceedings pursuant to sections 6(c) and 6(d) of the Commodity Exchange Act, making findings and imposing remedial sanctions', available at https://www.cftc.gov/sites/default/files/idc/groups/public/@lrenforcementactions/documents/legalpleading/enfrbsorder020613.pdf (accessed 4 May 2018).

26 Financial Services Authority, 'Final notice, The Royal Bank of Scotland plc', 6 February 2013, para. 51, p. 12, available at https://www.fca.org.uk/publication/final-notices/rbs.pdf (accessed 4 May 2018).

27 CFTC Docket No. 13–14, p. 9.

28 Ibid., p. 10.

29 Financial Services Authority, 'Final notice, The Royal Bank of Scotland', p. 15.

30 Ibid., para. 60, p. 16.

31 Ibid., p. 13.

32 Ibid., para. 51, p. 12.

33 CFTC Docket No. 13–14, p. 14.

34 Ibid.

35 Ibid.

36 Ibid., pp. 20–1.

37 Ibid., p. 21.

38 Ibid., pp. 26–7.

39 Ibid., pp. 27–9.

40 Financial Services Authority, 'Final notice, The Royal Bank of Scotland', para. 67, p. 18.

41 CFTC Docket No. 13–14, p. 22.

42 Ibid., p. 23.

43 Ibid., p. 24.

44 Financial Services Authority, 'Final notice, The Royal Bank of Scotland', para. 71, p. 21.

45 Ibid., para. 74, p. 22.

Chapter 4

Yet more banks are involved

In this chapter, I shall set out the ways in which other banks manipulated LIBOR, using the same techniques and for the same reasons. As the FSA final notice to UBS makes clear, the methods used followed in large part from one trader moving from one bank to another, so that networks of contacts were established. As in the last chapter, I have used both the FSA/FCA's final notices and the US CFTC orders to show that the evidence gathered by more than one regulatory authority led to the same conclusions.

Rabobank

The FCA issued its final notice to Rabobank on 29 October 2013. It set out in some detail the ways in which certain Rabobank submitters routinely took the bank's positions into account when making the bank's yen and, to a lesser extent, US dollar and sterling LIBOR submissions. The bank's traders requested particular rates as a matter of course, both via emails and orally. The submitters themselves made submissions which would benefit their own trading positions as money market traders. Furthermore, managers at various levels were often involved in these attempts at manipulation.

Rabobank identified certain traders as 'centres of competence', as they were considered to have extensive experience, wide market knowledge and expertise in cash instruments for a particular currency. The 'centres of competence traders' also had overall responsibility for managing the net risk from all of Rabobank's dealings in that currency. They advised Rabobank's submitters. From 2009 to November 2010, managers instructed yen LIBOR submitters to obtain 'market colour' from the 'centres of competence traders', ignoring the risk that this would be interpreted as an instruction to obtain and make LIBOR submissions at the levels suggested by traders, who indeed proposed levels that benefited their trading positions.

It did not stop there. As with other banks, there were attempts to manipulate the yen and the US dollar rates, by colluding with other panel banks, as well as with brokers. Between June 2005 and October 2008, at least one Rabobank trader and one submitter made at least 12 documented external requests to two individuals from other panel banks and the same submitter took into account at least two individuals at two other panel banks. Ten were for yen LIBOR and at least two individuals documented US dollar LIBOR external requests to at least one other panel bank and received at least seven documented yen LIBOR requests from that same panel banks as well as one other panel bank.

Altogether, the total number of documented internal requests between May 2005 and November 2010 came to 508, which includes at least 384 documented internal requests in relation to yen LIBOR, at least 112 in relation to dollar LIBOR and at least 12 in relation to sterling LIBOR. The FCA notes that at least 26 individuals were directly involved in these internal requests, seven of whom were managers. Two other managers should have known about these internal requests, as they were made by individuals who reported to them, and put a stop to the practice.

The FCA provides some examples of the various attempts to manipulate LIBOR, with traders making requests to submitters and managers:

On 15 September 2006, Trader 2 asked Submitter A for the 'USUAL FAVOURS, CAN YOU KEEP 3S AT 39 FOR THE NEXT FEW DAYS PLS MATE.'

Submitter A replied, 'will do', and then proceeded to keep three month USD LIBOR at 5.39 until 21 September.[1]

Managers also received internal requests such as:

On 6 October 2006, Trader 2 wrote to Manager 1, stating, 'HELLO SKIPPER, CAN U PUT 3S FOR ME TOMORROW PLEASE ... MANY THANKS'. Manager 1 replied, 'NEVER IN DOUBT!' Rabobank made a 5.37 three month USD LIBOR submission on 7 October.[2]

The FCA pointed out that some of the traders viewed themselves as the bank's de facto yen LIBOR submitters and gives this example:

When, on 14 December 2010, a Broker asked Trader 1 whether Trader 1 'set the libors for the bank', Trader 1 (who had never been a Submitter) replied, 'Till two weeks ago i was setting libors for rabo but due to BBA investigation someone outside of europe shudnt have any influence on libors then I cudnt be invol[v]ed in libors after then'.[3]

As already noted, both traders and submitters colluded with other banks to agree on a LIBOR submission. For example, on 19 March 2008, trader 1 asked submitter B to raise the bank's six-month yen LIBOR submission from 1.02 to 1.10. That submission was made for Rabobank but the submitter also contacted a submitter at another bank to ask if the external submitter would make the same 1.10 submission so that they could collectively alter the LIBOR for that day:

> Submitter B: [Trader 1] needs a high 6m libor if u can help skip – asked me to set 1.10!
> External Submitter 1: 00ps my 6s is 1.15!! [Trader 1 will] love me.
> Submitter B: hahaha so do i![4]

The FCA provides an example of submitter B's response to requests from brokers to adjust the submissions, in what the FCA points out is 'clearly part of a reciprocal process':

> Broker 2: Hello mate? What are you going to set your 1 month LIBOR today?
> Submitter B: I don't know what do you reckon?
> Broker 2: 65?
> Submitter B: I don't know. I ain't got a clue, 65. [Trader 1] wants me to set 98 in the 6's.
> Broker 2: That low yeah? What does [Trader 1] want you setting 1's then?
> Submitter B: Nothing [Trader 1] hasn't told me.

Submitter B then asked if the broker wanted him to set it at 65 and the broker replied that it should be as low as possible. The submitter then agreed to set it at 63:

> Submitter B: Well I'll set it to 63 if you want.... It makes no difference to me.
> Broker 2: Alright, cool.

Rabobank's one month JPY LIBOR submission was 0.63 that day.[5]

On 18 March 2011, Rabobank attested to the FCA that its arrangements for its LIBOR submissions were adequate and fit for purpose, when it had not yet formally implemented its policy nor disseminated it to its employees or trained them on it. The bank had failed to deal with the inherent conflict that exists when a panel bank allows its submitters to trade interest rate derivatives products linked to the very LIBORs for which they were responsible and had failed to address the need to retain sufficient records to allow the bank to properly audit its LIBOR submissions. The FCA noted that the way in which LIBOR submissions were made did not begin to change until 30 March 2011, when Rabobank put explicit policies in place to address LIBOR submissions. Even then, the new procedures were flawed and certain LIBOR-related compliance risks were not addressed until August 2012.

Deutsche Bank

In its summary of reasons, the FCA outlined the ways in which Deutsche Bank's manipulation of LIBOR was more extensive than was the case with the other banks it fined. Both managers and senior managers were involved; the 'culture of misconduct' was not confined to a small group of individuals, but extended to the Global Finance and FX Forwards Department (GFFX) of Deutsche Bank's investment bank, including its offices in London, Frankfurt, Tokyo and New York. Over at least five years, the money market derivatives (MMD) desks and the money market traders attempted to manipulate and improperly influence other panel banks' LIBOR submissions across a range of currencies, as well as EURIBOR. It was regarded as routine, involving a number of external parties and trading activities. It also included offering or bidding cash in the market to create an impression of an increased or reduced supply so that other panel banks would alter their submissions. Money market traders, derivatives traders and submitters were all sitting together on the same trading floor and were encouraged by managers to share information about currencies and markets without any restrictions.

In addition, Deutsche Bank's systems for identifying and recovering recordings of trader telephone calls and mapping trading books to traders were inadequate. No records were kept of which individuals made LIBOR submissions. Duties to make them on behalf of Deutsche Bank were nominally assigned to specific individuals by manager A, but these were often then sub-delegated without proper record-keeping. Nor was any rationale given for the rates submitted.

Furthermore, the trader audio system which Deutsche Bank introduced in 2007 was simply not fit for purpose. The system worked by recording the telephone calls of a single trader onto many digital audio tapes; it also recorded the calls made by many different traders. To find a particular call, it was necessary to cross-reference many detailed preservation spreadsheets with Deutsche Bank's DAT (digital audio tape) inventory. It was not fit for the purpose of scrutinising the behaviour of an individual trader over a period of time, which the bank's compliance team should have been able to do, let alone the regulatory authority. Deutsche Bank estimated that to identify and retrieve all calls for a single trader for a single month using the standard retrieval process would take 105 hours of machine time! This delayed the FCA's investigation, since it took over two years to retrieve the audio recordings of a large number of individuals, which the FCA had requested in December 2012.

The FCA includes in its final notice some examples of the improper requests and submissions made by derivatives traders, submitters and managers:

> On 4 April 2006, Derivatives Trader B made the following JPY LIBOR request: '…could u set 1m at 8bps pls, thanks'. Submitter A responded 'done mate'. Derivatives Trader B replied the following day, 'Thanks mate … the 1m back to 7bps [0.07] today pls' to which the Submitter A responded 'affirmative'. Deutsche Bank's JYP submissions exactly matched these requests.

On 29 December 2006, manager B and submitter C had the following exchange:

> Manager B: 'COULD I BEG YOU FOR A LOW 3M [EURIBOR] FIXING TODAY PLEASE … THAT WOULD BE THE BEST XMAS PRESENT;)'
> SUBMITTER C: '…BE A PLEASURE, NO PROBS WE HAVE NOTHING ON THE OTHER SIDE HERE. WILL PUT IN 71 [3.71] AT LEAST MAYBE WE CLD PUT IN 70 [3.70]…'
> Manager B: 'LOW AS POSSIBLE AS WE HAVE 2.5 YARDS [2.5 billion] ON IT TODAY, SO WOULD BE VERY HELPFUL'.[6]

On that day, Deutsche Bank's three-month EURIBOR submission was 3.70, three basis points lower than the day before.

Sometimes the submissions were made to benefit the submitters' own trading positions, as revealed in a discussion between two submitters on 31 August 2010 about a derivatives trader who had requested that the three-month sterling LIBOR be put down a tick because he had a fixing. Submitter D was concerned because the request did not suit the derivatives positions of the money market traders:

Submitter D: 'But I said we've got stuff up about 15th September we need higher libors, don't we?'

Colleague: 'Yeah'.

Submitter D: 'Yeah I said you know, he said [Derivatives Trader E] ok yeah just can you do it for me today...'

Colleague: 'Right okay fine'

Submitter D: 'So I've moved it down a tick to 73 [0.73] ... I've looked and I know we've got fixings on the 15th, haven't we, of September. We want it higher, we want 3s high, don't we?'

Colleague: 'We're going to get into trouble if we keep moving it up and down...'

On 31 August 2010 Deutsche Bank's three month GBP LIBOR submission was 0.73 compared with 0.74 the previous day.[7]

Examples of collusion between managers and external traders include an exchange on 13 November 2006, which manager B described as 'the big day' in discussions with external trader A:

Manager B: 'man, will you call [Panel Bank 2], please?'

External Trader A: 'yes and [Panel Bank 3]'

Manager B: 'don't tell them it's for me, because they hate me'

External Trader A: 'of course not'

Manager B: 'I am beeeeeeegging you'

Following that exchange, external trader A passed on the requests to external traders at the other two banks for a low one-month submission and the external traders agreed to act on those requests. He reminded the submitter at panel bank 1, who replied, 'No problem. I had not forgotten. The brokers are going for 3.372, we will put in at 36 [3.36] for our contribution'. On receipt of this reply from external trader A, manager B, replied 'I love you'.[8]

The FCA points out that manager B made most of his requests to external trader A at panel bank 1, knowing full well that external trader A was carrying out his instructions and that his doing so would increase the chances of EURIBOR being manipulated to benefit those of Deutsche Bank's trading positions for which manager B was responsible.

Derivatives traders colluded with other panel banks especially over yen LIBOR. Derivatives trader C colluded with an external trader B at panel bank 4, taking into account requests made by external trader B, knowing that these were made for his trading positions. On 26 June 2009, the two discussed their plans on Bloomberg:

External Trader B: basically i will help you in 2 weeks time ... i am the saem way

Derivatives Trader C: Perfect
External Trader B: but for the next 2 weeks i really really need you to put
6m higher ... after that i need 6m to crash off ... like you ... but please
move 6m up on Monday.
Derivatives Trader C: understood.
External Trader B: thx ... I need you in the panel on Monday
Derivatives Trader C: ok enough ... cheers.

On 26 June 2009, [Derivatives Trader C] increased his six month LIBOR
submission by 10 basis points to 0.65. On 29 June 2009, he increased his
submission by a further six bps to 0.71.[9]

Derivatives trader C's submissions were consistent with the request until 8 July 2009.

Derivative traders at Deutsche Bank also sought to influence LIBOR submissions through broker firms by influencing the market information they provided to their clients. One such attempt occurred on 27 February 2008, when manager A received a message from a broker firm about US dollar LIBOR, asking 'which direction do you want tom [tomorrow's] 1 mth libor pushed', to which manager A replied, 'lower and 3 mth higher'.[10]

These examples have been quoted in full to show that the claims made by the FCA are based on the actual behaviour of many of those involved in submitting their estimates of the cost of borrowing. The possibility of such behaviours going unchecked for such a long period of time will be discussed in the context of the introduction of the Senior Managers Regime in chapter 10.

UBS

This is the bank which Tom Hayes, the trader later imprisoned for his activities, joined and where he established his role as the person organising the largest number of traders, managers, submitters, brokers and other panel banks in seeking to fix LIBOR. All of this took place between 1 January 2005 and 31 December 2010.

The scale of the requests at UBS went far beyond that at other banks, as the FSA demonstrates in the figures given below, from its 'final notice' to UBS:[11]

- more than 800 documented internal requests were made in respect of yen LIBOR, in which at least 17 individuals were directly involved, four of whom were managers

- there were more than 115 documented internal requests in connection with other LIBOR currencies and EURIBOR
- in relation to sterling LIBOR, at least 90 documented internal requests were made, directly involving at least nine individuals, three of whom were managers;
- with regard to EURIBOR, at least 13 documented internal requests were made, in which eight individuals were directly involved, five of whom were managers.

The FSA concluded that, given the widespread and routine nature of making internal requests and the nature of the control features identified in the final notice, every LIBOR and EURIBOR submission in currencies and tenors in which UBS traded was at risk of having been improperly influenced.

The FSA's analysis shows that most of the efforts made by the traders were focused on manipulating Japanese yen (JYP) LIBOR, with at least 1900 documented internal requests, external requests and broker requests directed towards that end. These include 'open collusion', requests to 'spoof' the market and requests to manipulate screens. There is no record of such direct requests being made by other traders, although manipulation of LIBOR by other banks may well have resulted in false information being displayed on broker screens.

> Trader A asked certain brokers to manipulate their screens for the purpose of disseminating false information about prevailing market cash rates. The Brokers provided electronic screens to which certain Panel Banks had access for the purpose of obtaining information about cash rates in the market. At the request of Trader A, Brokers altered the information that those screens were showing and inserted false market information. For example, on 24 June 2009 in an electronic chat Trader A asked Broker E at Broker Firm B, 'pls try to keep 1y[ear] low on screen mate...'.[12]

The FSA identified three separate 'campaigns': in January–May 2007, in June 2009 and in July–August 2009. Extracts from the three campaigns are included here.

The January–May 2007 campaign

Throughout 2007, trader A made over 450 documented requests to manipulate yen LIBOR submissions. He had very large trading positions tied to three-month yen LIBOR that matured in each month

January–May 2007. As a result, trader A embarked on a coordinated campaign to influence the three-month yen LIBOR for the benefit of those positions, making internal requests, broker requests and external requests, but also offering to adjust UBS's yen LIBOR submissions to suit external traders. In an electronic chat on 2 February 2007, he explained the strategy to an external trader at a panel bank. He would take trading positions that would benefit from a reduction in the spread between the three-month yen LIBOR and another reference rate called TONAR (Tokyo overnight average rate, a yen-denominated reference rate published by the Bank of Japan every business day).

> His efforts to date were already producing results because he was: '... mates with the cash desks [Panel Bank 3] and i always help each other out' with the result that '3m libor is too high cause I have kept it artificially high' and that he was currently keeping that LIBOR rate one basis point too high.... In May 2007, he would manipulate three-month JPY LIBOR one basis point too low.

He intended to take spread trading positions that would benefit if the three-month yen LIBOR was high in January to early February 2007 and low from the end of March to the middle of May 2007. He also sought to manipulate the one-month and six-month yen LIBOR submissions.[13]

These were mostly internal requests made to trader-submitters, who agreed to help with every request. For example, on 24 January 2007, he contacted manager A, who supervised and provided input to UBS's yen LIBOR submission and asked him to 'try to keep 6m and 3m libors up', to which manager A responded 'standing order, sir'.

On the same day, trader-submitter A complained to manager A that trader A and trader B wanted conflicting submissions: 'As I said to you this is something majorly frustrating that those guys can give us shit as much as they like.... One guy [Trader A] wants us to do one thing and [Trader B] wants us to do another'.[14]

Between the end of March and mid-May 2007, trader A made at least 27 internal requests for low three-month submissions and all agreed in 26 cases. He also made at least 23 requests for the six-month tenor.

On 29 March 2007, trader A requested low three- and six-month LIBOR submissions from manager A and asked what yen submission UBS was going to set. Manager A replied: 'too early to say yet ... prob 69 would be our unbiased contribution'. Trader A repeated his request and manager A said, 'as i said before i don't mind helping you on your fixings but i'm not setting libor 7bp away from the truth i'll get ubs banned if i do that, no interest in that' and trader A replied that he did not either and was not asking for it to be seven basis points from reality. However, UBS's submission was two basis points less than the 'unbiased' figure of 0.69%.

> In recognition that his request might conflict with manager A's own trading positions, on 17 April 2007 Trader A said in an electronic chat: '... really need low libors today in everything, but esp 6 m, let me know if that suits or if not can we to an fra?' Thx. Trader A offered the 'fra' to Manager A as a facilitation trade in order to eliminate any conflict between their respective positions. In the event, there was no conflict, as reflected in Manager A's positive response: 'I've got nothing today, will keep 'em low'. On 17 April 2007, UBS's one month submission fell 1.5 basis points to 0.625%. The three month submission remained unchanged from the previous day at 0.65%. UBS's six month submission fell two basis points to 0.68%.

Indeed, over this period, 34 of the 36 three-month yen submissions made by UBS were lower than the published rate, consistent with trader A's requests for low submissions.

Trader A also made a number of requests to external traders; for example, on 20 April 2007, trader A followed up an earlier request in another electronic chat with a trader at another panel bank:

> Trader A: 'mate did you manage to speak to your cash boys?'
> External Trader C: 'yes u owe me they are going to 65 and 71'

The conversation resumed after the submission had been made by panel bank 4's submitters:

> External Trader C: 'mater [sic] they set [x]!
> Trader A: 'that's beyond the call of duty! I wish i was there!'[15]

The June 2009 campaign

By 23 June 2009, trader A held a large number of positions tied to the six-month yen LIBOR, due to reach maturity on 29 June. He would then benefit from a high six-month yen LIBOR, so he made two requests to external traders at another panel bank and at least 21 requests to brokers at four brokerages. In an electronic chat on 25 June 2009, trader A discussed his maturing trading positions with a broker, asking for 'a massive effort on the 6m tonight pls mate'. The broker confirmed that he was trying to assist and would involve other brokers. This was followed by an internal request on 29 June for a high six-month yen LIBOR because he had 'huge fixings' (maturity dates) with a value of US$2 million per basis point. The trader-submitter agreed and increased the submission from 0.72% on the previous day to 0.75%.[16]

The July–August 2009 campaign: 'operation 6M'

In a campaign which trader A dubbed 'operation 6m', he sought to manipulate the six-month yen LIBOR upwards and then downwards. It was during this time that he asked one of the brokers to manipulate his screen in connection with 12-month yen LIBOR. Other examples of collusion with both external traders and brokers are as follows.

On 14 July 2009, in an electronic chat with an external trader, trader A confirmed the plan to coordinate drops in their respective banks' six-month yen LIBOR submissions. Trader A said that after the end of the month, UBS would 'get 6M down alot, we will move from top to bottom [of the pack] and so will [Panel Bank 5] ... if you cld hold your 6m fix till [the end of the month] wld be a massive help'. The external trader agreed as this would suit him as well. Trader A was in almost constant contact with broker firms at this time, and made 39 requests to broker F alone. For example, in an electronic chat on 14 July 2009, trader A asked for a 'HIGH 6M SUPERMAN ... BE A HERO TODAY'. Broker F said, 'ill try mate ... as always'.[17]

The FSA also documents trader A's attempts to manipulate other currency LIBORs and EURIBOR submissions, with 90 documented internal requests in relation to sterling LIBOR and Swiss franc LIBOR. UBS systematically rounded all of these submissions by between 0.25 and 0.5 of a basis point to favour the bank's trading position, as well as those of others.

The whole approach can be summed up in the example of an email sent on 9 August 2007 by one of the managers to at least three senior managers:

> It is highly advisable to err on the low side with fixings for the time being to protect our franchise in these sensitive markets. Fixing risk and PNL thereof is secondary priority for now.[18]

'Fixing risk and PNL' refers to the financial exposure on derivatives positions and improving profits through LIBOR manipulation.

But a few months later one manager emailed another senior manager, frustrated by the low rates submitted:

How much pressure can we exert on MMC [money market and com-
modities] to raise our 3m yen fixing over the next week? We have 2 mio/
bp of fixing risk expiring on Dec imm. We have been riding a wave on this
trade, but everyone will be trying to influence the fixing next Monday
[17 December 2007] reflecting their positions. If we don't do the same we
risk an adverse PL [i.e. an adverse impact on UBS's profits]. Currently we
are in the bottom quartile. A move to the middle [of the pack] is worth
500k. There is some reluctance on their part to move it higher as they
are concerned about the reputational risks of putting in a high fix. I'd
agree with this if we were to set in the top quartile that may be the case,
but I don't think anyone's really got their eye on UBS's 3m yen fix. If our
position is bigger then [sic] MCC, we should be doing what's best for the
bank. What are your thoughts, please?[19]

A few days later, the same manager sent another email to the senior
manager, stating 'I need some assurance that they will put their rate
up please ... our rate input can make a significant difference'. On 17
December, UBS's submission increased by two basis points, resulting
in UBS's submission being included for the purposes of the calculation
of the published rate. The next day, UBS's submission decreased by 10
basis points, taking it back to the bottom quartile, where it remained
for a number of weeks.

As with other banks, UBS responded both to the media attention
and to speculation about LIBOR as the financial crisis worsened, and
especially to a Bloomberg article of 9 August 2007. The FSA noted
that the article had commented on the surge in the valuations of the
US dollar LIBOR submissions for the overnight tenor on that date of a
number of contributing banks, including UBS. The article commented
on UBS's submission because it was 65 basis points higher than its
previous day's submission, when its borrowing costs had increased
significantly, especially when compared with other panel banks. When
UBS investigated, it concluded that the submission had been made in
error. Erring on the low side was the decision made by the bank in the
months that followed, so that submissions would be lower, sending a
positive message about the bank's creditworthiness.[20]

The position had worsened by 2 April 2008, when UBS announced
additional losses of some $19 billion, which was followed by a down-
grading of UBS's credit worthiness on the same day with a warning
about possible future downgrades. The media attention turned to the
disparity between LIBOR submissions and rates on new issues of commercial paper and certificates of deposit. From then on, UBS's directives
moved to higher submissions, 'moving to issuance', until June 2008,

when an email from a manager to other senior managers pointed out that 'it seems we are the only bank trying to move in that direction'. Panel banks did not appear to be following it and this led to a return to being 'in the middle of the pack'. It was not, however, a foolproof means of avoiding media speculation, as one trader-submitter remarked:

> If you are too low you get written about for being too low … if you are too high, you get written about for being too high … and if you are in line with the crowd you get written about because the crowd is too low.[21]

It does, however, make it clear that UBS had abandoned its attempt to make its LIBOR submissions by reference to the cost of borrowing.

In its final assessment of what went wrong for UBS, the FSA notes that one cause of the LIBOR manipulation was the bank's complete lack of systems and controls. For example, during the whole period from January 2005 to September 2009 in relation to LIBOR and until October 2009 in relation to EURIBOR, UBS combined the roles of deciding on its submissions and proprietary trading in derivatives products depending on LIBOR and EURIBOR. This clearly involved a conflict of interest without any effective means of managing the conflict. Even when the trading and submitting roles were eventually separated in September 2009, the bank's systems and controls did not prevent traders from continuing their internal requests and attempting to influence submissions by describing them as 'market colour'. Trader-submitters themselves were able to try to manipulate the published rates for the benefit of their own trading positions. The analysis also makes it clear that managers were involved, even at senior levels, and that LIBOR submissions had little to do with reality and much more to do with ensuring that the bank appeared to be creditworthy or at least more creditworthy than its peers, or to do with maximising profits through manipulating LIBOR to support trading positions.

Citibank

In this case the action was taken by the Commodity Futures Trading Commission (CFTC) against Citibank over its attempts to manipulate LIBOR in two separate phases for different reasons. The first period was from the spring of 2008 through to the summer of 2009, when the bank's submitters based their US dollar LIBOR submissions on a desire to avoid generating negative media attention and to protect the bank's reputation in the market. This took place even when the bank knew that it was under investigation for its practices.

The second phase took place between February 2010 and August 2010, following the appointment of a senior yen trader in late 2009. Despite the fact that the bank was under investigation by CFTC's Enforcement Division, senior managers did not notify the compliance or legal departments about the appointee's statements after he was hired but before he had started work. During this period, the senior yen trader boasted about how he had tried to manipulate LIBOR at his previous place of employment.

Phase 1

During the financial crisis, Citibank's US dollar LIBOR submissions did not accurately or solely represent its assessment of the costs of borrowing on unsecured funds in the London interbank market. From August 2007, Citigroup, the parent company, faced financial uncertainties, including issues around liquidity. The US Federal Reserve required various financial institutions, including Citigroup, to make use of the discount window to obtain short-term money to alleviate temporary shortages of liquidity. As the crisis continued, liquidity in the London interbank market began to disappear. Citibank's US dollar submitters realised that it would be difficult to obtain deposits at or below LIBOR, especially for longer periods. They wanted to avoid Citi being seen as having to pay up for cash because of the effects on perceptions of the bank's soundness. The CFTC gives some examples of their concerns and the actions they took:

> February 14, 2008
> US Dollar Submitter 3: Things are very expensive over here. We posted 2.98 initially and got nothing. Went up to 3.01 and nothing. No surprise as cash is trading higher than libor.... No liquidity at all in the cash market. Didn't even bother putting a cash bid out there, as not paying over libor for it. Still need to do 200 MM.[22]

Citi finished 2007 short of its liquidity targets and facing increased funding costs. Its problems in finding low-cost funds in the market continued, so its submissions changed from being some of the lowest to among the highest by the end of March 2008. LIBOR fixings were increasingly scrutinised by the financial press during the spring and summer. Citi could not win with either high or low LIBOR submissions, since both attracted the attention of the media.

The issue of liquidity became even more sensitive for Citi, given that the bank drew heavily on the US government's financial support: it received $25 billion from the Term Asset Relief Program (TARP), followed by a loss-sharing agreement with the US government after a 60% drop in its share price. Further financial assistance was provided to the bank during December 2008 and January 2009. As a result of this and continuing financial support, the government had acquired one-third of Citigroup's shares. The Federal Reserve stress-tested the bank in March 2009, and directed Citi to raise additional capital, especially with the threat of a ratings downgrade.

In order to attract clients in other markets, Citi began offering increasingly higher interest rates. Clients' expectation to receive interest rates set at the LIBOR fixing or higher for their deposits created problems for the submitters:

August 6, 2008
LIBOR Manager [to a sales manager]: One thing that will cause a real issue is if we pay more than LIBOR because we are a LIBOR contributor, so if we ever pay more than LIBOR, we can be up in the press....

August 28, 2008
U.S. Dollar Submitter: If they [the BBA] find out that I paid a customer LIBOR [fixing], then obviously [the BBA] could strike us off putting in our LIBOR contributions – cause we should be saying our LIBORS are a lot higher. [...] Obviously, the last time we put our LIBORs too high [a Citi manager in New York said] [...] what are you doing? [...] We've asked the [sales] guys as well [...] just so that this, this thing is always creating issues [...] just get them to give the desk a call [...] just to advise if they've put a deal through, it's at LIBOR [...] for us to step up to LIBOR at 43 for 45 million dollars, I do, it does question the fact how much do we want to create pain in LIBOR fixings [...]'.

October 15, 2008
U.S. Dollar Submitter 1: I am a LIBOR contributor and so we put our LIBOR rates for dollars. We submit those to the BBA.... We are under some constraints because we, we are – you know, off the record, we are not allowed to be the highest setter.

December 8, 2008
LIBOR Manager: Even paying LIBOR causes an issue because of this whole LIBOR fixing stuff, because it will cause issue for the firm if we move LIBORS up...

March 24, 2009
U.S. Dollar Submitter 1: ... we as an institution have to be a little careful

about what rates we show in the market since we're LIBOR setters ... we monitor quite heavily what different Citi branches pay in the inter-bank market, and the reason is here in London we set the LIBORS, and the CFTC in the States have been very sharp on institutions that set LIBORs ... you were paying ... quite higher in the market than compared to where I would set LIBOR which kind of ties my hands a little bit so I am trying to work out what you are trying to do....

May 6, 2009
U.S. Dollar Submitter 1: At the moment everybody who sets LIBORS just doesn't want to be noticed, that's the way it is but anybody who is noticed or does make the big bold move has got to have something behind it.[23]

During this period, and despite everything that was going on in the London interbank market, Citibank's submitters did not raise their sub-missions, even though they knew that the bank's fundraising activities were sometimes at higher rates than the interbank rate. The submissions were in fact false and did not reflect the bank's assessment of the costs of borrowing unsecured funds in the interbank market. Instead, they were aimed at protecting the bank from any negative market perceptions concerning its liquidity, strength and creditworthiness.

Fixing Euroyen TIBOR

The Euroyen TIBOR, the Tokyo Interbank Offered Rate, is used for derivatives contracts, including interest rate swaps and futures contracts on exchanges around the world. An example of such a contract is the Chicago Mercantile Exchange's Euroyen TIBOR futures contract; during 2010, it was actively traded but by 2016, when the CFTC's order instituting proceedings was published, trading in that contract had ceased. But by the end of 2011, according to the BIS, the over-the-counter derivatives in yen consisted of contracts, such as swaps and forward rate agreements (FRAs), that amounted to US$66 trillion in notional value. It was therefore a sizeable market for some yen traders and their banks to exploit.

The contributing panel banks were supposed to provide the rates at which they believed a prime bank would transact in the Japan offshore market as of 11 a.m. Tokyo time. As with LIBOR, the rates should not represent the banks' own positions in the marketplace nor were they to be used in trading by the reference banks. The daily fixing was also calculated on the trimmed average methodology.

In April 2009, Citibank embarked on a strategic initiative of raising its profile in the derivatives markets in Japan. Given the possibilities in Japan, Citigroup Global Markets Japan Inc. (CGMJ) hired two senior traders in order to increase its market presence in Japan, to turn around its flagging Tokyo-based derivatives trading, increase customer flow and boost profits. They were a high-profile yen interest rates derivatives trader from UBS and his supervisor, a senior yen manager from the same bank. CGMJ's goal was to generate profits of US$50–150 million from interest rates derivatives trading.

The two new senior traders worked together to manipulate both the yen LIBOR and the Euroyen TIBOR, using the same tactics and contacts as they had during their time at UBS. As soon as he began trading in February 2010, the senior yen trader sent requests to interdealer brokers positioned to influence yen LIBOR panel banks, requests to traders at other panel banks and internal requests to Citi's yen LIBOR submitters. Generally, Citi's submitters did not act on these requests. From April 2010 to June 2010, the senior yen manager at times worked to manipulate Euroyen TIBOR by asking the TIBOR submitters at CJL European (Citibank's banking arm in Tokyo) to alter Citi's rate submissions for the benefit of his own derivatives trading positions. On a few occasions the submitters did take the trader's requests into account when submitting the bank's Euroyen TIBOR positions.

All the familiar ploys with the brokers were re-used in his new position, with the usual attempts to skew the fixings over a few days, or at critical times, such as the fixes for his contracts tied to yen LIBOR, even as far ahead as six months. Sometimes he and the brokers discussed targeting specific LIBOR panel members – including Citi – to optimise the senior yen trader's chances of manipulating the yen LIBOR fixing. Well versed in the senior yen trader's schemes from his time at UBS, the brokers often acknowledged his requests and reported to him on their efforts to accommodate him. Here are some examples, taken from the CFTC's order:

February 16, 2010

Senior Yen Trader: But I could do the high 6 month LIBOR ... like ... right now I don't have any fixes or anything, but just generally my position.

Broker 1: High, yeah.... Alright, okay. Well, Broker 2 seems to think that there's bugger all he can do, uh, is fix things at the moment. He says it doesn't seem to matter where he puts it. It just ... RBS moves it up or down 2 points when he's got a fix in. That's the only thing that seems

to move it ... your boys are sort of middle of the range ... so maybe
you ought to....[24]

March 19, 2010
Senior Yen Trader: i think after june i will push for higher libors and
lower tibors after june imm we are joining fixing panel in tibor and
will keep it high....
Deutsche Yen Trader: after June coolio
Senior Yen Trader: after june higher lib is OK for you? ... I selling june
ey will keep tibor high at least till june for year end I will need low
tibor and high libor.[25]

The senior yen trader tried to build on his previous relationships with
derivatives traders at UBS and Deutsche Bank by providing them with
key market colour and information about movements in yen LIBOR and
Euroyen TIBOR fixings and in return seeking information about their
yen submissions. He also sought to pressurise brokers and derivatives
traders at the same time, looking for a higher six-month yen LIBOR.
On one occasion he informed a trader at another yen LIBOR panel bank
that 'after June will push for higher esp 6m over the turn'. This was
followed by writing to a trader at another bank: 'next month we cross
the turn for 6 m any chance libor cld go higher then?'[26]

In all of these efforts to manipulate the rates, he was aided and
abetted by the senior yen manager, first pushing for the bank to join
the Euroyen TIBOR panel in order to increase the bank's standing and
prestige in the Tokyo financial market, then requesting the submitters
to the Euroyen TIBOR to adjust their submissions to assist the senior
yen trader's derivatives trading positions, which they did on a few occasions in 2010. The senior yen manager started pressurising the Euroyen
TIBOR submitters shortly after CJL European joined the panel, on 1
April 2010. They acknowledged the requests and understood the sensitivities, stating that they wanted to help the rates business. The senior
yen manager argued that CJL could influence the rates by a 'snowball'
effect, so that a slight change in CJL's submissions would be followed
incrementally. The overall effect would be to magnify alterations in the
official Euroyen TIBOR fixing. An example of the way in which the
senior yen manager influenced the thinking of the submitters is shown
in the following example from the CFTC order:

June 17, 2010
Euroyen TIBOR Submitter 2: ... we are not changing 3 months today ...
we think that only [one panel bank] followed us yesterday ... we were

talking the other day that there might be a snowball effect if one starts
to move down. But so far we have only seen [one panel bank] putting
the rates down for 3 month....

Senior Yen Manager: No, but the mega banks, they're not gonna move
it until the average moves, right? So the Western banks will all move
together and then once the average moves a point, then the mega banks
will move ... we're the highest foreign bank. So that's the point, right?
The point is the foreign banks will all move in concert with each other
and we're the highest one....

Euroyen TIBOR Submitter 2: ... But just please remember like two
months ago, you wanted the higher rate ... if we had quoted from the
first of April like [another panel bank], it would be much easier. But
you know, at the time, you guys had a position which rate is, higher
rate is better, so you know we just quoted TIBOR flat.[27]

What is interesting and different about Citibank is that both the
submitters and their manager grew tired of the increasingly aggressive
requests to alter the bank's submissions. The management acted and
instituted a 'firewall' between CGMJ and CJL to limit such requests
and exchanges of information between the senior yen manager or other
derivatives traders to the submitters.

The senior yen trader's magic began to fail. He was unable to
establish relationships with Citi's yen LIBOR submitters in London and
his attempt to use a junior interest rate swaps trader to convey messages
and requests to the submitters also failed. At the last attempt, on 25
June 2010, the senior managers elevated his conduct to compliance and
legal and he was dismissed. The bank then alerted the CFTC about the
behaviour and conducted an internal inquiry, the results of which were
reported to the CFTC in early autumn 2010.

Bank of Scotland/HBOS and Lloyds Bank

On 28 July 2014, the FCA issued its final notice against HBOS and Lloyds
Bank for manipulating LIBOR and the CFTC issued its order against
Lloyds Bank on the same day. Lloyds Bank routinely manipulated its
sterling LIBOR positions between September 2006 and June 2009, its US
dollar LIBOR between January 2008 and May 2009, and its yen LIBOR
submissions from May 2006 to June 2009, as well as colluding with
Rabobank from May 2006 to October 2008. It engaged in schemes of
'forcing' LIBOR to influence the sterling LIBOR submissions of other
LIBOR panel banks to benefit trading positions. Lloyds Bank engaged

in at least three such schemes from September 2006 to December 2006 and Bank of Scotland engaged in at least one such scheme in November 2006 and December 2006. At these firms there was a culture at the money market desks of trying to take financial advantage wherever possible. For example, on 19 July 2007, when a Lloyds manager was informed by a Lloyds trader about a request made to another Lloyds trader for a low yen LIBOR, the Lloyds trader commented that 'every little helps…. It's like Tescos', and the Lloyds manager replied, 'Absolutely, every little helps'.[28]

The FCA identified the ways in which Lloyds Bank and the Bank of Scotland, which was a LIBOR panel bank from September 2007 (when it took over the submissions from HBOS plc, a subsidiary HBOS Treasury Services plc) until 6 February 2009, following the merger with Lloyds, sought to manipulate LIBOR. The attempts to manipulate LIBOR took the forms used by other banks. When making their sterling and dollar LIBOR submissions, sterling and dollar traders from time to time took into account their own money market positions as well as requests from other traders.

After the Bank of Scotland ceased to be a LIBOR panel member, its sterling and dollar traders could not influence LIBOR, so they had to ask Lloyds Bank traders to take Bank of Scotland money market positions into account when making their LIBOR submissions, a practice which the FCA described as being 'casual and routine'.[29] The FCA gives a couple of examples:

On 11 May 2009, on receiving a Request for a low USD one month LIBOR submission from BoS Trader C, Lloyds Trader D automatically assumed it was because of BoS Trader C's 'fixings'. BoS Trader C also said: 'i will tell you when we have big resets as to be honest we [should] be co-ordinating the libor inputs to suit the books' to which Lloyds Trader D replied 'of course, that is very sensible … let me know on that day mate'.[30]

Another trader routinely took Lloyds' yen money market positions into account when making yen LIBOR submissions, and between May 2006 and October 2008 that trader also colluded with at least one person from Rabobank, making four documented requests and receiving at least 12 from Rabobank, and in turn taking at least eight Rabobank requests into account in making his own submissions. The traders acted not only to increase both the banks' profits but also the size of their own bonuses.

The FCA outlined at least two other schemes, which both Lloyds Bank and the Bank of Scotland set up, using somewhat different methods from the attempts by traders to manipulate LIBOR. Lloyds traders on the money market desks sought to 'force' LIBOR by entering into FRAs and then bid aggressively in the cash market. This scheme, which was in operation between September and December 2006, was designed to push up the one-month sterling LIBOR submissions of other LIBOR panel banks, 'forcing' them to increase the one-month sterling LIBOR, which would benefit those FRAs. This would be achieved by artificially inflating the one-month rate so that it was higher than the fixed rate of the FRA, thus increasing their profitability.

The FCA records how a Lloyds trader explained to one of the brokers, who had assisted in the scheme, that he had instructed one of the Lloyds traders to continue bidding on 25 September 2006: 'I have just told them my plan … I want to bid everything, so all LIBORs force up one month'. They were prepared to stand by their bids, but to avoid this they set up these schemes during times of market illiquidity on the grounds that 'you've got to do it when people can't lend', so that the likelihood of their bids being fulfilled was lessened. At 11.11 a.m. on that day, after LIBOR had fixed, the Lloyds trader stopped bidding and one-month sterling LIBOR fixed at 4.9575. As a result, Lloyds Bank made a gross profit of £266,063 on the £10 billion of FRAs. The broker who was assisting Lloyds arranged for a trader at another bank to be the counterparty to the FRAs, having explained in a telephone conversation on 31 August 2006 that: 'I'll have [bank] there as well … because that's what you want. You don't want the market to know what you're f*** doing'.[31] Two of the Lloyds traders and the broker engaged in two further schemes of 'forcing' LIBOR, in October and December 2006, which resulted in gross profits on the associated FRAs of £937,336.

The Bank of Scotland engaged in another scheme to benefit 'rolls'. It had a portfolio of assets (loans made to third parties generally), which were referenced to sterling LIBOR and refixed on a rolling basis for the term of the asset. The scheme was designed to take advantage of the fact that sterling LIBOR submitters at other banks took into account perceived conditions in the three-month sterling cash market. So the Bank of Scotland increased its bids for three-month sterling cash in order to influence the perception of the other sterling LIBOR banks so that they would increase their three-month sterling LIBOR submissions. The Bank of Scotland trader explained this to one of the bank's managers in an email in December 2006:

towards the end of the month our key focus became the reset of the large 3 month roll on the 1ˢᵗ of Dec where we had £6bn open so about a week before this I stared [sic] to gradually drive the 3's up, with a view that any funding achieved on the way would be useful … the net result was very successful on the libor front with … an increase of approx 3–4 bp on the week earlier.[32]

During the financial crisis, and especially after the collapse of Lehman Brothers in September 2008, interbank lending came to a virtual standstill and there was extreme dislocation in the global money markets. LIBOR submissions became a sensitive issue. Media scrutiny was focused on the financial strength of banks, as indicated by the increased costs of borrowing. Not surprisingly, the Bank of Scotland became concerned about its LIBOR submissions, especially after the announcement on 18 September 2008 that HBOS plc would be acquired by Lloyds TSB Bank plc.

On 24 and 25 September 2008, a Bank of Scotland trader made US dollar LIBOR submissions which represented large increases over the previous day's: on 24 September it was 40 basis points higher than the next highest submission, and on 25 September it was 55 basis points higher. On 26 September, the Bank of Scotland manager instructed the trader to lower his submissions in line with other LIBOR panel banks. In a Bloomberg message to a trader at another bank, the Bank of Scotland trader said, 'ive been pressurised by senior management to bring my rates down into line with everyone else'.[33] So its submission fell to the same level as the highest other submission, even though it was still 44 basis points above the published LIBOR. It then fell into line with the level of the LIBOR fix and remained within the pack of submissions until the merger was completed on 19 January 2009. An instruction given on 6 May 2008 by a Bank of Scotland senior manager had, it seems, eventually taken effect. He had then said:

> It will be readily apparent that in the current environment no bank can be seen as an outlier. The submissions of all banks are published and we could not afford to be significantly away from the pack.[34]

The CFTC published its order on the same day as the FCA's final notice to Lloyds Bank. Inevitably, therefore, they provide much the same evidence, but there are a few differences, providing a slightly different angle. The first section of the order describes the way in which the HBOS sterling submitter at first made false submissions occasionally to benefit his cash and derivatives trading positions. Between January and the summer of 2009, the Lloyds TSB sterling submitter and the former HBOS sterling submitter were located in different offices, but they were in communication by telephone about the necessity of adjusting the sterling LIBOR submissions to benefit themselves. The Lloyds TSB sterling submitter met the HBOS's submitter's requests, except of course when it did not suit his trading positions.

March 6, 2009

Former HBOS Sterling Submitter: I am paying on 12 yards of 1s today: a re-fix against Group, so if there's a way of making 1s relatively low, it would be helpful for us all. [...] I think it's going to be about 126 or something, maybe 128, it is a tricky one at the moment.

Lloyds TSB Sterling Submitter: Well I could, I mean I have left mine as 125 mate, I mean.

Former HBOS Sterling Submitter: Yeah, well that will be perfect. As long as you – you can't go lower than 125, if you are going at 125 that is what, that is what I am hoping to shape it down to, so if you can do that, that would be great.

Lloyds TSB Sterling Submitter: Yeah I have got a fixing small one nowhere near 12 yards, so yeah I do it at 25, alright?

Former HBOS Sterling Submitter: And I am a payer as well. I don't know what you were thinking of going in the 3s [...] I have only 500 quid in the 3s, so I am not that – it's not the end of the world, but if you're the other way around don't worry about it.

Lloyds TSB Sterling Submitter: No, no, no, I have got a small loan going out but it is less than that, alright I will probably have to go 90 – probably 96 but I will let you know before, I do 25 definitely at 1s and I will speak to you on –

Former HBOS Sterling Submitter: Yeah don't stress mate, go 25 in the 1s and just go with what you can in the 3s. No great stress.

Lloyds TSB Sterling Submitter: Yeah, no problem.

Former HBOS Sterling Submitter: Alright thanks.

March 31, 2009

Lloyds TSB Sterling Submitter: What do you need, and what was the other period, was it all 3s?

Former HBOS Sterling Submitter: No just 3s today and tomorrow

Lloyds TSB Sterling submitter: Okay, we will leave it at 67.

Former HBOS Sterling Submitter: Yeah cool. Just 1s as I am a small receiving today, tomorrow is a massive one in the 1s. I am paying but we'll worry about 1s tomorrow?

Lloyds TSB Sterling Submitter: Well luckily not today mate because I have got trillions and billions of 1s going out today, tomorrow I can set it slightly lower.

Former HBOS Sterling Submitter: Yeah that's cool, I am receiving 1s today in the yard, tomorrow I am paying on 11.5 yards [...] In the 1s but we will worry about it tomorrow, tomorrow.
Lloyds TSB Sterling Submitter: Yeah, okay mate no problem.[35]

The following day, a Lloyds TSB junior trader asked the former HBOS submitter on behalf of the Lloyds submitter what he wanted. The former HBOS submitter stated that he had a 'big liability fix, so as low as possible, please [...] But I have a massive asset fix in the 3s, so as high as you can in the 3s'. The junior trader relayed these requests to the Lloyds sterling LIBOR submitter.

The CFTC observed that from at least 2007 through to at least 2009, the Lloyds TSB and HBOS sterling LIBOR submitters attempted to manipulate their respective sterling LIBOR fixings on numerous occasions for the benefit of their own cash and derivatives trading positions: 'Lloyds TSB and HBOS, through their submitters, knew it was improper to consider trading positions in determining the bank's LIBOR submissions'.[36] The same considerations applied to their US dollar submissions. The submitters occasionally made false submissions and attempted to manipulate US dollar LIBOR to benefit their trading positions. The CFTC gave examples of this:

On May 11, 2009, the former HBOS U.S. Dollar LIBOR Submitter stated to the trader who assisted the Lloyds TSB U.S. dollar LIBOR Submitter, 'when we have big resets as to be honest we should be co ordinating the libor inputs to suit the books. for example, later this month i have a 5y 3 month liability reset so we should put in a low one there ill let you know'. Then, on May 19, 2009, the former HBOS U.S. Dollar LIBOR Submitter contacted the trader who assisted the Lloyds TSB U.S. Dollar LIBOR Submitter and specifically requested a lower three-month U.S. Dollar LIBOR submission to benefit his trading position. The Lloyds TSB U.S. Dollar LIBOR Submitter complied, stating on a telephone call, 'we got the LIBORs down for you'.[37]

The CFTC order also provides examples of the collusion between the Lloyds TSB yen submitter and a senior yen LIBOR submitter at Rabobank. Between mid-2006 until at least October 2008, the two yen submitters were frequently in contact over the rates each would submit for yen LIBOR, with the Rabobank submitter asking the Lloyds submitter to adjust his yen rates to benefit Rabobank's traders' positions.

June 27, 2006
Rabobank Yen Submitter: just for your info skip ... i need a high 1 mth today – so i will be setting an obseenly high 1 mth (6).

> Lloyds TSB Yen Submitter: sure mate no worries ... give us an idea where and I'll try n oblige....

The Lloyds TSB yen submitter maintained his relationship with and tried to meet the Rabobank yen trader-submitter's requests even when he was on an assignment in Tokyo and not making the submissions.

> On March 22, 2007 the Rabobank Yen LIBOR Submitter emailed the Lloyds Submitter: 'I need a high 1mth jpy libor set tomorrow please (val 27th) if you can ask your man to set a nice high one like today pls? Hugs skip'. The Lloyds s TSB Yen LIBOR Submitter forwarded the email to the two Lloyds TSB employees who were making the submissions in his absence, saying: 'We usually try and help each other out ... but only if it suits ... I think this will be OK for us anyway as we may have some month end Loans Admin roll overs?'[38]

> March 28, 2008
> Rabobank Yen Submitter: morning skip – [Rabobank Senior Yen Trader] has asked me to set high libors today – gave me levels of 1m 82, 3m 94 ... 6m 1.02
> Lloyds Yen Submitter: sry mate can't oblige today ... I need em lower!!!
> Rabobank Yen Submitter: yes was told by jimbo ... just thought I'd let you know why mine will be higher ... and you don't get cross with me.
> Lloyds TSB Yen Submitter: never get cross wiv yer mate.[39]

The Lloyds TSB yen submitter continued his relationship with the Rabobank yen submitter's LIBOR and tried to meet his requests even when he was on an assignment to Tokyo, through two Lloyds TSB employees who were making yen LIBOR submissions in his absence, stating, 'We usually try and help each other out ... but only if it suits ... I think this will be OK for us anyway as we may have some month end Loans Admin roll overs?'[40]

When he got back to London and resumed his duties, he received an internal request for a submission from a Lloyds TSB trader in Tokyo. The trader asked the Lloyds TS yen submitter on 19 July 2007 for a low three-month yen LIBOR submission, observing that he had a position worth Y83 billion that could benefit from an altered yen LIBOR fixing. The Lloyds TSB yen LIBOR submitter agreed to help and even offered to ask the Rabobank yen LIBOR submitter to assist as well. This went on from at least mid-2006 to October 2008, even though both the trader and submitter knew it was improper to consider their own bank's or another bank's trading positions in determining LIBOR submissions.

Before its acquisition by Lloyds TSB, HBOS lowered its US dollar and sterling LIBOR submissions to protect its market reputation.

During the financial crisis, HBOS faced serious funding and liquidity issues. On 16 April 2008 the *Wall Street Journal* featured an article questioning whether LIBOR panel banks were making submissions lower than what they were paying for funds in the money markets, to prevent the market from concluding that the banks were desperate for cash. The CFTC noted that, following publication of that article, an HBOS senior manager in an email to other senior managers pointed out that 'no bank can be seen to be an outlier'. He followed this on 8 August 2008 by circulating to HBOS managers and senior managers a presentation in which he stated:

> As a bank we are extremely careful about the rates we pay in different markets for different types of funds as paying too much risks ... in this climate, [giving] the impression of HBOS being a desperate borrower and so lead to a general withdrawal of wholesale lines.[41]

Just a few weeks later, Lloyds announced the terms for its acquisition of HBOS, in what was generally understood to be in effect a rescue of the bank.

The HBOS US dollar LIBOR submitter increased the three-month submission by 1.2% on 24 September 2008 and on 25 September his submission was higher than that of any other panel bank for that tenor. More senior managers advised him to lower his submissions to be in line with other banks, which he did the following day. On 21 October 2008, as the crisis worsened, the HBOS sterling LIBOR submitter began increasing his submissions until HBOS's became the highest in one-month through to six-month tenors. On that day, the HBOS LIBOR supervisor issued a directive to the submitters saying, 'I do not want to be an outlier in the BBA submissions – this could potentially create an issue with buyers of our paper'. He then instructed the submitters to submit '3–6 month Sterling LIBOR' 'at the expected BBA level for the time being'. The instructions were followed faithfully by the submitters, who then reduced the HBOS sterling LIBOR submissions over a period of several days. On 30 October, the HBOS LIBOR supervisor told the HBOS submitters that they should not make LIBOR submissions based on the 'expectation of where the funds will come' but should instead 'continue to post at levels at or slightly above the level we will pay for deposits or issue [certificates of deposit]'.[42] These instructions remained in force through to the acquisition of HBOS in January 2009. HBOS's submissions did not throughout this period reflect the bank's assessment of its borrowing costs in the relevant interbank markets.

The European Commission's investigation of the manipulation of EURIBOR

The UK FCA and the US CFTC were not the only regulators to impose fines on banks involved in LIBOR manipulation. Consequently, the same banks were fined in more than one jurisdiction. A full list is given in the Appendix. In the specific case of the euro area and EURIBOR, the European Banking Federation (EBF) is the benchmark administrator. Given the importance of EURIBOR, in terms of both its structure and the EBF's approach to misconduct, it is covered here. EURIBOR was established by the EBF in 1999, just before the introduction of the euro, with a large panel of banks, some 44 banks in September 2012, although it currently consists of only 20 banks, all obliged to conform with a code of conduct set out by the European Money Market Institute, its administrator. It is based on 'the rate at which euro interbank term deposits are being offered by one prime bank to another within the Economic and Monetary Union zone'. A term deposit in this case refers to one bank holding funds on behalf of another, where interbank deposit arrangements require that both banks hold a 'due to account' for another. The rate is published at 11 a.m. (central European time) and is a spot rate (T+2, i.e., transaction date and settlement date). Thus, it does not necessarily refer to interbank lending rates.[43]

The euro overnight index average (EONIA) is a transaction-based interest rate used for the euro area overnight segment of the money market. That rate is calculated by the European Central Bank (ECB), with the EBF as a benchmark administrator and Thomson Reuters as the publisher, as a weighted average of the interest rates on unsecured overnight lending transactions denominated in euro reported by a panel of contributing banks. The ECB is the calculation agent for EONIA. This is justified on the grounds of the need for confidentiality in the handling of individual banks' transaction data. The ECB is also there to ensure that the data are treated with careful security by an impartial third party. Because it is based on transactions, it reduces the risk of manipulation but it does not entirely remove it.

In the euro area EONIA is used for euro overnight interest rate swaps and EURIBOR is used as the benchmark for the usual wide swathe of financial instruments, from loans and mortgages to interest rate swaps. From the ECB's point of view, these two benchmarks are vitally important for the efficient functioning of the euro area, in forming euro money market interest rates, and in forming market expectations of the future value of short-term interest rates. They therefore play a vital role in interest rate policy.

The European Commission investigated several banks involved in the manipulation of EURIBOR. It began its investigations in 2011 with unannounced inspections and it opened proceedings in March 2013, which then led to fines being imposed on several banks, except Barclays because it had gained immunity by having revealed the existence of the cartel in EURIBOR and yen LIBOR. Other banks received a reduction in their fines because of their cooperation with the Commission. These included Deutsche Bank, RBS and Societe Generale. Even so, the fines totalled €1.49 billion.[44]

RBS also made an immunity application to the Commission, which at least saved it from further fines. The Commission brought two cases based on its anti-trust provisions: one for a cartel based on the Swiss franc LIBOR and the other for a cartel involving euro interest rate derivatives. The first set of fines was imposed on 21 October 2014, on a cartel involving RBS, UBS, JP Morgan and Credit Suisse:

> In this case, ... the banks did not collude to influence the benchmark. Rather, they directly agreed to collectively fix a pricing element which should have been determined by market forces alone.... Indeed, between May and September 2007, the four banks agreed on the so-called 'bid–ask' spread.... They agreed to quote wider, fixed spreads to all third parties on certain categories of derivatives, while maintaining narrower spreads between themselves.[45]

The other fine was for 'collusive practices by two banks, RBS and JP Morgan ... between March 2008 and July 2009 to influence the Swiss franc LIBOR'.[46] JP Morgan was fined €61.6 million.

After a two-year investigation, the European Commission fined Credit Agricole, HSBC and JP Morgan Chase a total of €485 million for their part in a cartel in euro interest rate derivatives. Those banks had chosen not to reach a settlement with the Commission in 2013, unlike Barclays, Deutsche Bank, RBS and Societe Generale. The Commission found that there was a cartel in place between September 2005 and May 2008, involving a total of seven banks over varying time periods. The 'participating traders of the banks were in regular contact through corporate chat rooms or instant messaging services'. They sought to manipulate EURIBOR by telling each other 'their desired or intended EURIBOR submissions and by exchanging sensitive information on their trading positions or on their trading or pricing strategies'.[47] They were fined a total of €485 million.

The European Commission's approach is unusual in its use of anti-trust legislation. LIBOR is, after all, a benchmark and not part of the market. The setting of LIBOR, even when manipulated, cannot be said to restrict competition. Only the potential effects in price fixing could be said to be anti-competitive, which might require the manipulation to be successful in obtaining the price set for some and not for others. This is quite different from the US approach, which based its proceedings on provisions in the Commodity Exchange Act, which prohibits financial institutions from making false, misleading or knowingly inaccurate reports concerning the costs of borrowing unsecured funds. The much more detailed accounts offered by the CFTC, the FSA and the FCA make both the legal basis clear and provide detailed evidence of wrongdoing.

Notes

1 Financial Conduct Authority, 'Final notice, Rabobank', 29 October 2013, para. 4.14, pp. 9–10, available at https://www.fca.org.uk/publication/final-notices/rabobank.pdf (accessed 4 May 2018).
2 Ibid., para. 4.16, p. 11.
3 Ibid., para. 4.20, p. 12.
4 Ibid., para. 4.25, p. 12.
5 Ibid., para. 4.20, pp. 13–14.
6 Financial Conduct Authority, 'Final notice, Deutsche Bank AG', 23 April 2015, para 4.28, pp. 13–14, available at https://www.fca.org.uk/publication/final-notices/deutsche-bank-ag-2015.pdf (accessed 4 May 2018). Some of the quotations of emails and chatrooms are in capital letters, together with grammatical errors, spelling mistakes, jargon and Cockney rhyming slang. They are recorded in this way by the FCA and I have retained them in the quotations from the FCA notices. The capital letters no doubt reflect the degree of urgency or even desperation on the part of the traders.
7 Ibid., para 4.32, pp. 14–15.
8 Ibid., para 4.41, pp. 17–18.
9 Ibid., para 4.45, p. 19.
10 Ibid., para 4.47, p. 20.
11 Financial Services Authority, 'Final notice, UBS AG', 19 December 2012, p. 13, available at https://www.fca.org.uk/publication/final-notices/ubs.pdf (accessed 4 May 2018).
12 Ibid., p. 13.
13 Ibid., p. 14.
14 Ibid., p. 15.
15 Ibid., p. 16.
16 Ibid., p. 17.

17 Ibid., p. 18.

18 Ibid., p. 20.

19 Ibid., p. 21.

20 Ibid., paras 113–16, p. 24.

21 Ibid., p. 26.

22 Commodity Futures Trading Commission, 'In the matter of Citibank, N.A.; Citibank Japan Ltd.; and Citigroup Global Markets Japan Inc.', CFTC Docket No. 16–17, 25 May 2016, 'Order instituting proceedings pursuant to sections 6(c) and 6(d) of the Commodity Exchange Act, making findings and imposing remedial sanctions', p. 15, available at https://www.cftc.gov/sites/default/files/idc/groups/public/@lrenforcementactions/documents/legalpleading/enfcitibanklibororder052516.pdf (accessed 4 May 2018).

23 Ibid., pp. 18–19.

24 Ibid., p. 8.

25 Ibid., p. 9.

26 Ibid., p. 10.

27 Ibid., p. 12.

28 FCA, 'Final notice, Lloyds Bank plc, Bank of Scotland plc', 28 July 2014, p. 4, available at https://www.fca.org.uk/publication/final-notices/lloyds-bank-of-scotland.pdf (accessed 4 May 2018). The firms are wholly owned subsidiaries of Lloyds Banking Group plc, which was formed following the merger of Lloyds Bank plc with HBOS on 19 January 2009. HBOS plc is the holding company for the Bank of Scotland plc.

29 Ibid., p. 12.

30 Ibid., para 4.35, p. 12.

31 Ibid., p. 13.

32 Ibid., p. 14.

33 Ibid., p. 16.

34 Ibid., p. 15.

35 Commodity Futures Trading Commission, 'In the matter of Lloyds Banking Group plc and Lloyds Bank plc', CFTC Docket No. 14–18, 28 July 2014, 'Order instituting proceedings pursuant to sections 6(c) and 6(d) of the Commodity Exchange Act, making findings, and imposing remedial sanctions', p. 8, available at https://www.cftc.gov/sites/default/files/idc/groups/public/@lrenforcementactions/documents/legalpleading/enflloydsorderdf072814.pdf (accessed 4 May 2018).

36 Ibid., p. 9.

37 Ibid., p. 10.

38 Ibid., p. 12.

39 Ibid.

40 Ibid.

41 Ibid., p. 14.

42 Ibid., p. 16.

43 A 'prime bank' was later defined as a 'credit institution of high credit worthiness for short-term liabilities, which lends at competitive and is recognised as active in the euro-denominated market instruments while having access to the Eurosystem's open market operations'. Unfortunately, during

and after the financial crisis a number of banks could not meet such criteria! An interbank deposit means a cash deposit between two credit institutions, maturing one year from inception.

44 European Commission, 'Amended – Antitrust: Commission fines banks €1.49 billion for participating in cartels in the interest rate derivatives industry', press release, 4 December 2013, available at http://europa.eu/rapid/press-release_IP-13-1208_en.htm (accessed 4 May 2018).

45 European Commission, 'Statement by Vice President Joaquín Almunia on 2 cartel decisions concerning Swiss franc related derivatives', press release, 21 October 2014, available at http://europa.eu/rapid/press-release_STATEMENT-14-330_en.htm (accessed 4 May 2018).

46 Ibid.

47 European Commission, 'Antitrust: Commission fines Crédit Agricole, HSBC and JP Morgan Chase €485 million for euro interest rate cartel', press release, 7 December 2016, available at http://europa.eu/rapid/press-release_IP-16-4304_en.htm (accessed 4 May 2018).

Chapter 5

Who knew what when?

In this chapter, I shall focus on the comments and claims made about LIBOR prior to the beginning of the formal investigations by the FSA and the CFTC. As usual, after any scandal, the question immediately arises as to why the regulators had not discovered the wrongdoing earlier and taken action against those involved. Market rumours had swirled around LIBOR at the very beginning of the financial crisis (and, some would claim, before that), but had apparently been ignored. Regulators should never overlook the possible significance of market rumours, but should take time to investigate the reliability of the sources and question the organisations concerned. On the other hand, the public outcry should not be directed at the regulators alone, but at the perpetrators. To focus on the regulators alone can result in the perpetrators not getting the attention they deserve. This chapter will therefore set out who knew what, and when, and consider the reasons both for the failure to detect what was going on with LIBOR and for the failure to take prompt action. The last part of the chapter will examine the actions taken to prevent the manipulation of LIBOR in the future.

Media speculation

A flurry of articles appeared in the *Financial Times*, *Wall Street Journal*, MarketWatch and Bloomberg, beginning with an article by Gillian Tett in September 2007, probably the first to direct attention to LIBOR, referring to the BBA's novel briefing mission as it had been bombarded with questions about the benchmark. It seems that the BBA may have had more explaining to do than it expected. Tett noted:

> as the credit squeeze has spread in recent months, the Libor benchmark has, at least until recently, risen relentlessly ... [but] while these pressures have propelled Libor into public view, it has come at the very moment

that some bankers are quietly starting to question its value ... prompting suggestions that Libor is no longer offering such an accurate benchmark as before.

According to Tett, the treasurer of one of the largest City banks had complained that 'Libor rates are a bit of a fiction. The number on the screen doesn't always match what we see now.' The banks used to quote rates that were almost identical but by the middle of September 2007 'the gap between these quotes had sometimes risen to almost 10 basis points for 3-month sterling funds', with the 'same pattern' for the yen, euro and sterling markets. Tett suggested a longer-term trend – banks borrowing from pension funds and large corporations, a trend which attracted very little attention. These differences in the quotes may simply have reflected the underlying credit risk (which is part of LIBOR) as credit conditions worsened and doubts about counterparty risk increased.[1]

Tett's article was followed by a series of articles published in the *Wall Street Journal*, starting in April 2008, including 'Bankers cast doubt on key rate amid crisis'.[2] Sterling LIBOR had declined somewhat, the *Financial Times* reported on 21 April 2008, but its US dollar counterpart continued to rise 'with sharp jumps last week, culminating in Monday's setting at 2.92%'. Moreover:

> at the very same time as institutions such as the Bank of England are trying to pull this rate lower, the credibility of Libor as a measure is declining ... threatening to inject a new element of volatility and investor distrust into the financial arena.[3]

Three days later, an article on Bloomberg reported:

> Interest-rate derivatives are signaling that the rate banks charge for loans in dollars in London may rise further as financial institutions remain reluctant to lend.
>
> The difference between the rate of three-month loans in London relative to the overnight index swap rate, known as the Libor–OIS spread, is 88 basis points, just below the year high of 90 basis points reached on April 21.
>
> The London interbank offered rate, or Libor, for dollar climbed to a seven-week high amid speculation the global credit crunch prompted lenders to manipulate the rate to prevent their borrowing costs from escalating.[4]

Further media attention followed. A news report and a newspaper article on 29 May attracted the most attention. The former, published by Bloomberg, quoted Tim Bond, a strategist at Barclays' Capital:

banks routinely misstated borrowing costs to the BBA [British Bankers' Association] to avoid the perception they faced difficulty raising funds as credit markets seized up. The rates the banks were posting to the BBA became a little divorced from reality ... we had one week in September where our treasurer, who takes his responsibilities pretty seriously, said, 'Right, I've had enough of this, I'm going to quote the right rates.' All we got for our pains was a series of media articles saying we were having difficulties financing.[5]

The newspaper article, by Carrick Mollenkamp and Mark Whitehouse in the *Wall Street Journal*, was based on a study which 'casts doubt on key rate'.[6] This was a comparison with LIBOR of the costs of default insurance. While two rates usually move in tandem, there may be important differences between, say, the interest on a credit default swap (CDS) and a LIBOR, for example between a three-month LIBOR and a six-month CDS, since the differences in the time period could well involve a different estimate of the risks involved. The seller of a CDS protects against the loss the loans the buyer of a CDS holds. The seller of a CDS is therefore taking on roughly the same risk exposure as a lender, but the buyer is entitled to request collateral from the dealer, who makes the transaction in an over-the-counter market, a market not noted for transparency. In their book *The Fix*, Liam Vaughan and Gavin Finch argue that the comparison of three-month LIBORs with six-month CDS prices showed only a 'minor error', which was enough for Tom Huertas, Director of Banking at the FSA, 'to justify dropping the matter'.[7] That was not in fact the case, but more of that later.

It is important to emphasise that banks are not obliged to borrow at LIBOR and a bank has no duty to lend to other banks at LIBOR. LIBOR is defined as an adjusted average of the rates submitted by members of the LIBOR panel. Each bank's submission is the rate at which the posting bank expects it will be able to borrow funds if it seeks funds in the market. It does not imply that the submitting bank will be willing to fund other banks at that rate. Even if the submitting bank is willing to lend to other banks, this may be at a level different from the rate it submits to the BBA for its own interbank borrowing, as well as different from the rate the borrowing bank expects to have to pay. But the use of this average creates the basis for the two variants: lowballing and level-fixing. For both, this point is important: LIBOR does not say anything about the actual cost of borrowing, so comparing a submission with a contemporaneous cost of borrowing may not be enough to prove lowballing. Mollenkamp and Whitehouse state:

the Journal's analysis doesn't prove that banks are lying or manipulating LIBOR. Analysts offer various reasons why some banks might report Libor rates lower than what other markets indicate ... since the financial crisis began, banks have all but stopped lending to each other for periods of three months or more, so their estimates of how much it would cost to borrow involve a lot of guesswork ... some U.S. banks, such as Citigroup and J.P. Morgan, have ample customer deposits and access to loans from the Federal Reserve, meaning that they might not need to borrow at higher rates from other banks.[8]

In addition to articles in the financial press, academic papers appeared that cast doubts on the reliability of LIBOR and they are discussed in the next section.[9]

Academic articles on LIBOR

Academic articles published during the financial crisis had examined the variations in the LIBOR daily rates and then compared them with other rates. Two appeared in the *BIS Quarterly Review* in March 2008. Jacob Gyntelberg and Philip Wooldridge examined the reasons for the unusual divergence of LIBOR from other reference rates, and argued that the design of the fixing mechanism moderated the influence of extreme quotes from contributor banks, as intended. They argued that banks were likely to behave in a strategic manner, by seeking to signal through their quotes information about either their credit quality or their liquidity needs, but noted that 'if there were any attempts to manipulate fixings during the recent turbulence, trimming procedures appear to have mitigated their impact'. They concluded:

> A comparison of different fixings in the same currency reveals that interbank rates diverged to an unusual extent in the second half of 2007. This divergence was not caused by shortcomings in the design of the fixing mechanism ... it reflected the dislocation in the underlying interbank markets. Changes in the credit quality of contributor banks and a deterioration in liquidity affected liquidity to varying degrees. Credit quality appears to have had an especially large impact on offshore fixings (including London), dominated by foreign banks. Liquidity was a significant factor in US dollar and euro fixings ... fixings are likely to be less representative when market conditions are volatile.... During volatile periods there can be significant dispersion because of greater uncertainty about credit quality and greater incentives to engage in strategic behaviour.[10]

In another article in the same issue of the *Quarterly Review*, François-Louis Michaud and Christian Upper drew on evidence from a LIBOR panel. They examined the reasons for the risk premium contained in interest rates on three-month interbank deposits at large internationally active banks, which increased sharply in August 2007 and remained high in 2008. Their analysis suggested that, in the short term, risk premia were mainly driven by short-term liquidity issues, that is, the ability to convert assets into cash, of individual banks. They noted the way in which spreads between LIBOR and the overnight index swap (OIS) rate increased during the months they studied and argued that the 'differences between maturities and sudden jumps point to the importance of bank liquidity needs' but noted that the OIS rate did not take much account of liquidity. It might be a useful indicator of expected future overnight interest rates, but 'the counterparty risk associated with these contracts is relatively small as they do not involve the exchange of principal'. Moreover:

> secondly, and perhaps more importantly, the liquidity premia contained in OIS rates should be very small as these contracts do not involve any initial cash flows. Under normal market conditions, OIS rates tend to be slightly below the corresponding Libor.[11]

The authors concluded that their results 'support the view that both credit and liquidity factors were behind the increase in risk premia in the interbank money market'.[12] Their analysis is careful to point out the differences in what each rate takes into account. This is important, because too often in these analyses the divergence between interest rates is assumed to show that LIBOR was, for that reason, being misused in some way. The comparison of one interest rate with another in the search for patterns is too blunt an instrument to identify the differences of one or two basis points in the false submissions.

In August 2008, Rosa Abrantes-Metz (with Albert Metz and others) published a paper querying LIBOR manipulation in response to the *Wall Street Journal*'s claims that banks were reporting costs that were significantly lower than the rates justified by bank-specific cost trend movements in the default insurance market.[13] The *Journal* had suggested that although this did not prove that banks were lying or manipulating LIBOR, the 'banks may have lowballing their borrowing rates to avoid looking desperate for cash'. Abrantes-Metz et al. looked at three separate periods: January to 8 August 2007; 9 August 2007 to 16 April 2008; and 17 April 2008. Their methodology involved examining structural breaks in the series of LIBORs and comparing them with benchmarks not suspected of manipulation. The comparison was with the Fed Fund effective rate (a weighted average of rates of the actual exchange between banks, usually overnight, so representing a short-term rate of borrowing between banks), 'making it a suitable benchmark' for their study. They compared one-month or three-month LIBORs with the Fed Fund effective rate, regardless of the different timescales involved, and concluded:

> although this study does not provide conclusive evidence of the existence of anti-competitive market behaviour (or for that matter, any effective manipulation of the Libor rate) on the part of banks, we do present statistical evidence of patterns that appear to be inconsistent with those that are normally expected to occur under conditions of market competition for certain of the periods under study.[14]

In addition, the FSA received a research paper by JP Morgan, dated 16 May 2008, which concluded:

> In our view, the LIBOR fixing process is not broken: BBA Libor broadly reflects the borrowing costs of the top tier large banks. Differences between Libor and other indices can largely be explained by the composition of the Libor panel. The main limitations of Libor are more due to lack of liquidity in the market rather than any bias in the fixing process.[15]

Before mid-2007, LIBOR tended to move closely with other short-term interest rates such as Treasury yields and OIS, but began, not surprisingly, to display greater volatility as the financial crisis deepened. A combination of counterparty credit risk and liquidity concerns pushed the three-month US dollar LIBOR to 5.62% on 31 August 2007, compared with an average of 5.6% during the previous six months, during a period of stable expectations for the overnight Fed Funds policy rate target for the Federal Reserve. The LIBOR–OIS spread is a measure of bank credit spread, term liquidity spread and term risk premia for interbank loans. LIBORs began to display greater volatility in relation to other rates in the second half of 2008 (after Fannie Mae and Freddie Mac were taken into conservatorship in June and the collapse of Lehman Brothers in September 2008). Liquidity began to dry up as banks were unwilling to lend to each other at all, still less to tie up funds for three months or more, and feared counterparty risk, since they were not sure of the value of each other's assets.

Some academic papers widened their focus from one average LIBOR–OIS spread to look at the panel dimensions of spreads, by including variations across banks, currencies and terms of the 'loans'. One such paper argued that this was 'essential from a statistical point of view', since the ' empirical results show that there are benefits from exploiting these panel dimensions in terms of increasing our understanding of liquidity and credit risk'.[16]

One further academic analysis was provided by Connan Snider and Thomas Youle. It examined the relationship between LIBOR and CDS rates, which, they argued, showed the bunching of LIBOR quotes around the fourth lowest, for which the explanation was that some banks had an incentive to alter the rate of overall LIBOR and the bunching was the result of these incentives interacting with the rate-setting mechanism. This was because of the nature of the portfolios of some banks in terms of their interest rate derivatives, though, as these banks were market-makers, it was likely that the outstanding notional value of their net positions was much smaller than their gross positions. This was regarded as 'new evidence corroborating concerns that LIBOR panel banks may be understating their true borrowing costs'.[17] Once again, the article rested on a comparison of LIBOR to CDS spreads as a proxy for banks' contemporaneous cost of funds, but these spreads represent much more than default risks and the CDS market is less liquid than the interbank lending market.

All the academic articles focused either on volatility in LIBORs or on comparisons of LIBOR with other rates rates based on entirely different foundations and so measuring or reflecting different economic realities). Even the latter analyses, though, failed to take account of the wider context of the financial crisis. That would have meant looking beyond all the major events to the responses of individual banks to their own particular situations and the impact of fears and rumours as well as government intervention during the crisis. Most of the articles were produced before the FSA and CFTC had completed their investigations. The only ones which had any bearing on the actions of the FSA and the Bank of England are the two articles in the BIS *Quarterly Review* and possibly the article by Abrantes-Metz et al. These provided some comfort, as indicated by the Governor of the Bank of England:

> We had no evidence of wrongdoing. None was supplied to us. The evidence you cite – there were plenty of academic articles that looked in[to] it and said they could not see in the data any evidence of manipulation.[18]

The Deputy Governor concurred:

> We didn't see it. I think there were other studies, including the one by the BIS, although I think I am aware of this after the fact, that didn't conclude that it was a problem. Maybe we were just too focused on the financial crisis.[19]

Furthermore, the Governor commented:

> I was very struck and surprised, when reading these three reports [from the regulatory authorities], to discover that changing LIBOR by one basis point was the kind of rigging that people were interested in. You would never have noticed that from market activity. We were worried by tens of basis points.[20]

Did the attempts at manipulation have any effect?

Most of the regulatory investigations were focused on whether there had been attempts to manipulate LIBOR, not on whether or not those attempts were successful. Even the regulators were not convinced that the manipulators could gain a clear advantage. For example, in its final notice to Barclays, the FSA merely stated that the bank '*could* have benefitted from this misconduct to the detriment of other market participants'.[21] The US Department of Justice's examination of Barclays concluded that the manipulation affected the rates 'on some occasions'.[22] These often had more to do with the settlement price, set four times annually, for interest rate futures contracts. The media (and a number of lawsuits) claimed that losses as a result of this manipulation were widespread, but such claims were hard to establish, and determining the level of damages was very difficult. This is not only because one basis point is unlikely to have had much effect. At the time, the calculation was based on what a bank's estimate of what its borrowing costs would be, not actual transactions. It is hard to see what the basis for a realistic counterfactual would be, since the claim would be that the borrowing costs would have been other than the bank's estimate if manipulation had not taken place. The claim would have to be about the amount of damages and it is impossible to assess that. Furthermore, if the attempted manipulation had worked, and that could be demonstrated, then there would be both winners and losers: what would have to happen to the winners? Did the attempted manipulation have a wider effect on the costs of mortgages, for example, as the media claimed? Maybe, but it is almost impossible to prove it.

When did the FSA realise what was happening with LIBOR?

The Bank of England was not the regulatory authority. That was the Financial Services Authority. Although the Bank had to know and understand what was taking place in the markets and, as a result of that obligation, had to maintain effective channels of communication with the FSA, and indeed with the major financial institutions, regulation and supervision were the responsibility of the FSA, not the Bank.

However, frequent references in the media to lowballing, and in particular Barclays' disclosure of the number of contacts it had with the FSA between 6 December 2007 and 30 September 2008 and references by external parties to their communications with the FSA about LIBOR, led to the decision by the FSA to conduct an internal audit. Lord Turner, then chairman of the FSA, asked for this to set out the facts relating to contacts with the FSA or awareness within the FSA relating to 'inappropriate LIBOR submissions to avoid negative media comment'. The team was also asked to form a judgement, if possible from the information available, on whether or not the FSA's response was appropriate at the time. This followed criticism of the FSA in the Treasury Select Committee's report *Fixing LIBOR* and the FSA's publication of its final notice imposing a fine on Barclays for breaches of a number of 'principles of business' on 27 June 2012.

The FSA's *Internal Audit Report* was published in March 2013.[23] The internal audit searched and reviewed electronic records from the FSA's management system from January 2007 to May 2009, loading 17 million documents and emails in the search software. The initial filter left 97,000 documents and emails, which were independently reviewed. The audit team searched for lowballing and trader manipulation but did not find any references to the latter. The report provides a great deal more information about the various communications the FSA received, and about its relationship to the CFTC and to the BBA. The BBA was of course the body responsible for the management of LIBOR and the FSA had no responsibility for LIBOR under the Financial Services and Markets Act 2000; nor did it have any supervisory powers. The internal audit lists at least 30 occasions on which various members of staff received inside information from banks and others. A selection of these references is set out here to indicate the type of information received and to whom it was given; the time periods are those of the four sections of the report's chapter 3.[24]

1 January 2007 to 31 December 2007

Against a background of deteriorating market conditions in the second half of 2007, when the subprime mortgage crisis was developing, a number of financial institutions experienced liquidity issues and the Bank of England announced on 14 September that it was providing a liquidity support facility to Northern Rock. In the USA, a number of subprime lenders either closed or filed for bankruptcy, but the bankruptcy of two well known mortgage banks, New Century Financial in April and American Home Mortgage in August, added to market anxieties. Bear Stearns's decision to stop redemptions in two of its hedge funds in June 2007 increased the uncertainty.

It is against that background that the various communications circulated within the FSA should be set. These are often 'Market conditions' and 'Market intelligence' updates from the Bank of England, which were circulated within the FSA to the Acting Managing Director of Wholesale and Institutional Markets, Director of the Wholesale Firms Division, Director of the Banking Sector, Director of the Major Retail Groups Division and the Financial Stability Sector and to staff below director level. This was the usual practice. The 'communications' also include emails and telephone calls from various financial institutions or notes on conference calls made by the FSA for updates on banks' liquidity and funding positions. These are itemised as a series of numbered and dated 'communications', which include the source of the information contained in the quotations. The *Internal Audit Report* also sets out the list of recipients in each case.

Communication 4, Market conditions update, 2 October 2007

> There is still a lack of offers in the dollar market, despite a few more from Hong Kong today, and therefore liquidity is reported as very thin. Several contacts noted that they think Libors should be higher, but banks are keeping them low.

This comment is taken from the 'Market conditions update' circulated by the Bank of England to the Acting Managing Director of Wholesale and Institutional Markets, Director of the Wholesale Firms Division, the Director of Major Retail Groups, the Director of Major Retail Groups and the Financial Stability Sector and staff within some of those groups. Similar comments are to be found in the later markets conditions reports.

Communication 10, Sterling Markets Division, Market Intelligence Summary, 29 November 2007

> The note included the following comment: [A broker reported in the context of sterling LIBOR–OIS spreads] 'increased talk that Libors were actually being slightly understated given that banks did not want to post a rate above the pack; others thought it had been a finger in the air exercise for months.

This note was attached to an email and circulated to the FSA mailing list entitled 'BoE Markets', which included the Managing Director of Wholesale and Institutional Markets, and the Directors of the Wholesale Firms Division, the Markets Division, the Strategy and Risk Division, and the Small Firms Division.

Communication 14, Barclays' first contact with the FSA regarding LIBOR, 6 December 2007
Barclays' Compliance contacted the FSA by telephone to express concerns about the levels at which other banks were setting the dollar LIBOR, but there is no record of the telephone call. The member of the supervision team replied the next day by email to the person within Barclays' Compliance, quoting from a newsletter which the FSA published on its website in October 2002 regarding conduct which was likely to breach the Code of Market Conduct. This stated that a breach of the Code would occur 'if one or more banks colluded to manipulate the fixing of Libor or Euribor to benefit a position they have in an interest rate future'; 'this could fall within the false or misleading impressions or distortion legs of the Code, though the extent to which this is possible varies according to the method of fixing which is used'. The FSA's final notice to Barclays' states that Barclays Compliance contacted the FSA on 6 December 2007 by telephone to relay a concern about levels at which *other banks* (my italics) were setting US dollar LIBOR, but there is no record of any further response on the part of the FSA.[25]

1 January 2008 to 31 March 2008

Market conditions worsened during this period, and stock markets fell. It was announced on 17 February that Northern Rock was being taken into public ownership. Bear Stearns was rescued by JP Morgan Chase following support from the New York Federal Reserve. During this period there were many more comments relating specifically to

LIBOR, including six from firms providing liquidity updates or views on the current state of wholesale funding. In this period, it seems that the circulation list was wider and included the Chairman, the Chief Executive, the Director of the Strategy and Risk Division, the Executive Committee (ExCo) and others, as well as staff below the director level. Apart from the market conditions reports, it is more useful in this context to list the communications from financial institutions, although these are sometimes indirect.

Communication 16, Market conditions update, 7 February 2008

> A similar story in the euro market, contacts expect spreads to widen, as Libors are forced higher on the back of cash offers in the market. Similar scenario to when they started widening in November, with several banks complaining that Libors are being set far too low.

This market conditions update was emailed to the Chairman, the Director of Major Retail Groups/Financial Stability Sector, the Director of the Banking Sector and others.

Communication 17, Email entitled 'More money market musings',
8 February 2008
An email from a member of staff below director level in the Strategy and Risk Division read:

> it is likely that the reported 1-month spreads for high quality names and ABCP spreads versus LIBOR are not adequately reflecting the increased stresses we are hearing about in the market.

This email went to the Chairman, the Directors of the Banking Sector, the Major Retail Groups Division, the Financial Stability Sector, the Wholesale Firms Division, the Retail Intermediaries Sector, and the Strategy and Risk Division.

Communication 18, 19 February 2008

> LIBORS generally continue to be non-representative of true prices going through the market.

This email summarises certain financial institutions' views of the wholesale funding conditions, including the above comment from a LIBOR panel bank. The email was circulated to all the directors of the various divisions listed above.

Communication 22, 27 February 2008

Barclays advise further that in general, cash is expensive; however, this is not being reflected in LIBOR rates. A member of staff commented that the diversion between interbank lending rates and LIBOR is a known effect, which has fluctuated. LIBOR is not based on transactions and therefore may not be reflective of the true interbank market. LIBOR is used for the pricing derivatives, and loans.

This communication is in fact a note of a 'market conditions' meeting within the FSA. Chaired by the Director of the Banking Sector and attended by staff below director level of all the major divisions, including the Asset Management Sector team and the Wholesale and Prudential Policy Division. A note of the meeting was circulated among the directors of all the major divisions with the addition of the Director of the Retail Policy Themes Division/Asset Management Sector, the Director of the Treating Customers Fairly Division, the Director of the Communications Division, the Bank of England and the Treasury, as well as to other staff. The wide range of people on the circulation list and the fact the meeting itself was not attended by directors suggest that the purpose of the meeting was unclear.

Communication 24, LIBOR panel bank, 11 March 2008

LIBOR fixings are becoming increasingly divorced irrelevant to the reality of the pricing in the market.

The above comment was in an email from a LIBOR panel bank.

Communication 25, Barclays, 17 March 2008

There is little to no cash available where LIBORs are setting, the few lenders around in the market are increasingly name sensitive.

To this was added two days later, 'We feel that some banks are posting artificially low reference rates so as not to draw attention to themselves'. (This email from Barclays was disclosed by Barclays to the Treasury Select Committee but was not in the FSA's system.) These emails were circulated to staff below director level in the Barclays supervision team.

Communication 27, Market conditions update, 27 March 2008

Contacts are still suggesting that Libors should be even higher and spreads wider at the moment.

Communication 28, Barclays, 27 March 2008

> There has been comment that Libors are 'too low' and the calculations
> of Libor benchmarks migt be causing apparent distortions.... Barclays
> advise that they have seen divergence between cash and Libor of over
> 5 bps on occasion, but caveat that the methodology of using 16 contrib-
> utors and dropping the top 4 and bottom 4 quotes, might be a factor
> depending on where the top and bottom quotes are.

This email referring to the discussion with Barclays was circulated to the
Chairman and the Chief Executive, as well as to the other Managing
Directors, and the Bank of England, the Treasury and staff below
director level in these divisions, including the Prudential Risks Division.

Communication 29, Barclays, 28 March 2008

> There are few cash offers to support where LIBORs are being set and the
> few lenders in the market are increasingly name sensitive.

This was yet another email from Barclays. It was sent to staff within the
supervision team within the Major Retail Groups Division.

1 April 2008 to 25 June 2008

Once again, the focus will be on communications received from external
sources, from banks and other financial institutions. The first of these
was from a non-LIBOR panel bank.

Communication 30, a non-LIBOR panel bank, 1 April 2008
A compliance officer at a non-LIBOR panel bank advised his supervisor
as follows:

> It appears to us that something is wrong when a panel of contributor
> banks is supplying LIBOR at below what the banks can achieve in the
> market. It may be worth investigating to see if the contributor banks are
> making profits on the back of these quotes.

In the end, the compliance officer was referred back to the BBA. Some
staff, it seems, had begun to recognise the risks involved and that the
LIBOR fixing was going wrong. One staff member in the Prudential
Risk Division pointed out that 'the implications if someone wanted to
challenge the "fairness" of the fixes are massive'. This comment was
circulated to the managing director of Wholesale and Institutional

Markets, the Director of the Banking Sector, and staff below director level in the Prudential Risk and Wholesale Firms Divisions. At the same time, the advice from the General Counsel's Division was that the FSA did not regulate the BBA and any concerns about LIBOR fixings should be raised with that body. That advice was relayed to the Directors of the Markets Division and of the Banking Sector. This is all covered in communication 30.

Communication 32, Non-LIBOR panel bank, 7 April 2008
Another non-LIBOR panel bank mentioned as part of a conference call:

> US LIBOR appears to be low compared to US Cash. European investors make use of FX arbitrage to swap US LIBOR ... back to £ sub-LIBOR.

This note of a conference call was circulated to staff in the Major Retail Groups Division.

Communication 34, Note of market conditions meeting, 9 April 2008
The internal audit team included a note of the meeting sent by the Director of the Markets Division to a member of staff in his Division, asking:

> What are our thoughts on Libor fixing – ie is this now a broken process?

The reply included the following comments:

> No more broken than it has been for some time.

> As an aside, there is some concern around Bank's [sic] used in the fix deliberately misquoting for the fix in order to put pressure on the Bank. The BBA who own this process are looking at this. It's very difficult to tell if this is a real issue (if it were there may be market manipulation issues).

Communications 37 and 38, Barclays, 17 April 2008
'Manager D' from Barclays made the following comment (communication 37) in a routine liquidity telephone call with the FSA:

> We've always been at the top end and therefore one of the four banks that's been eliminated. Um, so I would, I would sort of express us maybe as not clean clean, but clean in principle.

A further email (communication 38), not in the FSA's management system, added:

USD Libor fixings came under renewed scrutiny following an article earlier in the WSJ [*Wall Street Journal*]. The story suggested something we have long known, which is that USD Libors are fixing too low.

This was a liquidity telephone call between Barclays and two members of staff in the supervision team at the Major Retail Groups Division, but the note of the call did not refer to what Barclays said about LIBOR.

Communication 39, Bank of England, 18 April 2008
This update recorded the expectation that US dollar LIBORs would see 'similar increases to yesterday's marked step-up following the BBA's warning to banks about submitting accurate fixings' but noted that LIBOR–OIS spreads 'have widened further ... the widest level since the crisis started' and that 'At the longer end of the curve there still looks as though Libor levels are too low compared to cash with [LIBOR Panel Bank 1] willing to pay [xx] bp and [LIBOR Panel Bank 2] [xx] bp above Libor!'

Communication 41, Barclays, 23 April 2008
The following email came from someone in Barclays' Compliance:

> USD Libors are still fixing below where cash would be available, currently the only offers of 3 months are 3.20 and 1 year at 3.50 compared with Libors of 2.92 and 3.11 respectively, although when the US starts trading we expect to see money market funds looking to buy CDs around 3.00 in 3's and 3.35 in 1 y.

Once again, the email went to staff in the Major Retail Groups Division, but was not found in the FSA's files.

26 June 2008 to 31 May 2009

From September 2008, market conditions deteriorated significantly; LIBOR–OIS spreads widened sharply following the collapse of Lehman Brothers on 15 September and the sale of Merrill Lynch to the Bank of America the same day. Many financial institutions clearly experienced severe difficulties. The FTSE 100 index fell by 381.7 points on 10 October 2008, its most serious one-day fall since the crash of 1987. The US dollar LIBOR–OIS spread reached 365 basis points on 10 October and the sterling LIBOR–OIS spread reached 299 basis points on 6 November. Central bank interventions meant that towards the end of 2008 spreads begin to fall, bringing about some improvements in market conditions.

For its part, the Bank of England reduced the base rate to 0.5% and introduced the quantitative easing programme on 5 March 2009. Hence, towards the end of 2008, LIBOR–OIS spreads began to fall.

By this time, the focus of attention for the FSA regarding LIBOR had shifted to a BBA review and subsequent report and to communications from the US CFTC. But there were still a number of communications from financial institutions and from Barclays. They are as follows.

Communication 52, Market conditions update, 11 September 2008

> Several contacts have highlighted the theory that Libor is not truly reflective of actual inter-bank lending offer rates for many institutions.

This comment, in the context of US dollar LIBOR fixings, was circulated to the Chairman, the Director of the Banking Sector and the Director of the Financial Stability Division, among others.

Communications 53–55, emails from panel member banks, 22–23 September 2008
A series of emails included the following:

> USD Libor rates are described as 'wide and wonderful' – they are no guide to where the cash is being dealt.

> The O/N [overnight rate] is trading okay and there is some turnover in periods out to 1 week. In other periods there are no offers to support the Libor fixings.

> USD Libors are 'nonsense' and do not relate to cash levels – they noted 1 month Libor at 5.0%/4.5%, which is well away from where they were bidding.

> We had the latest round of $TAFs [Term Auction Facility] earlier [...] the stand-out detail was the [stop-out] rate which at 3.75 was 55bp above the 1 month BBA Libor, probably more evidence that Libors are fixing too low.

These emails were from two panel member banks, one of which was Barclays. They were circulated to staff in the Major Retail Groups Division, including supervisory staff.

Communications 58, 59 and 61, 25 September, 30 September and 15 October 2008
Again, the following emails were from Barclays Compliance:

If $ Libors were more market reflective (at least of the bid side for cash), the spread would be much higher.

Since the start of the month 3 month Libors have risen, USD 124 bp, EUR 31 bp and GBP 55bp. At the same time, OIS yields have fallen, USD 45 bp, EUR 28 bp and GBP 22 bp on accelerating cut views. That rise in the 3 month $ Libor still does not reflect the true USD liquidity conditions as cash is bid 50 bp to 150bp higher than the fixing without any real offer.

Barclays note that some UK banks are posting low for GBP Libor, but they know they are not attracting funds at these levels.

These emails went to staff in the supervision team in the Major Retail Groups Division.

Communication 62, LIBOR panel bank, 16 October 2008
Another LIBOR panel bank observed:

LIBOR fixings – although lower – are not reflective of market activity.

Communication 63, Non-LIBOR panel bank, 17 October 2008
A non-LIBOR panel bank made two comments on wholesale funding conditions:

Current GBP Libor fixings do not reflect the true picture of offers in the interbank market if and when they do materialise.

All Libor fixings have also registered large reductions but where they are fixing and where they are trading is a wholly different story.

These emails went to an FSA mailbox which was monitored by staff in the supervision divisions and the Prudential Risk Division.

Communication 64, Update on positions of two LIBOR panel banks, 22 October 2008

They [Barclays] believe that the improvement in Libor is an overstatement, and indicate that firms are not necessarily funding where they post for the fixing.

This was a discussion with firms on their funding positions. The email went to the Director of the Major Groups Division and staff in the Financial Stability and Prudential Risk Divisions.

Communication 66, Note for record, 6 November 2008
This note for the record relating to a supervisory visit to review a building society's treasury function included the following comment:

> The society were concerned at the way LIBOR rates were set. The society felt that the rates did not have any resemblance to real market activity, and in particular where the large banks were prepared to take deposits.

This note was not circulated.

Communication 68, Note for record, 11 December 2008
In a record of a liquidity meeting with Barclays, it was noted that:

> Barclays described their LIBOR settings as 'honest', something they don't believe to be the case for all participants. They see elevated funding cost as a small price to pay for term funding. They continue to be at the higher end for $ though £ has fallen back in line. They questioned whether some firms had been somewhat disingenuous with their LIBOR fixings.

Communication 70, Update from Barclays, 4 February 2009
In an update of the funding position of Barclays, it was recorded that:

> Barclays note that while GBP Libors are unchanged, that the market still has fully priced in a cut of 50bps tomorrow. They note that perhaps the Libor settings are not reflecting their purpose.

This note went to the Bank of England and to staff below the director level in the Major Retail Groups Division and Prudential Risk Division.

Communication 71, Update on funding position of a LIBOR panel bank, 9 March 2009

> LIBOR fixings do not represent what is going on in the market.

This email was circulated to staff below the director level in the Major Retail Groups, Wholesale Firms Division.

Communication 72, Note providing information on a LIBOR panel bank's liquidity position, 17 March 2009

> Sterling Libors have crept lower, but this is purely on market sentiment and not indicative of levels traded ([the LIBOR Panel Bank] comment that Sterling Libors do not reflect true levels).

This was circulated to staff below the director level in the Major Retail Groups, Wholesale Firms and Prudential Risk Divisions.

Communication 73, Market conditions update, 18 March 2009

> Contacts were unsure why Libors continued to edge down, with the fixings remaining disconnected from the small volume of lending in the market.

This note was attached to an email and circulated to the Bank of England mailing list for its market conditions update.

Communication 74, Update on funding position of Barclays, 20 March 2009

> Libors continue to edge down, but Barclays question their reliability given that there is little activity to support them.

This email was circulated to the Director of the Major Retail Groups Division and staff in the Financial Stability, Wholesale Firms and Prudential Risk Divisions. This comment was included in an FSA internal email, 29 March 2009, to the Chairman's office, the Chief Executive and Directors.

Barclays and the FSA: an example of the limitations of the FSA's response

What is clear from the above communications, some internal, some from external institutions, is the extent to which Barclays dominates the input regarding submissions to LIBOR, most of which come from Barclays' own compliance team. It is interesting to speculate about the reasons for this. No other bank, even panel member banks, chose to go on the record in the same way, it appears from the available evidence. Barclays frequently referred to the fact that other banks were not submitting the correct rates, but that did not seem to attract the attention it deserved. Nor did it help Barclays, which, ironically, was the first bank to be formally investigated.

Some of the comments made by staff below director level showed that they understood the relevance of the comments made about LIBOR, such as one comment by a member of staff in the Prudential Risk Division: 'the implications if someone wanted to challenge the "fairness" of the fixes are massive'. A member of staff in the Enforcement Division noted that the FSA did 'have prudential supervisory responsibility over the FSA authorised banks providing the information to the BBA' and a staff member in the Markets Division said 'we can visit any banks which have made significant increases in their returns to the BBA'.[26] It seems that there was wide knowledge that LIBOR was being misused, though mostly through lowballing, rather than manipulation, as reflected in emails circulated throughout the FSA. The problem was that the communications were not appropriately targeted. It was entirely unclear who, if anybody, had overall responsibility for collating the information received from various sources and who had responsibility for taking action. There was some understanding on the part of some members of staff that, although the FSA was not responsible for the BBA's management of LIBOR, nevertheless lowballing may well have indicated prudential implications and did conflict with the FSA's Principles for Business.

The FSA ought to have clarified the roles and responsibilities within the organisation for dealing with external bodies, especially in view of the information about LIBOR being circulated by the Bank of England. The FSA should also have looked for clarification of the roles and responsibilities of those external bodies, as well as the relationships between the tripartite authorities – that is, the FSA, the Bank of England and the Treasury, which were bound by a memorandum of understanding to share information with each other. All in all, one can only agree with the conclusion of the internal audit:

> the FSA's focus on dealing with the implications of the financial crisis for the capital and liquidity positions of individual firms, together with the fact that contributing to or administering LIBOR were not 'regulated activities', led to the FSA being too narrowly focused in its handling of LIBOR-related information.

All was not lost, however, since once the FSA and the CFTC recognised that there was a problem, the long and arduous task of investigating the panel banks began and the FSA was able to fine the banks concerned on the basis of its Principles for Business.

Did the FSA listen to the CFTC?

It is sometimes alleged that the FSA simply ignored warnings and approaches from the CFTC. The first communication from the CFTC, communication 40 in the FSA *Internal Audit Report*, dated 22 April

2008, referred to 'possible false reporting of information to the BBA', together with two press articles,[27] one of which referred to 'Concerns [which] emerged this week that some banks may have been under-reporting'. These were circulated to members of staff below the director level and also to staff in the Banking Sector Team and Prudential Risk Division and later (25 April) to the Director of Markets Division (Wholesale), the Managing Director of Wholesale and Institutional Markets, and the Directors of the Banking Sector and of the Financial Stability Division. A member of staff below the director level emailed the CFTC saying the FSA would look into it, but 'The FSA does not have supervisory responsibility for the BBA rate setting mechanism although [...] we do have prudential supervisory responsibility over the FSA authorised banks providing the information to the FSA'. He was correct on both points. The Director of Banking asked what jurisdiction the CFTC had in the matter, which was a genuine request for information but which was never forwarded to the General Counsel Division of the CFTC and therefore never provided.

Further to the approach in April, the CFTC again contacted the FSA regarding media coverage of LIBOR under-reporting by certain banks. On 26 June 2008, the CFTC emailed a member of staff within the FSA's Enforcement Division, attaching the article by Mollenkamp and Whitehouse in the *Wall Street Journal* from 29 May, which referred to five contributor banks. The staff member referred the CFTC to the Director of Markets Division and to another member of staff in Prudential Risk. It was decided then that the person responsible was the Director of Banking and the email was also circulated to other divisions. The CFTC's request was then discussed at ExCo, with a note that the CFTC wanted to 'reach out' to the five banks mentioned to ask them for information on a voluntary basis to assess whether there was any deliberate under-reporting or collusion. This would be taken forward as part of the CFTC's false-reporting statute, which applies to inter-state commerce, which, in the CFTC's view, 'includes the world'.[28] However, it turns out that Dr Huertas, then Director of Banking at the FSA, was right to ask questions about the CFTC's jurisdiction in the matter. The worldwide application was not obvious. The long-standing interpretation is that 'Neither the Commodity Exchange Act nor its legislative history specifically authorises extraterritorial application of the statute' but that the Act does allow the CFTC 'to pursue' individuals and entities that violate the Act through 'domestic' transactions executed on US exchanges. Wholly extraterritorial conduct, though, is outside its remit.[29]

The *Internal Audit Report* notes that on 27 June 2008 the CFTC finally called the Director of the FSA's Enforcement Division, following up with an email on 30 June 2008, again attaching the article in the *Wall Street Journal* on 29 May. The CFTC was then referred to the Director of Banking. A conference call took place between the FSA, the BBA and the CFTC on 9 July but there is no record of the contents of the call. From then, on the FSA and the CFTC cooperated, with the FSA facilitating contact between the CFTC and the BBA, though it has to be said that the BBA's responses were often slow. Part of the reason for the delay was the CFTC's scatter-gun approach in sending emails to various members of staff below director level, who would not have had the authority to suggest any formal contact. The initial requests should have been addressed to one of the directors or indeed to the Chief Executive. However, once the requests were made to the appropriate directors, cooperation did follow, resulting in the FSA's and the CTFC's imposition of fines on various LIBOR panel banks.

The BBA: limitations and weaknesses exposed

LIBOR was also discussed at a Bank of England Governor's Advisory Group, with representatives from the six largest UK banks, including Barclays, of the BoE and of the BBA, when it met on 25 April 2008. The Bank's note for the record refers to the BBA 'currently undertaking a charm offensive to explain their recent intervention on the process for setting US dollar LIBOR fixings'. At that meeting, Angela Knight, then Chief Executive of the BBA, confirmed that, beyond the dollar issue, a full review of how the LIBOR fixings were set was under way. Longer term, Knight 'thought it would be necessary to explore whether a trade association was best placed to continue to provide what represented a key piece of market infrastructure'.[30]

Knight was right but unfortunately too far ahead. Both Sir John Gieve, the Deputy Governor for Financial Stability at the Bank of England, and Paul Tucker, the Deputy Governor, welcomed these initiatives. The note was released to the Treasury Select Committee on 23 July 2012, for its report *Fixing LIBOR*, with an accompanying letter in which the Bank stated:

> its preferred approach was (and is) for there to be a gradual move away from systems based on self-reporting. And the Bank, having no regulatory authority, was not prepared to lend its imprimatur to a system that

it was not able to control or enforce ... and the BBA did want to use the
Bank's name to bolster confidence in Libor.[31]

On 16 April 2008, the BBA's response to growing criticism was to
bring forward its annual review of LIBOR fixings and to publish on 10
June a consultation paper entitled *Governance and Scrutiny of LIBOR*.
The FSA noted that a Bank of England markets conditions update
reported the announcement of the review and pointed out that the BBA
asserted that 'it could ban any member deliberately misquoting.... This
is mainly thought to be aimed at European banks understating their
US $ fixings, given that they do not want to publicly acknowledge their
higher business rates'.[32] At first, some thought that the BBA may have
intended to publish only the usual annual review, but its consultation
paper of 10 June and the subsequent feedback put paid to that idea.

The BBA had frequent contacts with the US regulators, especially
during 2008. The BBA received on 3 June the Federal Reserve Bank of
New York's recommendations, which had been forwarded to the BBA by
the Bank of England. They were considered by the BBA to be broadly in
line with its own proposals, following a conference call between the BBA
and the New York Fed. In October, the BBA sent a draft of a 'governance
and scrutiny' document to the New York Fed and met with it to discuss
the review, followed by a meeting in November with the Office of the
Comptroller of the Currency.[33]

Prior to the publication of the BBA's consultation paper, two meetings
took place between the FSA and the BBA in May. The FSA's *Internal
Audit Report* notes that the FSA had recorded that, for example, the
BBA had written to LIBOR panel contributor banks to ask them to
ensure that the figures they were inputting were correct and really were
the rates that they could borrow at in the cash market. But 'the banks
have indicated to them [the BBA] that the BBA should not rock the
markets by substantially changing the way in which LIBOR is fixed'.
The FSA noted that 'it is evident that [the BBA representative] doubted
whether the LIBOR fixing process would change significantly after the
review [...] since the advantages of alternative options were not clear'.[34]

According to the *Internal Audit Report*, in a previous meeting (22
May 2008), the FSA had stressed its 'central concern':

> some banks have on occasion been posting Libor fixings which do not
> accurately reflect their cost of funding [and that a] credible oversight
> process that promotes accuracy should ... incorporate several monitor-
> ing devices to guard against and detect 'gamesmanship' of the quotes.

The BBA needs to utilise mechanisms which will detect several banks collectively (i.e. as a pack) submitting off-market quotes.[35]

After a further meeting on 30 May 2008, a briefing provided by a staff member included suggestions on enhancing the BBA's monitoring process, and commented: 'Likely course of action is to strengthen the review panel, give review panel greater reference to actual transactions so as to control outliers'.[36] These meetings were attended by staff below the director level but the notes were widely circulated to staff at and below director level.

The FSA's *Internal Audit Report* documents further discussions that took place between the FSA and the BBA before the publication of the consultation paper. The issues which were discussed included governance, transparency and clarity over the way in which submissions would be scrutinised and what instruments should be eligible for scrutiny in LIBOR fixings but the main concern was that the 'scrutiny process for Libor remains light'. Finally, it was noted that though the draft consultation paper had been 'much improved', it was not 'optimal'.[37] The consultation paper (which seemed to have been confused with the annual review) was finally published on 10 June 2008.[38] The FSA recorded how a Bank of England market intelligence summary at the time had reported that it was:

> widely seen as a 'damp squib' with the Libor panels for all currencies remaining exactly the same, and the BBA just committing to strengthening the 'oversight of BBA Libor' (with further details expected to emerge shortly). Radical reform had not been expected, but this was seen as the bare minimum that would be done.[39]

Those consulted included panel member banks, non-contributing banks, several brokers, hedge funds, money market funds and other asset managers, and others in the public sector. Not all of those listed would be interested parties in the sense of being able to influence submissions to LIBOR. Those consulted urged caution, as BBA LIBOR then supported a swap market estimated at $310 trillion and a loan market of $10 trillion. Much of the consultation document provided a detailed description of LIBOR. It pointed out that it was not to be confused with the overnight index swap (OIS) or the Fed Term Auction Facility rate, as they used quite different methods.

The responses to the consultation were published in August 2008, and contained the following significant statements, according the FSA's *Internal Audit Report*:

The respondents all supported the enhancement in the governance and scrutiny procedures for BBA LIBOR and the BBA will be releasing further details as soon as is practicable.

Respondents [...] considered that BBA LIBOR is a fundamentally robust and accurate benchmark with contributors inputting rates that they believe to reflect future funding costs.

A number of respondents noted that BBA LIBOR has been the subject of inaccurate and misconceived commentary in some areas of the media and that needs to be addressed.

... although recent comments have focused on US Dollar LIBOR, this has been due to a period of unprecedented stress in the market.

The BBA's paper on governance and scrutiny was eventually published on 17 December 2008 but the FSA had reviewed it prior to publication. As it had been sent to the Director of the Markets Division, a member of that team requested a meeting with the BBA, commenting:

governance and scrutiny were key areas which we raised [...] during the initial consultation [...] as areas which would benefit from much greater transparency and certainty. Your proposals, on first reading, certainly appear to go a long way towards addressing these issues.[40]

The FSA met with the BBA on 9 December 2008. The FSA asked for a reference to the FSA to be removed and commented: 'Otherwise we're actually reasonably impressed with these proposals as they may address many of the concerns we raised originally'.[41] The final report proposed changes in the governance and membership of the BBA's FX & MM Committee and established two subcommittees: a fixings committee and an oversight committee.[42] The committee would now consist of individuals representing their own firms, as well as a representative of a non-panel US bank, a representative of a non-panel European bank, a representative from LIFFE and the Chicago Mercantile Exchange and two rate-takers. It also set out disciplinary procedures, including requirements for audits and the possibility of removing the contributing banks from the panel.

Thomson Reuters, as the designated distributor of LIBOR, was given a significant role in terms of scrutiny, checking the consistency of the data by examining the spread between the top and bottom quotes for each maturity, with outliers open to challenge. Post-publication checks were to be undertaken by the LIBOR manager from BBA Ltd, based on the data Reuters provided, covering the major currencies and on 1-, 3-,

6- and 12-month tenors. That would include unexplained submissions which moved the contributor more than two standard deviations from the previous fix for that maturity, for example. Day-to-day monitoring of the internal consistency of the submissions would be carried out by the fixings team at Reuters and analysts at the BBA. If a bank insisted on submitting a rate that would still trigger an alert, Reuters would contact the line manager at the BBA, who would ask the bank to justify its position and log the circumstances. If unsatisfactory, then it would be referred to the fixings committee and ultimately to the FX & MM Committee. LIBOR panel banks would receive an unannounced visit from the LIBOR manager and it would be possible for participants to provide email comments on a secure website to be investigated by the LIBOR manager.

Part of the problem for the BBA was that the attempts to tighten up procedures did not seem to work, as can be seen, for example, from the FSA's final notice to UBS, issued in 2012, which refers to UBS's 'misconduct relating to the calculation of LIBOR and EURIBOR' between 1 January 2005 and 31 December 2010.[43] It is also possible that there was too much concern about 'lowballing' and the reasons for that, combined with a lack of awareness of the other uses to which altering a submission could be put. However, this failure led to further discussions about the future of LIBOR and ultimately the transfer of the supervision and regulation of LIBOR to the Financial Conduct Authority (FCA) as part of the Financial Services Act 2012.

Despite all the efforts made to improve the oversight of LIBOR and its governance, the fact remains that the BBA, with the best will in the world, lacked both the authority and the powers of a regulator. It lacked the resources to visit the banks sufficiently frequently or to require reports from overseas subsidiaries of global banks. Even with a more competent management of LIBOR than appears to be the case, the BBA could not demand that a bank be 'open and honest with its regulator', as required by the FSA's Principles of Business. A contributor to the panel was not authorised by the BBA. Even more important, perhaps, is the fact that the BBA could not demand to see internal emails or online chat rooms, or the layout of the trading rooms. When the FSA took regulatory action over the manipulation of LIBOR, it proceeded on the basis of the connection between LIBOR submissions and other regulated activities. That, as shown in the previous chapter, was the only source of *evidence* on which the FSA could rely for the imposition of fines. But there was no specific regulatory regime covering LIBOR submissions.

The Wheatley review

Chancellor George Osborne announced a review of LIBOR in an emergency statement to Parliament after the FSA issued its final notice against Barclays on 27 June 2012 and the order issued by the CFTC on the same day. In his statement, he raised two principal questions:

- How was it that such failures were allowed to continue undetected and unchecked, especially two years before the financial crisis?
- What changes are needed to our regulatory system to prevent such abuses occurring again and to make sure that the authorities have every power they need to hold those responsible fully to account?

He also asked what further investigations were required into the activities at Barclays, what sanctions were available and what questions the Chief Executive should answer. The latter questions were in fact covered in the Treasury Select Committee report and the Barclays' Chief Executive Officer, Bob Diamond, did resign on 3 July 2012. The issue of sanctions and punishment is one to which I shall return in this book, especially in the last chapter.

However, the Chancellor's main focus was on a 'review of LIBOR and the strength of the financial regulatory architecture', including 'examining if there are any gaps in the criminal regime inherited by this government and we will take the necessary steps to address that', but 'the scope of the FSA's criminal powers granted by the previous government does not extend to be able to impose criminal sanctions for the manipulation on LIBOR'. On 2 July 2012, the Chancellor appointed Martin Wheatley, Managing Director and Chief Executive Officer designate of the Financial Conduct Authority, to conduct a review, with a view to reforming the framework for setting and governing LIBOR.

Wheatley's review was completed in September 2012. His recommendations were as follows:

- there should be statutory regulation of the administration of LIBOR and submissions to LIBOR;
- the BBA should transfer responsibility for LIBOR to a new administrator, responsible for the compilation and administration of the rate as well as for credible governance and oversight;
- the new administrator should fulfil specific obligations as part of its oversight of the rate, having due regard to transparency and fair and non-discriminatory access to the benchmark (this would

include surveillance and scrutiny of the submissions, publication of a statistical digest of rate submissions, and periodic reviews addressing the issue of whether LIBOR continues to meet market needs, credibly and effectively);

- the new administrator should as a priority introduce a code of conduct for submitters that should clearly define guidelines for the explicit use of transaction data to determine submissions, as well as the systems and controls for submitting firms;
- there should be transaction record-keeping responsibilities for submitting banks;
- there should be a requirement for regular auditing of submitting firms.[44]

His review noted that the European Union's market abuse regulation did not cover attempts to manipulate benchmarks. Negotiations about a new market abuse regulation were already under way. It was eventually agreed and published in the *Official Journal* on 16 April 2014, to take effect on 3 July 2016. Section 44 of the Market Abuse Regulation (596/2014) for the first time brought benchmarks into the scope of regulation to ensure fair and non-discriminatory access to them. It prohibits:

> manipulation of the benchmark itself, the transmission of false or misleading information, false or misleading inputs or any other action that manipulates the calculation of the benchmark.

It applies to transactions, orders to trade, or other behaviour relating to benchmarks where any transmission of information input or calculation likely to affect the benchmark. It provides an essential underpinning to the market abuse regime, together with the Market Abuse Directive (2014/57/EU), which made market abuses criminal offences. But, at the time of the investigations, the FSA could take action only on the basis of the connection between LIBOR submissions and other regulated activities. Wheatley's review proposed making submitting to and administering LIBOR regulated activities, as well as the calculation of the benchmark.

Wheatley's recommendations were accepted and incorporated into the Financial Services Act 2012. The Act abolished the FSA and replaced it with two regulatory authorities: the Financial Conduct Authority (FCA) and the Prudential Regulatory Authority. Aspects of the Wheatley report were included in the FCA's rule book. Section 91 of the Act created a new offence of making 'misleading statements' in relation to benchmarks. The Wheatley review argued that such an offence was necessary:

> any attempts to manipulate LIBOR constitute sufficiently serious conduct to merit this being a criminal offence ... this conduct is likely to occur in full awareness of the potentially serious and wide ranging impact that the manipulation of LIBOR may have in light of its global use.[45]

(There is, however, little indication in the traders' exchanges as quoted in the final notices or orders that they ever gave such issues a thought!) The criminal offence takes two forms: making misleading statements or impressions in the course of setting a benchmark; and a reckless statement or giving a misleading impression relating to the price of any investment or transaction with an interest rate that may affect the setting of the relevant benchmark. The statements or impressions may be deliberate or reckless but, in either case, they are criminal offences with a maximum prison sentence of seven years or a fine.

The Act also covers 'dishonest concealment of any material facts if the person intends to induce or is reckless as to whether he or she may induce another person to offer to enter into or refrain from entering into a relevant agreement'. This means any agreement which involves a regulated activity, such as an investment agreement, and a misleading impression as to the value of an investment given with the intention to produce gains for oneself or loss to another.

The new regulations established the 'benchmark administrative function' within a bank, that is, the management responsible for the staff who administer, collect, analyse and process benchmark submissions. Managers responsible for the submission function have to be separately authorised to carry out that function. They are expected to put in place effective controls to manage potential conflicts of interest. The Act came into force on 1 April 2013. It is impossible not to reflect that had such rules been in place for the FSA, then greater note would have been taken of the various external comments and perhaps action would have followed, even in the midst of the financial crisis.

Current administration of LIBOR

One of Wheatley's aims was to remove the supervision of LIBOR submissions from the BBA and to transfer it to an administrator regulated by the FCA for each specified benchmark so that all the organisations that succeed the BBA are subject to the FCA's oversight. The newly appointed administrator would have to set up an oversight commit- tee, composed of benchmark users, market infrastructure providers, benchmark submitters and at least two independent members. It would be responsible for 'considering matters of definition and scope' of the benchmark, scrutinising benchmark submissions and notifying the FCA of those submitters who fail to meet the required standards.

ICE Benchmark Administration (IBA) became the administrator for ICE LIBOR on 1 February 2014. LIBOR is now produced for five curren- cies (the Swiss franc, the euro, the pound, the yen and the US dollar) and seven maturities. LIBORS with few transactions or underused curren- cies were phased out. The IBA published its first consultation in October 2014, following the Financial Stability Board's proposed reforms, the most important of which was that 'reference rates should be based exclusively on actual transactions.[46] The Financial Stability Board also noted that in many cases insufficient transactions will be available to do this, so the degree of dependence on transactions should vary by currency and will depend on 'market liquidity, depth and data suffi- ciency'. If there are insufficient transactions, rates should be promoted which depend on a 'waterfall of different date types: underlying market transactions first, then transactions in related markets, then committed quotes, and then indicative quotes'.[47] In the introduction setting out the principles and detailed requirements for strengthening the major reference interest rates (LIBOR, EURIBOR and TIBOR), the Financial Stability Board points out that:

> Because the major reference interest rates ... are widely used in the global financial system as benchmarks for a large volume and broad range of financial products and contracts, uncertainty surrounding the integrity of these reference rates represents a potentially serious systemic vulnerability and systemic risk.[48]

It is that dimension which adds to the heinous nature of the crimes committed. The Board also noted that, even then, LIBOR is the most referenced benchmark in US dollars, sterling and Swiss franc, with EURIBOR as the dominant rate in euro products. The total outstanding amount for LIBOR is estimated at about $220 trillion, for EURIBOR, $150–180 trillion and for TIBOR the figure is about $5 trillion.[49]

The experience of the IBA over the first few months of 2014 showed that the interbank lending market had declined considerably since the financial crisis and the levels still remained too low in some tenors to support an entirely transaction-based rate, for a number of reasons, of which the most important is the perceived risk of bank counterparty default. Having got their fingers burnt once, the banks are unwilling to risk lending to each other again. Banks are required to hold more regulatory capital and have higher liquidity coverage ratios (the highly liquid assets held by financial institutions to meet short-term obligations), which has modified the demand and supply of interbank funding, as the banks move towards longer maturity.

The IBA published its road map on the evolution of LIBOR in 2016, where it set out reforms aimed at reducing the risk profile of LIBOR and creating the conditions for more banks to participate. Prior to the publication of the road map, the IBA had consulted widely and held roundtables chaired by the Bank of England, the Bank of Japan, the Banque de France, the Board of Governors of the Federal Reserve Bank of New York and the Swiss National Bank.

To anchor LIBOR to the greatest extent in transactions, as well as to reflect changes in banks' funding models, the IBA 'has designed a waterfall of submission methodologies' to ensure that LIBOR panel banks use funding transactions where possible.[50] This will also ensure that panel banks make a submission even if activity levels are low on a particular day. The 'waterfall' consists of three levels:

- Level 1: The volume-weighted average price of eligible transactions. These will only be unsecured deposits, commercial paper (fixed-rate primary issues only) and certificates of deposit.
- Level 2: Submissions derived from transactions (including adjusted and historical transactions).
- Level 3: Expert judgement, appropriately framed.[51]

Level 3 is based on the panel bank's internal procedures, and formulated using the inputs allowed by the IBA, together with full documentation of the rationale.

Before the financial crisis, LIBOR was to a great extent driven by interbank lending, which has declined sharply since then. ICE Benchmark takes a much wider set of wholesale funding sources. In calculating their LIBOR submissions, panel banks use the following types of transaction: funding from other banks, central banks, or corporations as counterparties to funding transactions (only with maturities of more than 35 calendar days), government entities (including local/ quasi-governmental organisations, multilateral development banks, and non-bank financial institutions, including money market managers and insurers), sovereign wealth funds and supranational corporations. An 'Approved List of Funding Locations' will be owned by the LIBOR Oversight Committee and will be based on major centres in Canada, the USA, the EU, the European Free Trade Association (EFTA), Hong Kong, Singapore, Japan and Australia.

The IBA had to tackle two further issues: the length of time for submissions and the transaction size, which had just been defined as a 'reasonable size' in the previous definition of LIBOR. LIBOR remains as a rate set at 11 a.m. London time, but the period for submissions has been extended so that the collection window is open to previous submissions. The size has been defined by setting a minimum of 10 million dollars, euros, pounds or francs, or 1 billion yen, and two trades with different counterparties.

There are times when expert judgement has to be used – when a LIBOR panel bank does not have enough transactional data to provide a level 1 or level 2 submission, but the judgement now has to be made by a submitter acting in accord with the Code of Conduct for submitters and based on the panel bank's internally approved procedure and agreed by the IBA, formulated using the inputs approved by the IBA and accompanied by full documentation of the rationale and with supporting evidence. It is a far cry from the days in which requests for a particular submission were shouted across the room to submitters by traders.

The final major issue to be addressed is the publication of the submissions. A three-month embargo had already been imposed by the regulators on individual submissions, but LIBOR panel banks expressed 'concern that not only commercially sensitive data would become public but also that day-on-day volatility in LIBOR rates could lead to false inferences about a bank's financial stability and credit quality'.[52] The IBA publishes submissions on a non-attributed basis, although individual submissions continue to be available to the IBA, the FCA and, as appropriate, to the Oversight Committee.

By 2016, LIBOR was referenced by an estimated US$350 trillion of outstanding contracts in maturities, ranging from overnight to over 30 years. It is still the primary benchmark for short-term interest rates globally. All seemed set fair for the future of LIBOR.

Notes

1 Gillian Tett, 'Libor's value is called into question', _Financial Times_, 25 September 2007, available at https://www.ft.com/content/8c7dd45e-6b9c-11dc-863b-0000779fd2ac (accessed 4 May 2018).

2 Carrick Mollenkamp, 'Bankers cast doubt on key rate amid crisis', _Wall Street Journal_, 16 April 2008, available at https://www.wsj.com/articles/SB120831164167818299 (accessed 4 May 2018).

3 Gillian Tett and Michael Mackenzie, 'Doubts over Libor widen', _Financial Times_, 21 April 2008, available at https://www.ft.com/content/d1d9a792-0fbd-11dd-8871-0000779fd2ac (accessed 4 May 2018).

4 'Libor to rise as banks stay wary', Bloomberg, 24 April 2008.

5 'LIBOR banks misstated rates, Bond at Barclays says', Bloomberg, 29 May 2008.

6 Carrick Mollenkamp and Mark Whitehouse, 'Study casts doubt on key rate', _Wall Street Journal_, 29 May 2008, available at https://www.wsj.com/articles/SB121200703762027135 (accessed 4 May 2018). The analysis suggested banks may have reported flawed interest data for LIBOR.

7 Liam Vaughan and Gavin Finch, _The Fix: How Bankers Lied, Cheated and Colluded to Rig the World's Most Important Number_ (John Wiley & Sons, 2017), p. 57.

8 Mollenkamp and Whitehouse, 'Study casts doubt on key rate'.

9 In addition to those cited above, the press articles include 'LIBOR cracks widen as banks struggle with reforms', _GATA_, 27 May 2008, available at https://www.gata.org/node/6328 (accessed 4 May 2018); 'Libor to be set by more banks as BBA boosts scrutiny', Bloomberg, 10 June 2008.

10 Jacob Gyntelberg and Philip Wooldridge, 'Interbank rate fixings during the recent turmoil', _BIS Quarterly Review_, March 2008, p. 71, available at https://www.bis.org/repofficepubl/arpresearch_dev_200803.02.htm (accessed 3 May 2018).

11 François-Louis Michaud and Christian Upper, 'What drives interbank rates? Evidence from the Libor panel', _BIS Quarterly Review_, March 2008, pp. 48–9, available at https://www.bis.org/publ/qtrpdf/r_qt0803f.pdf (accessed 4 May 2018).

12 Ibid., p. 58.

13 Rosa Abrantes-Metz, Michael Kraten, Albert D. Metz and Gim Seow, 'Libor manipulation?', 4 August 2008, available at https://papers.ssrn.com/sol3/papers.cfm?abstract_id=1201389 (accessed 4 May 2018). A version of this paper was later published in _Journal of Banking and Finance_, 36:1 (2012), pp. 136–50.

14 Ibid., p. 15.

15 Quoted in Financial Services Authority, _Internal Audit Report: A Review of the Extent of Awareness with the FSA of Inappropriate LIBOR Submissions_ (FSA, March 2013), p. 67, available at https://www.fca.org.uk/publication/corporate/fsa-ia-libor.pdf (accessed 3 May 2018).

16 Deborah Defang, Gary Koop and Simon M. Potter, _Understanding Liquidity and Credit Risks in the Financial Crisis_ (Research & Statistics Group,

Federal Reserve Bank of New York, May 2011), available at http://citeseerx. ist.psu.edu/viewdoc/download?doi=10.1.1.307.3757&rep=rep1&type=pdf (accessed 4 May 2018).

17 Connan Andrew Snider and Thomas Youle, 'Does LIBOR reflect banks' borrowing costs?', 2 April 2010, p. 18, available at https://papers.ssrn.com/sol3/papers.cfm?abstract_id=1569603 (accessed 4 May 2018).

18 House of Commons Treasury Committee, *Fixing LIBOR: Some Preliminary Findings, Second Report of Session 2012–13, Volume I: Report, Together with Formal Minutes* (Stationery Office, August 2012), p. 27, available at https://publications.parliament.uk/pa/cm201213/cmselect/cmtreasy/481/481.pdf (accessed 4 May 2018).

19 Ibid., p. 28.

20 Ibid., p. 15.

21 Financial Services Authority, 'Final notice, Barclays Bank plc', 27 June 2012, para. 11, p. 3 (emphasis added), available at https://www.fca.org.uk/publication/final-notices/barclays-jun12.pdf (accessed 3 May 2018).

22 US Department of Justice, 'Statement of facts', 2012, para. 20, p. 9, available at https://www.justice.gov/iso/opa/resources/9312012710173426365941.pdf (accessed 4 May 2018).

23 Financial Services Authority, *Internal Audit Report*.

24 The communications cited below can easily be found in the FSA's *Internal Audit Report* by the number of the communication and the time when it was received. The latter shows that the nature of the communications inevitably changed as the financial crisis developed.

25 FSA, 'Final notice, Barclays Bank', para. 173.

26 Financial Services Authority, *Internal Audit Report*, communications 30 and 40.

27 Alistair Barr, 'BBA to start Libor review earlier as rate spikes', Market-Watch, 17 April 2008, available at https://www.marketwatch.com/story/review-of-libor-brought-forward-as-closely-watched-rate-spikes (accessed 4 May 2018); and Carrick Mollenkamp, Serena Ng, Laurence Norman and James R. Hagerty, 'Libor's rise may sock many borrowers', *Wall Street Journal*, 19 April 2008, available at https://www.wsj.com/articles/SB120856108868827857 (accessed 4 May 2018).

28 Financial Services Authority, *Internal Audit Report*, p. 70.

29 A full account of the issue is provided by Michael L. Spafford and Daren F. Stanaway, 'The extraterritoriality reach of the Commodity Exchange Act in the wake of *Morrison* and Dodd-Frank', *Futures and Derivatives Law Report*, 37:7 (July 2017).

30 Formal minutes, Bank of England/BBA meeting, 25 April 2008.

31 Letter from the assistant private secretary to the Governor of the Bank of England to the Clerk of the Treasury Committee and accompanying notes, 23 July 2012.

32 Financial Services Authority, *Internal Audit Report*, p. 46.

33 Details of meetings between the Federal Reserve Bank of New York and the Office of the Comptroller of the Currency were given in response to a request from the Treasury Select Committee and are in House of

Commons Treasury Committee, *Fixing LIBOR: Some Preliminary Findings, Second Report of Session 2012–13, Volume II: Oral and Written Evidence* (The Stationery Office, 9 August 2012), available at https://publications.parliament.uk/pa/cm201213/cmselect/cmtreasy/481/481ii.pdf (accessed 4 May 2018).

34 Financial Services Authority, *Internal Audit Report*, p. 47.
35 Ibid.
36 Ibid., p. 48.
37 Ibid., pp. 49–50.
38 British Bankers' Association, *Understanding the Construction and Operation of BBA LIBOR – Strengthening for the Future* (BBA, June 2008).
39 Financial Services Authority, *Internal Audit Report*, p. 52.
40 Ibid., p. 74.
41 Ibid.
42 British Bankers' Association, 'LIBOR governance and scrutiny – proposals agreed by the FX & MM Committee', 17 November 2008.
43 Financial Conduct Authority, 'Final notice, UBS AG', 19 December 2012, p. 1, available at https://www.fca.org.uk/publication/final-notices/ubs.pdf (accessed 4 May 2018).
44 HM Treasury, *The Wheatley Review of LIBOR: Final Report* (The Stationery Office, October 2011), p. 47 (all documents of the Wheatley Review are available at https://www.gov.uk/government/publications/the-wheatley-review).
45 Ibid., p. 18.
46 Financial Stability Board, *Reforming Major Interest Rate Benchmarks* (FSB, 22 July 2014), p. 12, available at https://www.fsb.org/wp-content/uploads/r_140722.pdf (accessed 4 May 2018).
47 Ibid.
48 Ibid., p. 3.
49 Financial Stability Board, *Market Participants Group on Reforming Interest Rate Benchmarks: Final Report* (FSB, March 2014), available at https://www.fsb.org/wp-content/uploads/r_140722b.pdf?page_moved=1 (accessed 4 May 2018).
50 ICE Benchmark Administration, 'Roadmap for ICE LIBOR', 18 March 2016, p. 4, available at https://www.theice.com/publicdocs/ICE_LIBOR_Roadmap0316.pdf (accessed 4 May 2018).
51 Ibid.
52 Ibid., p. 17.

Part II: A decade or more of change in the foreign exchange market

Chapter 6

A rapidly changing foreign exchange market

This chapter is designed to show how much the foreign exchange market has changed over the years. The days of noisy currency trading floors where dealers shouted at each other have long gone, replaced by computers and people tapping at keyboards or talking quietly to each other. When did the foreign exchange market start to change and why does this matter?

A different market begins to emerge

As with LIBOR, there are suggestions that rigging or manipulating the foreign exchange (FX) market began in 2005. To look for explanations, it is worth beginning with the changing structure of the foreign exchange market during the 2000s. Interpreting these changes might provide an explanation as to why attempts to manipulate the market became not only possible but also financially worthwhile from the point of view of the traders.

Changes began with the extensive use of computers in FX from 2000 onwards. Networks principally connected brokers to banks but a number of competing companies allowed their FX customers to see prices from many banks simultaneously and, through these multi-dealer platforms, they could see a blended rate on one screen, such as a bid from Deutsche Bank and an offer from UBS. Although the percentage of flows transacted through these APIs (application programme interfaces) was only about 5% at first, it was the beginning of much more dramatic changes.

In his interesting account of his life as a banker, Kevin Rodgers explains the impact of two changes which occurred in 2005. The first step was taken by Barclays, which involved an additional decimal point, which hardly seemed an earth-shattering move. Barclays used its computer system to quote, for example, the US dollar rate as 1.32783, whereas everyone else would be quoting 1.3278; this enabled Barclays to undercut other banks. If one bank quoted prices with 3 pips (as they are called), the only way the bank could go to a narrower spread would be to go to 2 pips, a 33% reduction. But Barclays could go to 2.9 pips (a tighter spread, at only 3%). That could mean for other banks the loss of customers with large sums to change into another currency, such as major companies operating in more than one country.

Rodgers and his team at Deutsche Bank noticed a change in the behaviour of one large American fund and eventually discovered that it was engaged in 'latency arbitrage':

> Its computers would constantly monitor the market, wait for a large order or information release to move prices on EBS [Electronic Broking Services] or elsewhere. Then its computers would 'look' around the prices shown by its banking counterparties and deal on any rate that was too slow to respond. Deutsche Bank's ARM, its computer system, was programmed to alter prices in this event in a fraction of a second, but the fund was faster.[1]

He also explains why the American fund turned away from latency to 'relative value'. By observing the bids and offers deals in the market, a fund's computers would predict future prices over a very short period and would get ahead of market moves before they happened. The fund was helped by the vast amounts of information available and by the availability of decimal pricing. For example, if the fund's algorithm showed that the US dollar was likely to weaken in the next split second, it could enter an offer to sell a tenth of a pip under the best offer in the market and be paid before the predicted move happened. 'Decimalisation is a gift for high frequency traders', one of Rodgers's colleagues remarked sourly.[2] That turned out to be the case, when Electronic Broking Services (EBS) launched its decimalised/fractional pip pricing for major currency pairs in March 2011, since human beings cannot handle the extra digit easily, while algorithms can.

In April 2006, EBS was sold by its bank shareholders to the brokerage house ICAP for $825 million. EBS and Reuters accounted for 60% of all the flows between banks at that time and the sale meant that neither company had any bank representatives on their boards. A broker's revenues depended more and more on the volume of sales, so their platforms were designed in such a way as to encourage more trades and it was the high-frequency trading (HFT) that enabled that to take place.

The impact of electronic trading on the foreign exchange market: the BIS Triennial Surveys

The developments in the FX market are reflected in the Triennial Central Bank Surveys produced by the Bank for International Settlements. The first one which is relevant is the 2004 survey, the results of which were published in March 2005.

Triennial Survey 2004

The survey showed a sharp increase in the traditional FX markets compared with 2001: a 57% increase, to $1.9 trillion, more than reversing the fall in global trading volumes between 1998 and 2001, especially in the spot and forward markets. The BIS concluded that there were three factors responsible: more active asset managers; investors' interest in foreign exchange as an asset class and as an alternative to equity and fixed income; and the increasingly important role of hedge funds.

The growth in turnover was driven by all kinds of counterparties, but especially by trade between banks and financial customers (up from 28% to 33%), probably due to the activities of hedge funds, asset managers and commodity trading advisers. The share of trading between reporting dealers[3] continued to fall, from 59% in 2001 to 53% in 2004, reflecting continuing global consolidation in the banking industry. The BIS considered it might also be due to 'efficiency gains from the use of electronic brokers in the spot interbank market'.[4] The UK continued to be the most active trading centre, with 31% of total turnover, followed by the USA with 19%, Japan with 8%, Singapore with 5%, Germany with 5%, Hong Kong with 4% and Switzerland with 3%.

The strong growth in turnover in the FX market was apparently due to the presence of clear trends and higher volatility in the FX markets which led to 'momentum trading', where investors took large positions in currencies that followed persistent appreciating trends. Interest rate differentials encouraged 'carry trading', where investments in high-interest currencies was financed by short positions in low-interest currencies, for example if a target currency like the Australian dollar tended to appreciate against a funding currency like the US dollar. These strategies fed back into prices and supported the persistence of trends in exchange rates. In spite of the use of the Australian dollar, the US dollar continued to be the most traded currency, being on one side of 89% of all transactions, with the euro remaining at 37% and the yen at around 20%.

Banking mergers led to a reduction in the number of market participants, as consolidation continued. For example, in the USA, the number of banks accounting for 75% of the foreign exchange market was only 11 in 2004, compared with 13 in 2001, and 20 in 1998 and 1995. In the UK, 16 banks accounted for 75% of the foreign exchange market in 2004, compared with 17 in 2001, 24 in 1998 and 20 in 1995. The BIS notes that the reporting banks covered by the turnover part of the Triennial Survey are individual offices of trading firms rather than banking organisations on a consolidated basis.

Triennial Survey 2007

The market continued to develop rapidly and grew in size between 2004 and 2007. Certain elements of the changing structure which have already been noted are quantified in the BIS survey. First of all, the average daily turnover grew by 69%, to $3.2 trillion, a surprisingly high rate of growth, a 71% increase since the previous survey. The BIS notes that the growth was across all financial instruments but that over half the increase in turnover was due to foreign exchange swaps, which rose by 80% compared with 45% over the previous three-year period. The increasing importance of FX swaps could have been due to the changes in hedging activity. Growth in the turnover of forward contracts also grew by 73%.

First of all, a shift in the source of the trading activity took place, so that transactions between reporting dealers and non-reporting financial institutions, such as hedge funds, mutual funds, pension funds and insurance companies, more than doubled between April 2004 and April 2007, and contributed more than half of the increase in the aggregate turnover. This growth was based on spot, forward and FX swaps. Part of the reason for this was attractive investments for those with short-term investment horizons. The returns were apparently less risky because foreign exchange and financial market volatility was at relatively low levels. Longer-term investors, such as pension funds, were also seeking to diversify their portfolios internationally and so they contributed to the increase in FX turnover. These included hedge funds using 'carry trade' strategies, in which the trader stands to make a profit out of the difference between the interest rates of two countries as long as the exchange rate between the currencies does not change. The profits can be very large when leverage is taken into account. If, for example, traders use a leverage factor of 10:1, then they may make a profit of 10 times the interest rate difference.[5] Hedge fund activity at that time was concentrated in the USA and London.

Other changes in the market included the development of algorithmic trading. All this means is that computers are programmed to follow a certain set of instructions to place orders for trades at speeds and frequencies which are impossible for a human being. The rules programmed into the computer are based on timing, price, quantity or any other mathematical model decided by the company. Such programmes are designed to increase profits for the trader but, it is claimed, make markets more liquid and trading more systematic by excluding emotional and intuitive aspects of trading. This style of trading makes use of high-frequency movements in exchange rate quotes that are available electronically, based on a set of rules. The growth in this market segment is a result of the advances in electronic trading systems, especially in the spot market. This all makes algorithmic trading sound straightforward and uncontentious, but as part of HFT that may not be the case, as I shall indicate later.

That and the spread of electronic broking platforms are factors involved in the falling share of interbank FX transactions. The electronic broking platforms were apparently more important in Germany and Switzerland but less so in the UK and the USA. What might be more interesting is the reduction in the number of banks in the USA and the UK, down from 11 to 10 in the USA and from 16 to 12 in the UK, but they still accounted for 75% of the FX turnover. Some of the remaining dealing banks, in order to face the competition, linked up with the multi-bank trading platforms, allowing their retail customers to access prices and to trade with any of the participating dealers with whom they had an established trading relationship. This development would continue to increase turnover by providing access to retail margin traders.

The sober language and the statistics in the BIS survey reflect what Rodgers describes in more colourful language:

> Banks dealt directly with each other through EBS and Reuters, with computer-to-computer APIs increasingly bypassing human involvement altogether. Customers' computers could also deal directly with those of

banks, and the way had been opened, via the magic of prime brokerage, for customers to deal in the interbank market, albeit cloaked in another name. The barriers preventing the market from becoming a playground for high-frequency traders were now almost down.[6]

The extent to which the latter comment was true will emerge as we look at further developments in the market.

Triennial Survey 2010

This survey covers the years of the financial crisis. It would be natural to expect a fall in the average daily turnover in the global FX market, but in fact it increased by 20%, to $4 trillion, compared with $3.3 trillion in 2007. The increase was driven by a 48% growth in the turnover of spot transactions, up to $1.5 trillion in April 2010 from $1.0 trillion in April 2007. Turnover in FX instruments was relatively modest.

The interesting question is, who was trading? Other financial institutions, non-reporting banks, hedge funds, pension funds, mutual funds, insurance companies and central banks again contributed to this growth to a large extent, up 42%, to $1.9 trillion in April 2010 compared with $1.3 trillion in April 2007. Not surprisingly, FX trading with corporates and governments fell to 13%, the lowest since 2001, reflecting the impact of the financial crisis on the economy. Transactions between dealers in the interbank market also slowed down, partly due to the reduction in the number of banks in the FX market and also because of the increasing use of electronic broking platforms.

In their analysis of the 2010 survey, King and Rime ask the '$4 trillion question': what explains the FX growth since the 2007 survey?[7] It is not obvious that the FX market should be so large, given that the survey covers the worst years of the financial crisis. Their analysis suggests that the increased turnover was driven by high-frequency trading, more trading by the smaller banks (which were increasingly dependent as clients on the top dealers for major currency exchanges) and the emergence of retail investors, both individuals and smaller institutions. The increased participation of the retail investors was due to the increase in electronic trading and electronic brokering. High-frequency trading is a type of algorithmic trading that profits from incremental price movements with frequent small trades executed in milliseconds.

The FX business of the largest dealers grew as they invested heavily in their single-bank proprietary trading systems, with banks such as Barclays and Deutsche Bank making huge investments in their IT systems.[8] The tight bid–ask spreads and guaranteed market liquidity on such platforms made it unprofitable for smaller players to compete for customers in the major currency pairs. Many smaller banks became clients of the top dealers for these currencies, while continuing to make markets for customers in local currencies. These banks with their client relationships can profit from their local expertise and comparative advantage in the provision of credit. They could not afford the costly investments necessary to compete in the spot market for major currencies. Lastly, the electronic execution methods allow small retail investors to make a significant contribution to the growth in spot FX deals.[9]

The BIS survey itself gives very little indication of the effect of the financial crisis on the FX market, but the analysis offered by King and Rime does. FX activity peaked just after the collapse of Lehman Brothers, but after that activity sharply declined and began to recover only after October 2009. With limited liquidity in various asset classes, many investors looked to the spot FX market to hedge risk exposures; for example, downside risk in US equities was apparently hedged by buying Japanese yen. A strategy of this kind may have had limited success but at least it was available, even if expensive, because the bid–ask spreads for the major currencies widened during the crisis by a factor of four to five.

The other way in which investors were hit was by the rise in FX volatility and the increased risk aversion of investors. This manifested itself in the rapid unwinding of currency trading positions, with funding currencies increasing sharply and many investors suffering large losses. The Japanese yen, for example, appreciated by 7.7% against the Australian dollar on 16 August 2008. King and Rime report that despite the unwinding of carry trades during 2008 and 2009, market participants stated that this was not a significant factor explaining FX turnover during April 2010. They conclude that 'despite the widespread financial market disruptions, most parts of the FX markets continued to function relatively smoothly, although FX swaps were severely disrupted'.[10] They put this down to the role of the CLS Bank, which operated the largest multi-currency cash settlement system, in mitigating settlement risk for its members and customers.

The crisis changed the focus of the FX markets and attracted the attention of the regulators. Clients began to be more concerned about minimising transaction costs, while demonstrating best execution. The management of counterparty credit risk obviously became much more important, and that had an impact on FX swaps since these create counterparty risk exposures, and the constraints on dealers' balance sheets and restrictions on the availability of credit took their toll. Regulators increased capital requirements for retail FX brokers and reduced the leverage available to individuals, as well as increasing the use of central counterparties.

Some argue that the impact of the crisis on the FX market was more severe, especially on the 'carry' trade, in the early stages of the financial crisis, that is, August 2007. Many currency investors were short on Japanese yen and long on Australian and New Zealand dollars, but the unwinding of that particular trade occurred then. The one-day change in the yen price of Australian dollars was –7.7% compared with an average daily change of only 0.7% before 15 August. Many currency managers lost out.

Extreme volatility in exchange rates followed increasing anxieties about the US subprime market. From November 2007 onwards, credit concerns increased and this hit hedge funds in particular in relation to carry trades and other FX investments. Hedge funds use a prime broker to provide financing for their funds, to give them their required leverage, but prime brokers impose risk management controls on their clients, which could trigger calls for the fund either to deposit additional cash or to liquidate positions, so these are unwound in an illiquid market at the worst time. The forced sale of Bear Stearns in March 2008 disrupted the markets. Liquidity dried up. As a result, the FX market experienced unprecedented levels of volatility. For example, a quoted spot spread prior to the failure of Lehman Brothers could have been 1.1525–1.1529 but thereafter[11] this widened to 16 pips, and in general spreads were at least 400% wider than normal.

Triennial Survey 2013

This survey has been included for two reasons: first, it covers the aftermath of the financial crisis; and secondly, it records further structural changes in the market during the period in which the manipulation of the FX market occurred. The FCA's fines applied to a period from 2008 to 2013 in each case, and it is important to understand the market at the time at which the relevant FX dealing took place.

The survey was published in 2013 and refers only to foreign exchange, unlike previous surveys.[12] Global FX market activity reached $5.3 trillion a day, up from $4.0 trillion in 2010, but the growth rate did not hit the record increase of 72% between 2004 and 2007.

The category of 'other' financial institutions continued to contribute the most to the growth in global FX turnover between 2010 and 2013. In 2010, 'other financial institutions' had for the first time overtaken 'other reporting dealers', that is, trading in the inter-dealer market. FX transactions with this group of customers grew by 48%, to $2.3 trillion in 2013, up from $1.9 trillion in 2010. 'Other financial institutions' were separately identified in this survey. The non-reporting banks (i.e. those not included in the survey conducted by their central banks) are the smaller banks and regional banks that serve as clients of the large FX dealing banks but do not engage in market-making in major currencies. They accounted for 24% of the global turnover; institutional investors, hedge funds and proprietary trading firms had a share of about 11% each. The official sector, such as central banks and sovereign wealth funds, accounted for less than 1%.

Inter-dealer trading grew by 34%, to $2.1 trillion in 2013, up from $1.5 trillion in 2010. Its share remained more or less constant over the three years. The survey points out that this figure could be misleading, because the relative importance of inter-dealing trading in the global FX market had fallen by almost 25% since 1998. This apparently happened for two reasons: the increased concentration and market share allowed dealers to match larger quantities of customer trades on their own books by internalising trades; secondly, vast investments in technology by the top-tier dealers over the previous few years had allowed the warehousing of inventory risk, reducing the need to get rid of the accumulated inventory in the inter-dealer market quickly. That had reduced the number of trades, but, on the other hand, the ability and willingness of banks to 'warehouse' risk by acting as market makers was a very significant source of liquidity in the foreign exchange market. Market makers do have the ability to absorb flow and therefore warehouse risk.

The counterparty segment which had contributed the most to growth in global FX turnover between 2010 and 2013 was 'other financial institutions', including small banks, institutional investors, hedge funds and proprietary trading firms, as well as official sector financial institutions, among others. Transactions of FX dealers with this group of customers grew by 48%, to $2.8 trillion in 2013, up from $1.9 trillion in 2010. Trading activity with these counterparties expanded most in FX options (82%), the outright forward market (58%) and the spot market (57%). Trading with other reporting dealers rose at a similar rate as the aggregate FX market between 2010 and 2013, but trading with non-financial customers had declined considerably over the three years.

Trading increased in all the main FX instruments. Spot market trading increased by 38%, to $2 trillion per day in April 2013, contributing about 40% of the rise in global FX activity between 2010 and 2013, a more moderate increase than in the previous survey. FX swaps remained the most actively traded FX instrument, generally used by banks to raise liquidity across money markets denominated in different currencies. Their daily volume of $2.2 trillion amounted to 42% of all transactions but trading volumes in forwards and FX options also increased. The vast majority of trading in FX instruments, including spot transactions, consisted of over-the-counter trading.

Trading in the FX market reached an all-time high, but what were the drivers behind the growth? The so-called 'non-dealer' financial institutions all played their part. They included the smaller banks working as clients of the large banks dealing in foreign currencies. They could not compete with rival dealers offering competitive quotes in major currencies, so they focused on niche markets. Like dealers, they traded short-tenor FX swaps, with a maturity of less than a week, often used for short-term liquidity management. The next group were institutional investors such as mutual funds, pension funds and insurance companies, and hedge funds. The former group focused on forward contracts, which they used to hedge international bond portfolios. Hedge funds were especially active in options markets, since these enable them to take leveraged positions and 'invest' in exchange rate movements and volatility. They were also behind increases in the spot market and forward contracts. Trading by the institutional investors and hedge funds was concentrated in London and New York (a combined 60% share of global turnover), where major dealers have their desks.

Prime brokerage was typically offered by the major investment banks in London or New York, enabling other non-financials to gain access to the institutional platforms, such as Reuters Matching, EBS or other electronic currency networks, and trade anonymously with dealers and other counterparties. Prime-brokered trades accounted for 23% of the total FX volume in the USA and the UK. The rapid increase in electronic and algorithmic trading also contributed to concentration in centres because, for certain types of algorithmic trading, milliseconds matter.

Electronic trading now dominates the market. It was the preferred trading channel in the 2013 survey, with a share of above 50% for all customer segments. Spot was the part of the market with the highest proportion of trades conducted electronically, at 64%. Voice and relationship trading is still the preferred method in some contexts, such as providing advice on alternative order execution strategies or ways to implement a trade idea. Voice is obviously the preferred way of dealing with more complex FX derivatives. Non-financial institutions prefer to deal directly with their relationship bank, whereas the financials trade directly with dealers electronically, for example via Bloomberg Tradebook or various multi-bank platforms and electronic brokerage systems.

Finally, Dagfinn Rime and Andreas Schrimpf point out that one of the reasons for the growth of the FX market was that foreign currency was becoming regarded as an asset class in its own right, especially by hedge funds buying and selling vast quantities of multiple currencies. The carry trade is one example of this, and the best-known, although it has become less popular as interest rate differentials have shrunk. Other strategies include momentum trading – a bet on the continuation of exchange rate trends – and buying currencies thought to be undervalued and selling those perceived to be overvalued. However, since these are familiar strategies, Rime and Schrimpf argue that the rise in the international diversification of asset portfolios is the explanation, with currency trading as an obvious by-product of that. It also gave rise to a greater demand for hedging currency exposures. The FX market picked up most for countries which also saw significant equity price increases. These factors, taken together, especially the greater variety and number of non-dealer market participants, have increased the possibility of more gains from the trade, and have expanded the FX market.[13]

Triennial Survey 2016

For the first time in 15 years, FX trading volumes shrank in the survey period: average daily turnover fell to $5.1 trillion in 2016, with spot trading being especially hard hit, falling from $2.0 trillion in 2013 to $1.7 trillion in 2016.[14] Nonetheless, most FX derivatives, especially swaps, continued to grow. That partly reflects lack of growth in the global economy, which had still not returned to pre-financial crisis levels. The reasons include a fall in prime brokerage as banks had been reassessing the profitability of that business, the fall in hedge fund activity and the principal trading firms reaching saturation point with their aggressive fast trade execution and short-term arbitrage. Hedge funds had had a difficult time and were trading less.

The organisations that had been doing more trading, such as pension funds and life insurers, had been doing so in search of returns. In countries such as Germany and Japan, these institutions, although taking less risk, had been buying foreign bonds to get some returns, so that they could meet their obligations on the policies they sold, and pensions. Their swap trades increased by 80%.

It is interesting to note that FX turnover by prime brokers (banks) fell sharply, by 22% overall and by almost 30% in the spot markets. The BIS survey makes no reference to the revelations of manipulation and collusion in the FX spot market, although the fines imposed on the banks involved were public knowledge by 2014 at the latest, with media speculation long before that. Instead, the reasons for the decline suggested by the BIS included post-regulatory reforms, low overall profitability and the shock given to the market by a Swiss announcement that it would no longer buy euros to hold against the franc at SFr1.20 against the single currency. The banks put the barriers up by raising capital requirements and raising fees. The dealer banks appear to have focused more on retaining a relationship-driven market structure where bilateral over-the-counter trades dominate. This takes place mainly through proprietary single-bank trading platforms operated by FX dealing banks or electronic price streams via API connectivity. Further changes took place in the FX market from 2013 onwards, but the most important ones are the changes in the approach of the large dealer banks, especially after the discovery of manipulation and collusion. As a result, apart from meeting new regulatory requirements, they want to focus on customer relationships, rebuild trust and cut costs.

High-frequency trading and the foreign exchange market

As can be seen from the BIS surveys, the role of high-frequency trading (HFT) has increased considerably over the years, to account for 90% of spot foreign exchange dealing by 2014. It is best defined as a subset of automated trading. It takes two forms: algorithmic execution, in which an electronic trading programme completes the trade after a trading decision has been made (this is often used for larger orders); and algorithmic trade decision-making, in which a firm builds a computer model to initiate trades based on order-book imbalance, momentum or correlations in or across markets (to mention but a few). A bank's automated risk management tool may use HFT to offset risk automatically. Hedge funds use similar strategies.

HFT firms make their earnings from a large number of small trades with small profits with a very short risk-holding period, usually under

5 seconds and often less than 1 second. Given its nature, HFT requires a liquid underlying market. HFT players can detect and act on profitable trading opportunities even in 1 millisecond, compared with 5–10 milliseconds for most players without HFT. (Apparently it takes about 150 milliseconds for a human being to blink.) Further declines in 'latency' will result from too many players and other players upgrading their systems.[15]

Although there are many small firms, several large and well capitalised firms, the majority in Chicago, New York and London, account for most HFT. The HFT traders access the various electronic trading platforms through their prime brokers, usually the large investment banks. These banks are responsible for the credit they provide to clients, but they also carry out smaller transactions and hold on to risk very briefly. Although the individual transactions are small, the use of HFT increases the fundamental risks associated with trading in the financial markets, such as market risk, counterparty risk and operational risk, and can materially increase the build-up of intraday positions.

Not surprisingly, the banks are ambivalent about HFT. On the one hand, they find that HFT firms can detect the bank's orders in the early stages of its completion. The extra pip (see above) further increases the scope for HFT players to outprice the banks. Banks found that they had to devote considerable resources to 'monitor customer relationships closely and screen out any predatory (and thus loss-yielding) practices by HFT firms' so that they can retain their clients and their profits. They see HFT firms as 'opportunistic liquidity-takers'.[16] On the other hand, some banks view HFT firms as useful clients, and take advantage of the constant flows generated by them to develop and improve their own risk management. But, in general, banks have been investing heavily in IT and in algorithms to ward off competition in an environment in which the HFT firms need the banks more than the banks need them. The HFT firms ultimately need other players, especially the FX dealing banks, which continue to take larger risk positions, in order to trade.

The extent of the impact of HFT can be deduced from the BIS Triennial Survey. For April 2010, it was been estimated that three-quarters of the growth in the daily average growth in global FX turnover came from the increase in spot transactions, mostly in the UK but also in the USA. Most of this took place through multi-bank platforms and electronic brokers, such as Reuters and EBS.[17]

The FX market is a largely decentralised OTC market without statutory regulation, so trading practices, including those of HFT firms, are governed by self-regulation. For non-bank HFT companies this consists of three elements: (i) their internal risk management systems; (ii) the risk management controls of their prime brokers; and (iii) any trade controls imposed by the trading platform. The last includes the management of credit risk, as this is relevant to whether or not the HFT firm is in a position to trade.

If it is possible to identify any predatory HFT behaviour, counter-parties will seek to limit their exposure to those firms, with the ultimate sanction of cutting off trade with the counterparty. That is possible only if the trading is not completely anonymous, for example if the counterparty is identifiable by a code on a trading platform. In 2011, the various codes of conduct were being reviewed to take account of the increase in HFT.

Self-regulation often suggests a lack of control, but one aspect of an HFT company's strategy is the effective reduction or at least man-agement of their market risk, including ceasing to trade in extremely volatile markets. From the company's point of view this is essential, since the owners' capital is at risk. They back-test their trading al-gorithms before actual trading and seek to use a broad range of trading strategies. Prime brokers are incentivised to monitor and control HFT clients' market access, since it is the bank's reputation which is at risk. Many prime brokers work together with the trading platforms to create an efficient process for limiting or cutting off credit to clients across the platforms if necessary. However, despite the controls set out below, the responsibility for risk control for the HFT participants lies with the prime broker or bank.

A BIS study of HFT points out that the trading platforms used also have controls to influence participants' trading behaviour. EBS and Reuters, for example, have controls which set a minimum amount of time a quote has to remain active, controls on the percentage of actual trades carried out relative to the total amount of quotes submitted, and a limit on the maximum number of quotes that can be submitted in a given time. The Chicago Mercantile Exchange has similar controls. The study also raises the question of whether the existence of so many HFT companies affects the functioning of the market. The application of technology has aided the functioning of the market by providing liquid-ity and compressing spreads, for smaller trade sizes at least. It arguably makes the market more competitive. But HFT-generated liquidity could vanish in times of market stress. The concern expressed by the BIS is the possibility of systemic risk:

HFT may not be the trigger of market malfunction but rather an accelerator once the initial problem has been precipitated.... HFT has systemic implications because of its potential to amplify and propagate a shock, even if the shock itself does not originate from HFT.[18]

That issue was addressed after the revelations about FX manipulation discussed below.

That completes the picture of a rapidly changing, largely unregulated and vast market with its turnover of trades valued at over $5 trillion dollars daily. It is a market in which exchange rates can vary within a few seconds, which paints an entirely different picture from the rates posted by bureaux de change on a daily basis or even with checking those published in newspapers or online, but even there the rates are delayed by 15 minutes before publication (for the *Financial Times* online currency converter, for example). In this context, both market participants and their customers seek a fixed point of reference, a benchmark, a fix. Contracts are based on such a benchmark and, for the seller of services, it provides a demonstrable exchange rate. Without such a reference point, customers would demand proof that the exchange rate was as the bank or other seller of services claimed.

The 4 p.m. Reuters fix and the 1.15 p.m. ECB fix

WM/Reuters Fx Benchmark[19] publishes a series of rates for various 'currency pairs', with the first-listed currency as the base currency and the second as the quote currency, at different times in the day, but 4 p.m. UK time is of particular importance. The published rates always include the major currency pairs (euro–US dollar, dollar–yen, sterling–dollar and dollar–Swiss franc) and other G10 currencies as well. The 4 p.m. Reuters fix was regarded as the standard closing spot rate in the major currency pairs. It was calculated by capturing the rates for single executed trades and orders, taken from Thomson Reuters Matching or EBS, given that 17 trade currencies use Thomson Reuters Matching as a single data source.

The choice of the rate lies with WM/Reuters Fx Benchmark, on the basis of which is most appropriate to represent the market. Sixty-one single snapshots of trade and order rates are taken over 1 minute 30 seconds before to 30 seconds after the fix time. The snap from Thomson Reuters Matching takes the current/last trade and current/last best-order trades at the capture time. A trade is identified as being on one side of the market, 'sell' or 'buy', depending on whether it is hitting a 'bid' or lifting an 'offer'. The bid–offer spreads are calculated from the difference between the best bid and the best offer for each valid snap. This spread is then applied to the captured trade data in that particular second to establish the opposite side of the market. The result is a bid and offer rate for each trade. Once the data have been verified and subject to further calculations, WM/Reuters publishes a bid and offer rate to four decimal places. The methodology is complicated but it uses data from three transaction systems and four key data points to publish the fixing rates – best bid, best ask, last traded bid and last traded ask. It was presumably thought to be quite foolproof at the time and yet traders found ways of manipulating it.

The European Central Bank (ECB) also establishes reference rates for various currency pairs, rates which, according to its website, are 'based on the regular daily concertation procedure between central banks across Europe'.[20] This is an agreed exchange of information between the banks. This usually takes place at 1.15 p.m. UK time and the reference rates are published soon after that. In the FX markets, this rate is generally known as a 'flash' fix, because it reflects the rate at that particular time. Rates established at these fixes are used in the global financial markets by banks, asset managers, pension funds and corporations for valuing different currencies. They are used in the valuation of assets and liabilities denominated in foreign currencies, the valuation and performance of investment portfolios, the compilation of equity and bond indices and in contracts of different kinds, including the settlement of derivatives.

The FCA gives some examples of fix orders, which is helpful in understanding how the fix was manipulated.[21] A bank may receive and accept multiple client orders to buy or sell in a particular currency pair for a fix on a given day, and agrees to transact with the client at the fix rate on that day, whatever it is. In practice, opposing client orders (say sterling–dollar and dollar–sterling) are 'netted out' as far as possible, that is, offsetting the gains in one position against losses in another.

A bank does not charge commission for its trading or act as an agent on behalf of the client. Instead, the bank acts as principal, so it is the bank which makes a profit or a loss. It could work like this:

- A bank with net client orders to buy a currency for a forthcoming fix will make a profit if the fix rate (i.e. the rate which it has agreed to sell a certain amount of currency to a client) is higher than the average rate at which the firm buys the same amount of that currency pair in the market. A loss will be made by the bank if the fix rate is lower than that average rate.

- A bank with net client orders to sell a currency for a forthcoming fix will make a profit if the fix rate (i.e. the rate at which it has agreed to buy a quantity of the currency pair from the client) is lower than the average rate at which it has agreed to buy a quantity of the currency pair in the market. A loss will be made by the bank if the fix rate is higher than that average rate.

A bank legitimately managing the risk arising from its net client orders may make a profit or a loss from its associated trading in the market. The bank will have an incentive to manipulate the fix in a direction which will profit it. For instance, a bank with net client 'buy' orders for the forthcoming fix can make a profit if it trades in a way that moves the fix rate higher. This is just one example of the attempts at manipulation which are more fully described in the next chapter, in the UK in the final notices issued by the FSA and then the FCA, and in the USA by the CFTC and the Department of Justice.

A similar attempt at manipulation can occur with 'stop loss' orders. The FCA explains that a client will place a stop loss order with a bank to help manage the risk arising from movements in the spot FX market.[22] For example, in circumstances where a client has bought euros with dollars he may place a stop loss order with a bank to sell euros for dollars at or around a specified rate below that of his original purchase. By accepting the order, the bank agrees to transact for the client at or around a specified rate if the currency trades at that rate in the market. No binding agreement is made until the agreed rate has been 'triggered' (i.e. when the currency trades at that rate in the market).

How is it that traders at a particular bank can influence such a vast market? The answer lies in the changing structure of the market, as shown in the BIS Triennial Surveys. Despite the huge impact of algorithmic trading and HFT, the spot market, with its $2 trillion daily turnover, is dominated by fewer than 100 individual traders at a small group of global banks. Why such a small group? The impact of technology meant that whole departments of traders disappeared. Kevin Rodgers, in his account of his career as a banker, recalls the early days when trading rooms were full of clamouring traders and gesticulating salesmen. During his time at Deutsche Bank, decades later, 'voice' traders had left and had not been not replaced. The only expansion was in e-trading and the derivatives (options) team. The only sound heard over more recent years was the gentle tapping of keyboards.[23]

By 2013, the spot trades undertaken by the major dealers, UBS, Deutsche Bank and Citibank, were 64% of the daily turnover, up from 20% less than 15 years previously. Nevertheless, voice trading, despite the small number of banks involved, was thought to be a way of retaining major clients, such as pension funds, large corporations and mutual funds, by offering them a cut-price service, with spreads often only a fraction of a basis point. After the financial crisis, the number of voice traders at the spot foreign exchange desks of the leading banks was probably less than a dozen. From the results of the official investigations, by regulators and others, into alleged manipulation of the FX fixes by bankers, it is clear that many of the traders had worked with their counterparts in other banks and moved from one bank to another. These traders took orders from their clients in the 30 minutes or so before the fix, and therefore they knew how much they would need to buy or sell at the fix price. Because the market could move against them, they saw this as a risk for the bank and so they might decide to trade ahead of the fix to hedge it. That is one possibility. In the next chapter, we shall examine the ways in which traders sought to manipulate the fix and the extent of the collusion. The official investigations meant that, once again, regulators had to trawl through mountains of emails and chat room tapes to find the evidence. It took months and years of work, but find it they did.

Notes

1 Kevin Rodgers, *Why Aren't They Shouting? A Banker's Tale of Change, Computers and Perpetual Crisis* (Random House Business Books, 2016), pp. 68–71.
2 Ibid., p. 72.
3 The survey is based on the returns from the reporting central banks, which in turn depend on a wide range of financial institutions 'reporting' to them: hence the difference between reporting dealers, for example, and non-reporting financial institutions.
4 Bank for International Settlements, *Triennial Central Bank Survey: Foreign Exchange and Derivatives Market Activity in 2004* (BIS, March 2005), p. 8, available at https://www.bis.org/publ/rpfx05t.pdf (accessed 4 May 2018).
5 In addition to access to relatively cheap funding and benign conditions in that period, hedge funds benefited from prime brokerage services, whereby a customer, such as a hedge fund, could obtain liquidity from a variety of

sources while at the same time maintaining a credit relationship, placing collateral and settling transactions with a single bank – the prime broker.

6 Rodgers, *Why Aren't They Shouting?*, p. 63.

7 Michael R. King and Dagfinn Rime, 'The $4 trillion question: what explains FX growth since the 2007 survey?', *BIS Quarterly Review* (December 2010), pp. 27–42, available at https://www.bis.org/publ/qtrpdf/r_qt1012.pdf (accessed 4 May 2018).

8 Rodgers, *Why Aren't They Shouting?*, ch. 3.

9 King and Rime, 'The $4 trillion question'.

10 Ibid., p. 32.

11 Michael Melvin and Mark P. Taylor, 'The crisis in the foreign exchange market', working paper no. 2707 (CESifo, March 2009), available at https://papers.ssrn.com/sol3/papers.cfm?abstract_id=1437408 (accessed 4 May 2018).

12 Detailed analyses of the 2013 Triennial Survey results were published in the December 2013 issue of the *BIS Quarterly Review*.

13 Dagfinn Rime and Andreas Schrimpf, 'The anatomy of the global FX market through the lens of the 2013 Triennial Survey', *BIS Quarterly Review*, December 2013, available at https://www.bis.org/publ/qtrpdf/r_qt1312e.pdf (accessed 4 May 2018).

14 Detailed analyses of the 2016 Triennial Survey results were published in the December 2016 issue of the *BIS Quarterly Review*.

15 Latency is defined as the delay between the transmission of information from one source and its receipt by another.

16 Bank for International Settlements, *High-Frequency Trading in the Foreign Exchange Market* (BIS, September 2011), p. 9, available at https://www.bis.org/publ/mktc05.pdf (accessed 4 May 2018).

17 Ibid., p. 10.

18 Ibid., p. 24.

19 Reuters acquired the FX benchmark rate calculation business of the World Markets Company (WM) from the State Street Corporation in 2016. WM/Reuters FX Benchmark is regulated by the FCA.

20 See the web page https://www.ecb.europa.eu/stats/policy_and_exchange_rates/euro_reference_exchange_rates/html/index.en.html (accessed October 2018).

21 Financial Conduct Authority, 'Final notice, Barclays Bank plc', 20 May 2015, annex B, available at https://www.fca.org.uk/publication/final-notices/barclays-bank-plc-may-15.pdf (accessed 4 May 2018).

22 Ibid. A stop loss order is a contingent order that triggers a buy or sell order for a specified notional amount when a reference price has reached or passed a predefined trigger level.

23 Rodgers, *Why Aren't They Shouting?*

Chapter 7

Manipulating the foreign exchange market

As we saw in the last chapter, the BIS Triennial Surveys show that dealers generally take orders from clients but executed them in the market as principal, bearing the consequent price risk, rather than executing in the market as agent acting for the client. To manage the risks associated with the flow of client orders, dealers hedge by executing FX transactions in and around the calculation window, which results in a large spike in the trading volume. This creates a market in which the dealer is agreeing to execute the orders at an unknown price, which is subsequently established during the fixing calculation window. That price should be the clearing price, which reflects the balance of supply and demand going through the market at that time, and therefore the prices should move as necessary, even if only temporarily, in response to these flows. Mostly the dealer gives the client the mid-rate of this as yet unknown fix price, whether the customer is buying or selling.

At a minimum, this market structure creates the impression of dealers 'trading ahead' of the fix even where the activity is essentially under client instruction. Worse still, it can create an opportunity and an incentive for dealers to try to influence the exchange rate, either by collusion or by inappropriate ways of sharing information. The aim is to try to ensure that the market price at the fix is a rate which gives the dealer a profit. It is both an incentive for and an opportunity for improper trading. It is, then, trading behaviour, rather than the method of computing the fix, which creates the possibility of making a profit from fix trading. However, the two interact, and can lead to adverse outcomes for clients. The evidence collected by the regulators shows that this is what happened.

Final notice to Barclays issued by the FCA, 20 May 2015

Barclays was the first to admit wrongdoing but was nevertheless fined by the FCA. In its final notice, issued on 20 May 2015, the FCA stated that over the five years between 1 January 2009 and 15 October 2013, Barclays failed to control its London voice trading operations in the G10 spot FX market.[1] Barclays put its interests ahead of the interests of its clients, other market participants and the wider UK financial system. Similar failings occurred in other areas of Barclays' FX voice trading in London, including various transactions in currencies of countries in emerging markets and the G10.

What did Barclays do by way of manipulation?

- It made attempts to manipulate the WM Reuters and the ECB fix rates, in collusion with traders at other firms, for Barclays' own benefit and to the potential detriment of its clients and of other market participants.
- It attempted to trigger clients' stop loss orders for Barclays' own benefit and to the potential detriment of those clients and of other market participants.
- It inappropriately shared confidential information (e.g. specific client identities and information about clients' orders) internally and with third parties, including other market participants.

Traders made use of electronic messaging services, including chat rooms. They formed tight-knit groups or one-to-one relationships based on mutual benefit and often focused on particular currency pairs. The participants tightly controlled entry to such groups, using electronic communications to exchange confidential information with and from traders at other firms regarding the size and direction of net orders at a forthcoming fix and used the information to determine the likely direction of the fix. They were then in a position to decide on their trading strategies and to attempt to manipulate the fix in a certain direction.

The typical strategies were as follows:

(1) The traders in a chat room with net orders in the opposite direction to the desired outcome at the fix sought to 'net off' their orders with third parties outside the chat room rather than with traders in the chat room. This maintained the volume of orders in the required direction held by traders in the chat room and avoided orders being transacted in the opposite direction at

the fix. Traders within the market have referred to this as 'leaving you with the ammo'.

(2) The traders in a chat room with net orders in the same direction to the desired outcome at the fix sought before the fix to do one or more of the following:

- net off these orders with third parties outside the chat room, so reducing the volume of orders held by third parties that might otherwise be transacted at the fix in the opposite direction (traders called this 'taking out the filth' or 'clearing the decks');

- transfer these orders to a single trader in the chat room, to increase the likelihood of successfully manipulating the fix, as one trader had much more control over the trading strategy during the fix than a number of traders acting separately;

- transact with third parties outside the chat room to increase the volume of orders held by them in the right direction (more than the volume necessary to manage the risks associated with the firms' net buy or sell orders at the fix – i.e., over-buying or over-selling).

The effect of these actions was to increase the influence that these traders had on the forthcoming fix and so the likelihood of them being able to manipulate the rate in the direction they wanted.

The FCA provides two examples of Barclays manipulating the foreign exchange market: an attempt to manipulate the WM Reuters fix for a particular currency pair; and an attempt to trigger client stop loss orders. The second example from the final notice is quoted in full here, as it is complicated, but it demonstrates the manoeuvring which took place between the traders and the necessity for the FCA to decode the exchanges.

Barclays attempted to trigger a client's stop loss order. The client had placed a stop loss order to buy £77 million at a rate of 95 against another currency, but the bank took a decision not to trigger the order until the market had traded at a rate of 97. Barclays then executed the order, that is, sold £77 million to the client at 96.5, as it knew it would make a profit if the average rate at which it bought sterling for the client was in accordance with the stop loss order. Between 10.37 and 11.37, Barclays attempted to trigger the client's stop loss order, but Barclays disclosed details of the order to traders at other companies and provided a commentary to them about the attempt. Here are the various stages, as reported by the FCA:

(1) At 10:38, Firm X asked Barclays and Firms Y and Z if they had any stop loss orders ('u got ... stops?'). Barclays responded that it had a stop loss order for '80 quid' at a level of 95. Barclays noted it was 'primed like a coiled cobra ... concentrating so hard ... [as if] made of wax ...[haven't] even blinked'.

(2) At 10:46, the rate increased to 84 and Firm X commented '... is higher sint it'. Barclays responded 'watch out ... will be soon . The FCA considers this to be a reference to the intention on the part of Barclays to attempt to manipulate the rate to trigger the stop loss order. Firm X responded that it did not believe that Barclays could trigger the stop loss order.

(3) As a first attempt, between approximately 10.46 and 10.49 Barclays purchased GBP66 million at rates between 78 and 95. Barclays then placed an order to buy GBP5 million up to 97, which was above the best offer price prevailing in the market at that time which was 95. This order resulted in Barclays buying GBP2 million at 95 and GBP3 million at 96, before the rate fell back lower.

(4) At 10:49, Firm X commented 'hope that was a o.t' (i.e. a one-touch order).[2] The FCA considers this to be a reference to the stop loss order at 95 which if it had been a one-touch order would have been executed. Firm Y also stated 'i was just about to say that'. Barclays replied 'errr ...long some ... here'. The FCA considers this to be a reference to Barclays buying the currency pair but not being able to trigger the stop loss order by trading at a rate of 97 and thereby selling GBP to the client. Hence it is left with a 'long' position.

(5) At 10:51, Firm X told Barclays 'we pick up a seller ... guy i like ... and just above the print u need'. Barclays responded ('ok ... ta').

(6) At approximately 10:58, the rate increased to 94. As a second attempt, Barclays placed an order to buy GBP10 million up to 97. Again this was above the best offer price prevailing in the market at that time, which was 95. This order resulted in Barclays buying GBP10 million at 95, following which the rate fell to 85 and Barclays noted 'foooooooooooookkkkk'. By approximately 11:09, the rate had fallen to 78, by which time Barclays had reduced its long position by selling GBP and noted it was 'dead'. The FCA considers this to be a reference to Barclays not being able to trigger the stop loss order and incurring a loss on the long position it had established as a result of the rate falling.

(7) Barclays also confirmed to the other firms that the stop loss order would not be triggered until the rate reached 97 and that it had been unable to achieve this ('... cudnt get the 97 print ... despite trying super hard'). Barclays noted that there were 'algos galore at 96'. The FCA considers this to be a reference to selling interest from algorithms at a rate of 96 which Barclays perceived had prevented the rate from going higher.

(8) The third and final attempt took place approximately 20 minutes later. At approximately 11:37, transactions occurred in the market

at rates 94–96 and the prevailing best offer rate increased to 97. Firm X noted 'attemot number 3'. Barclays then placed an order to buy GBP2 million at up to 97. As a result of this order, Barclays bought GBP1 million at 96 and at 97. The purchase at 97 enabled Barclays to execute the stop loss order. Barclays then confirmed this to the other firms ('done').

(9) Barclays' purchase of GBP1 million at 97 was the only trade at that rate on the trading platform at that time. The currency pair did not trade at this rate again until approximately 16:00.

4.69. Barclays then executed the stop loss order by selling GBP77 million to the client at a rate of 96.5. Barclays' trading was aimed to manipulate the spot rate for the currency pair such that the stop loss was triggered. Barclays' trading in this example generated a loss equivalent to USD63,84515.[3]

4.70. Following the triggering of the stop loss order, Firm X commented, ironically, that Barclays would have 'one happy cleitn!'. Barclays responded 'he shud be as he wants minimal protection and really cud have been done with 96 print ... but we held him in'). The FCA considers 'held him in' to be a reference to Barclays not executing the stop loss order for the client when the currency pair traded at 96.

4.71. Although Barclays did not execute the stop loss order at 95 or 96, Barclays traded in a manner that was intended to move the rate to 97. Therefore, as noted by the other firms, instead of holding the client in, Barclays attempted to trigger the stop loss order. At 11:39, Firm Y responded to Barclays: 'hahahah ... hardly [Barclays] ... thats not holding him in ... gd work though'. Firm X concurred: 'helkd him in ... with a lot of cursingf ... u tried to carve him ... and eventually succeeded'. Firm Z stated that Barclays' comment about holding the client in 'might have to go in the quote book'. Barclays responded 'hehe'.[4]

CFTC investigation of Barclays

The CFTC found examples of similar abuses in relation to Barclays. For instance, traders in one chat room had to decide whether or not to ensure that a new member – a Barclays trader – would put the interests of the group first:

> Bank Z trader: 7.49:55 are we ok with keeping this as is
> 7.50:27 ie the info levls & risk sharing?...
> Bank Z trader: 7:50:30 that is the qu[estion]
> Bank X trader: 7:50:32–7:50:43 you know him best obv ... if you think we need to adjust it then he shouldn't be in chat
> Bank Y trader: 7:50:54 yeah that is the key
> 7:51:00 simple question [Bank Z trader]
> 7.51:08 I trust you implicitly [Bank Z trader]

7:51:13 and your judgment
7:51:21 you know him
7:51:21 will he tell the rest of the bank stuff
7:51:26 or god forbin his nyk...
Bank X trader: 7:51:46 yes
Bank X trader: 7:51:51–7:52:46 that's really imp[ortant] q[uestion]. Don't want other numpty's in mkt to know but not only that is he gonna protect us like we protect each other against our own branches ie if you guys are rhs ... and my nyk isihs ... ill say my nyk lhs in few.
Bank Z trader: 7:53:52 what concerns me is that I know he'll never tell us when at risk....

After further discussion of whether the Barclays trader would 'add huge value to this cartel', the traders decided to invite the trader into the chat room for a '1 month trial' with bank X.[5]

Final notice to UBS AG issued by the FCA, 11 November 2014

The FCA provides an example of the way in which UBS sought to manipulate the ECB fix.[6] During the time leading up to the ECB fix, UBS increased the 'built' volume of euros that it would sell for the fix to €211 million through a series of additional trades conducted with other market participants, much more than necessary to manage UBS's risk associated with net client orders at the fix.

> 4.42. From 12:35pm to 1:14pm, UBS sold a net amount of EUR132 million. At 1:14:59pm (i.e. 1 second before the ECB fix), UBS placed an order to sell EUR100 million at 1.3092, which was three basis points below the prevailing best market bid at that time.
>
> 4.43. This order was immediately executed and accounted for 29% of the sales in EUR/USD on the EBS platform during the period from 1:14:55 to 1:15:02pm.
>
> 4.44. The ECB subsequently published the fix rate for EUR/USD at 1.3092.
>
> 4.45. The information disclosed between UBS and Firms A, B and C, regarding their order flows was used to determine their trading strategies. The consequent 'building' by UBS and its trading in relation to that increased quantity at the fix were designed to decrease the ECB fix rate to UBS's benefit. UBS undertook the selling of Euros prior to the 1:15pm ECB fix in anticipation that the fix rate at which it would buy Euros would be lower than the average rate at which it had sold. The placing of a large sell order by UBS immediately prior to 1:15pm was designed to achieve this outcome. UBS's trading in EUR/USD in this example generated a profit of USD513,000.

4.46. In the immediate aftermath of the ECB fix, UBS was congratulated on the success of its trading by Firms A, B and C ('hes sat back in his chaoir [sic] … feet on desk … announcing to desk … thats why i got the bonus pool' and 'yeah made most peoples year').

CFTC order issued to the Royal Bank of Scotland, 11 November 2014

In this example, an RBS trader has a client order to sell the sterling–dollar pair at the WM Reuters fix.[7] The RBS trader shares this information with other traders and learns that they also have orders to sell at the fix. After the fix, the chatroom participants discuss the trading.

> 15:45:357 RBS Trader: im getting abt 80 quid now … fixing
> 15:45:54 Bank U Trader: my ny 100 quid….
> 15:51:19 RBS Trader: getting more than u now [Bank U Trader] betty
> 15:51:26 Bank U Trader: ok thx
> 15:52:23 Bank W Trader: nice job gents
> 15:54:16 Bank U Trader: [RBS Trader], just matched with [Bank 1] and [Bank 2] for 100, still lhs in about 140
> 15:54:26 RBS Trader: cool….
> 16:00:58 Bank Z Trader: i don my hat….
> 16:01:08 Bank W Trader: what a job
> 16:01:23 Bank Z Trader: welld one lads
> 16:01:28 Bank W Trader: bravo
> 16:07:03 RBS Trader: 1.6218 … nice
> 16:07:33 Bank U Trader: worked ok that one….

CFTC order issued to HSBC, 11 November 2014

The CFTC uses some of the same examples of misconduct as the FCA does. The example reproduced here from the CFTC order, though, is not included by the FCA.[8] A trader on HSBC's London G10 FX trading desk discusses the fact that they are net sellers ('lhs') in 'cable'.[9]

> Bank W Trader 1: 2:50:21 pm: early days but im a seller cable at fix […]
> Bank S Trader: 3:11:43 pm: here also
> Bank R Trader: 3:24:50 pm: u got much to do in fix [Bank Trader W]
> Bank W Trader 1: 3:25:07 pm: im seller 130 cable that it […]
> Bank W Trader 1: 3:28:02 pm: hopefulyl a few more get same way and we can team whack it
> Bank R Trader: 3:28:17 pm: ill do some digging […]
> Bank W Trader 1: 3:36:13 pm: im seller 170 gbp atmofix
> Bank R Trader: 3:36:26 pm: we sellers of 40

HSBC Trader: 3:38:26 pm: lhs in cable at the fix
HSBC Trader: 3:38:29 pm: good amount
As the 4 p.m. fix period closes, the participants in the chat room made
the following statements:
Bank R Trader: 4:00:35 pm: well done gents
Bank W Trader 1: 4:01:56 pm: hooray nice team work
HSBC Trader: 4:02:22 pm: nice one mate

The HSBC trader does not confine the information shared to one chat
room but to another three chat rooms. In a separate private chat room,
the HSBC trader informs bank W trader 2, just before the close of the
fix period, that he should buy cable at the fix, and shortly after that the
HSBC trader tells bank W trader 2 that he has a net sell order of about
400 million cable at the fix and bank W trader 2 says he is a seller of 150
million cable at the fix. At the same time, the HSBC trader discloses he
is selling at the fix in yet another private chat with a trader at bank V, at
3.28 p.m., and in a fourth chat room, HSBC disclosed his position with
traders at other banks. Before the fix in another private chat, bank W
trader 1 warned him that a firm outside the chat room was 'building' in
the opposite direction to them and that he had taken action to net off
against this order, which would be in the opposite direction at the fix
from his and HSBC's positions. In another chat room, the HSBC trader
and yet another trader from bank W discuss unloading their positions
just before the fix and were apparently successful in doing so. The HSBC
trader's practice of communicating confidential information (i.e. the
size and direction of orders) and similar information soliciting and
directing banks to follow his actions during the fix period continued on
various days in 2011 and 2012 until he left HSBC in mid-2012. His were
complicated manoeuvres, involving a number of traders in different
tactics, leaving a question as to whether or not the traders in the various
chat rooms continued to trust him.

CFTC order issued to JP Morgan Chase Bank, 11 November 2014

In one example, a JP Morgan Chase (JPMC) FX trader and a 'bank W'
trader coordinated their trading in an attempt to manipulate the 4 p.m.
euro–dollar fix.[10] At 3.43.50, the bank W trader asked the JP Morgan
Chase trader whether he needed to buy euros in the market in the forthcoming fix. The JPMC trader replied that he had a net buy order for the
fix, which he subsequently confirmed as €105 million. At 3.44.04, the

JPMC trader offered to transfer the net buy order to the bank W trader. The bank W trader replied 'maybe' and then stated that he had a net buy order for €150 million. The traders then had the following exchange:

> Bank W Trader: 3:46:53 i'd prefer we join forces
> JPMC Trader: 3:46:56 perfick
> 3:46:59 lets do this...
> JPMC Trader: 3:47:11 lets double team them
> Bank W Trader: 3:47:12 YESsssssssssss

Immediately after the fixing window, the traders congratulated themselves:

> Bank W Trader: 4:03:25 sml rumour we haven't lost it
> JPMC Trader: 4:03:45 we
> 4:03:46 do
> 4:03:48 dollarrr

CFTC order issued to Citibank, 11 November 2014

In this example, a Citibank trader coordinated with traders from banks W, Y and Z to attempt to manipulate the euro–dollar and dollar–Swiss franc fixes.[11] The fix discussion began at about 3.16 p.m. that day, with traders sharing position information and rumours about several currencies. Between 3.31 and 3.40, the chat room participants matched off their Australian dollar positions so they were 'all good'. They then turned their attention to other currency pairs:

> Citibank Trader:3:53:35 can anyone help in chf fix
> 3:53:38 i lose 130 total
> Bank Y Trader: 3:53:46 arb it for more ammo
> Citibank Trader:3:53:55 [Bank Z trader] ur guy want it?
> Bank Z Trader: 3:54:09 nope he's flatish i think
> Bank W Trader: 3:54:16 buy the eurchf and les hammer eur
> 3:54:18 come on
> Bank Y Trader: 3:54:29 [Citibank trader] ill do it of u want
> 3:54:33 ive nothing else to do....
> Citibank Trader:3:54:53 ok 130 usdchf mine
> Bank Y Trader: 3:54:57 ok 130 u buy

Having offset their CHF positions, the traders turned their attention to the EUR in the remaining minutes before the fix:

> Bank Y Trader: 3:55:01 u want small eurusd?
> Bank W Trader: 3:55:19 so [Bank Z trader] u get eur now?
> Bank Z Trader: 3:56:00 checkin
> Bank Y Trader: 3:56:04 right who wants 40 eur

Bank Z Trader: 3:56:06 sub 30
Bank Y Trader: 3:57:53 gd lk fellas

At 4:00:44 the Bank Y trader stated 'no surre any winner there.' Three minutes later, the Citibank trader replied with 'wmr is impossible.'

Other investigations and penalties

The banks listed here faced fines not only from the FCA and the CFTC but also from the US Department of Justice, the US Federal Reserve and the New York Department of Financial Services. In the last case, the press releases regarding Barclays and UBS provide further information about the ways in which the banks manipulated the foreign exchange market or treated their customers.

Barclays

The press release detailing the reasons for the New York Department of Financial Services' imposition of a further fine on Barclays of $2.4 billion sets out efforts to cheat the bank's clients (original emphasis below):[12]

> On numerous occasions, from at least 2008 to 2014, Barclays employees on the FX Sales team engaged in misleading sales practices with clients. Sales employees applied 'hard mark-ups' to the prices that traders gave them without their clients' knowledge. A hard mark-up represents the difference between the price the trader gives a salesperson and the price the salesperson shows to the client.
>
> FX Sales employees would determine the appropriate mark-up by calculating **the most advantageous rate for Barclays that did not cause the client to question whether executing the transaction with the Bank was a good idea**, based on the relationship with the client, recent pricing history, client expectations and other factors.
>
> As one FX Sales employee wrote in a chat to an employee at another bank on December 30, 2009, **'hard mark up is key ... but i was taught early ... u dont have clients ... u dont make money ... so dont be stupid.'**
>
> The practice of certain FX Sales Employees when a client called for a price quote was to mute the telephone line when asking the trader for a price, which would allow Sales employees to add mark-up without the client's knowledge.
>
> Mark-ups represented a key revenue source for Barclays and generating mark-ups was a high priority for sales managers. As the future Co-Head of UK FX Hedge Fund Sales (who was then a Vice President in the New York Branch) wrote in a November 5, 2010 chat: 'markup is making sure you make the right decision on price ... which is whats the worst price i can put on this where the customers decision to trade with me or give me future business doesn't change ... **if you aint cheating, you aint trying.'**

On June 26, 2009, after one FX Sales employee appeared to admit to another Sales employee that he 'came clean' about charging a hard mark-up after a client called him out on it, the second employee stated 'i wouldnt normally admit to clients if you pip them. i think saying you rounded is fine.' The first employee agreed, and replied that he didn't actually come clean to the client, but rather 'said i was rounding.'

On September 23, 2014, another FX Sales employee applied a mark-up to a client's trade. The client called and asked if had applied a mark-up, and **this Sales employee lied and said that he had not.**

Another misleading sales practice was giving a client the worst (or a worse) rate that was reached during a particular time interval, even if the trader was able to execute the order at a better price. The more favorable fill generated a profit, which Barclays would keep, in whole or in part, without providing disclosure to the client.

A similar practice was to tell clients that their orders had been only partially filled, when in fact the FX Sales employees were holding back a portion of the fill as the market moved in Barclays' favor, permitting Barclays to generate an undisclosed profit at the client's expense.

UBS

Citicorp, JP Morgan Chase, Barclays, the Royal Bank of Scotland and UBS all pleaded guilty in connection with the FX market and agreed to pay more than $2.5 billion in criminal fines. A press release from the US Department of Justice cites collusion between euro–dollar traders at Citicorp, JP Morgan, Barclays and RBS, self-described members of 'The Cartel', using an exclusive electronic chat room and coded language to manipulate benchmark exchange rates between December 2007 and January 2013.[13] The same evidence was used in connection with all the banks listed here, apart from UBS. This bank was singled out particularly, presumably because it violated its December 2012 non-prosecution agreement resolving the LIBOR investigation.

The focus in the plea agreement[14] was on sales and trading practices, including misrepresentations about sales mark-ups. For example:

> On May 3, 2013, a UBS FX sales person based in London, in an electronic chat with a customer, stated, 'ALL of your business today we have filled completely flat and on 1 clips of gbp we took pip loss – we have not made any money out of each clip whatsoever … I can assure you no hard mark-up is taken on yr business'. [This was simply untrue.]

On occasion, some UBS customers requested that a UBS FX sales-person provide them with an 'open line' while the salesperson consulted with a UBS FX trading desk, to ensure the price they were offered was indeed the 'trader price' and did not include any sales mark-up. However, this facility was misused as well. Certain UBS FX salespeople and traders used hand signals during certain customers' 'open line' calls; for example, a salesperson would hold up two fingers to signal that the trader should add a mark-up of 'two pips' to the quoted price. Or with advance knowledge or expectation of an imminent 'open line' request by a particular customer, salespeople and traders made a prior arrangement to add an undisclosed mark-up to the prices quoted by traders over the open line. For example:

> On July 19, 2013, a UBS FX salesperson based in Stamford, in an electronic chat with a UBS FX trader in Stamford, said, 'so the game plan is: I will ask for the price over the hoot [i.e an internal communication system that enabled the sales staff and traders to communicate with one another over a speaker, but the conversation could be heard by someone on the end of a phone if the phone was close enough to the hoot] and I will leave the phone line open for the customer to hear the hoot. So we (you and I) and [a UBS colleague] will need to coordinate on pricing'. The sales person went to say, 'so because you and I will have an open hoot, the price you give me will have the spread included'.

'Working' FX customers' limit orders at altered prices

A limit order is an order to buy or sell a currency pair when the market hits a price specified by a customer. UBS staff would 'work' or track certain limit orders at a price level different from the one specified by the customer to add an undisclosed mark-up. This practice of tracking and executing limit orders at a level different from the customer's level happened at UBS's FX sales desks. One example of this is presented in the same plea agreement:

> On July 17, 2013, a UBS FX salesperson based in Stamford sent the following email to colleagues on UBS's London and Singapore FX desks: 'Please note that [customer] has an order to buy EUR 150 mio at 1.3070. I split the trade into three pieces; EUR 50 mio flat = 1.3070, EUR 50 mio at 1.3069 and EUR 50 mio at 1.3068.' Later in the same email, the UBS FX salesperson added, 'If he trades, I would like you to try and take two pips…. Three would be even better, but I'll leave that up to you.'

Barclays' 'last look' system

An electronic trading platform for the FX market called BARX allows traders to execute FX trades with Barclays. Such a platform might be able to exploit latencies in the flow of information by requesting trades at prices that reflect information that Barclays and other market makers may not have. Orders like this, which seek to outflank and exploit a market maker's less nimble trading system, are known as 'toxic order flow' or 'toxic flow'. For example, a sophisticated electronic trading business might detect a market movement some milliseconds before Barclays' system has, and so benefit from trading with Barclays' systems before they properly adjust their prices.

Barclays made use of a common practice in the foreign exchange market, the 'last look' system, which creates a small gap between client orders and the execution of trades; this is to its own advantage, as it can ensure the profitability of a trade for the bank. In an internal email, Barclays employees emphasised that 'Our Team generally does not share this information with the client'.[15] Barclays would then compare the BARX price of the customer's order at the start of the hold time against the BARX price at the end of the period. If, following the order, the price had moved against Barclays and in favour of the client beyond a threshold set by Barclays, Barclays would reject the trade.

Barclays did not try to distinguish toxic order flow from instances in which prices merely happened to move in favour of the customer and against Barclays after the order was placed in Barclays' systems. It applied 'last look' to all FIX/API trades as well as a handful of GUI customers. If prices moved against Barclays in this holding period and in favour of the customer beyond a certain undisclosed loss threshold, Barclays treated the trade as toxic flows. It was seen as a means of protecting the bank's profit, instead of using 'last look' as a 'purely defensive measure'.[16]

Thus, Barclays' 'last look' system was used to automatically reject client orders that would be unprofitable for the bank because of subsequent price swings during milliseconds-long latency (hold) periods. When clients questioned Barclays about these rejected trades, Barclays failed to give the reason for the rejection, citing technical issues or providing vague responses.

From 2009 to at least 2014, certain Barclays staff provided insufficient or incomplete information to its customers about 'last look'. Instead, the client would receive a simple rejection message: NACK (not acknowledged). The New York Department of Financial Services produced both a press release and a 'consent order' relating to the matter.[17] Both provide examples of misconduct.

The consent order records the following:

On December 15, 2010, a Barclays client wrote, '[w]e have noticed that there were over 300 rejected orders with you today and the reason is "NACK", could you pls have a look at them and advise what's causing it?' After failing to receive a substantive response, the client followed up two days later, writing, '[w]e have not heard anything back with regards to the rejections. And this has become quite a serious matter.... We kept receiving top of the book rates from you and hitting your rate, but we got rejected by you 9 times out of 10 where we could have been well filled by other liquidity providers who have been providing competitive rates.... Could someone from your side shed some light on the rejections? Whether they are due to technical difficulties or business decisions?' There is no evidence that Barclays ever responded to these queries.[18]

Possibly Barclays just lost the client!

The press release notes that some sophisticated customers monitored their rejection rates and turn-around times at Barclays and other banks:

> On certain occasions, some of these sophisticated customers raised concerns about their high rejection rates at Barclays. Upon such complaints, Barclays engaged in discussions with customers concerning their rejection rates, and sometimes adjusted hold times and thresholds to decrease rejection rates.[19]

Finally, the New York Financial Services Department noted that the Barclays Managing Director and Head of Automated Electronic FX Trading wrote: 'Do not discuss Last Look with Sales. If there has been a spurt [in rejected trades] just blame it on the weekend IT release and say it's being fixed'.[20]

Interestingly enough, this was not a line of enquiry which the Department pursued again. It did, though, make an announcement on 11 December 2014 that an investigation was being pursued against Deutsche Bank as to whether FX algorithms were being used to manipulate exchange rates.[21]

On 20 April 2017, the US Federal Reserve announced that it was fining Deutsche Bank $156.6 million for violating FX rules and running against the Volcker Rule. Reuters noted at the time that the bank still faced an investigation into whether its automated trading platform was programmed to manipulate foreign exchange rates.[22]

Was the Bank of England involved?

As details emerged from the FCA's investigation about the extent of manipulation of the FX market, attention turned to the Bank of

England, especially when journalists realised that regular meetings took place between the chief FX dealer at the Bank of England and the chief dealers of 11 banks, the Foreign Exchange Joint Standing Committee (FXJSC) and the chief dealers' subgroup (CDSG), established in 2005.[23] These lunchtime meetings took place at various restaurants, such as Gaucho and the Don Bistro, depending on which bank was hosting the lunchtime meeting, until 2008, when they were held in offices in the City and Canary Wharf.[24] It was easy for the media to paint the meetings as evidence that the Bank knew what was going on but turned a blind eye or, worse still, condoned it. From the outside, it is easy to interpret such meetings in this way, but they are essential if a central bank is to understand what is going on in the market and it will always be one source of information, but not the only one. The Bank of England (in the Grabiner report discussed below) published the minutes of the meeting of the CDSG on 5 March 2014. The only references in the minutes which could possibly be taken to indicate that the representatives from the banks were engaged in the kind of misconduct under investigation by the FCA are as follows:

4 July 2006 CDSG meeting

...

11) It was noted that there was evidence of attempts to move the market around popular fixing times by players that had no particular interest in that fix. This was not in the interest of customers if the market was forced away from where it should be when the fixing snapshot was taken. It was noted that 'fixing business' generally was becoming increasingly fraught due to this behaviour.

12) The discussion then widened to cover ... formulation and treatment of benchmark services. It was noted that it was no longer uncommon to be selling/buying to/from a customer at a fixing price that could not be obtained in the market.... The Chair noted that this was largely a competitive issue.[25]

A few months later, on 9 October 2006, the same group discussed order management around the fixings with 'some unease about the methodologies used, latency in publications and how new matching technology proposed by some service providers, so-called "dark room netting", might change the dynamics of fixing flows'.[26] It was proposed that the chairman invite a fixing company to give a presentation at a future meeting, which was eventually arranged for 6 July 2008.

When the CDSG met on 16 May 2008, 'the large majority of members [expressed] concern about the lack of transparency among some methodologies and the impacts in managing order flow and pricing liquidity at times of concentrated benchmarked interest such as the 4pm London fix'.[27] It was after that meeting that the presentation of the fixing methodology to its members finally took place.

However, enough questions had been raised for the Oversight Committee of the Bank of England to investigate whether, between 2005 and 2013, any Bank of England official was involved in, or aware of, the conduct which is the subject of the FCA's investigations into the FX market. On 14 March 2014, Lord Grabiner was appointed by the Oversight Committee to investigate the role of bank officials in relation to conduct issues in the foreign exchange market. The investigation was to focus on whether any Bank official between July 2005 and December 2013 was:

> (i) involved in the attempted or actual manipulation of the foreign exchange market (including the WMR FX benchmark), or (ii) aware of any attempted or actual manipulation of the foreign exchange market, or (iii) aware of the potential for such manipulation, or (iv) colluded with market participants in relation to any such manipulation or aware of any such collusion between market participants.[28]

The report was published on 12 November 2014. In the event, it was narrowly focused and it was not concerned with the nature and extent of FX manipulation, which was the subject of the investigation conducted by the FCA. Dealing in spot foreign currency exchanges was not a regulated activity under the Financial Services and Markets Act 2000, and nor did the statutory market abuse regime apply at that time; indeed, the Bank of England was not a regulatory authority until 1 April 2013.

The Bank of England is involved in the FX market through its FX Desk, members of which trade currency in the market. The Foreign Exchange Division (FED) is part of the Markets Directorate of the Bank. It contains a number of subdivisions, one of which is the FX Desk. Members of the FX Desk gather market intelligence about the FX market, which is then distributed through the Bank to assist in its policy decisions. Gathering market intelligence and the general oversight of the FX Desk was the responsibility of Mr Mallett, the chief dealer for the period in question (2005–13). The FX Desk is itself involved in trading foreign currencies both for the Treasury Exchange Equalisation Account and for the Bank's own account.

Mallett, the chief dealer, was the market intelligence 'champion' together with his team of analysts. They gathered market intelligence from a number of sources, but in particular Bloomberg chat rooms, through conversations with market participants. But the only written 'escalation policy' before 2012 was in the FED manual, which stated:

> If staff become aware of any activity that may constitute market abuse either internally in the Bank or externally, this should be brought to the attention of the line manager or Head of Department who may alert the appropriate authorities.[29]

It did not apply to the spot FX market.

Lord Grabiner also refers to three conversations which took place after a meeting of the CDSG on 16 May 2008. One was in a chat room on 19 May, in which Mr O'Riordan (UBS) described the CDSG meeting to his superior as one in which the 'BoE showed a little concern with banks openly chatting to each other on reuters/bloomie about the upcoming fixes and matching them off'.[30] O'Riordan, when questioned later, said the BoE reference meant Mr Mallett. Lord Grabiner cites a number of telephone calls between October 2011 and November 2012 from a member of the CDSG, from a trader and from a market commentator, as well as a meeting with a senior FX trader and a salesman. The calls indicate that Mallett clearly had concerns about the matching process and feared that this could lead to collusion and to market participants being disadvantaged. In the first telephone call (3 October 2011), which Lord Grabiner suggests was not understood, there was a clear reference to 'building a book' and 'spoofing' (not genuine sales), and Mallett recognised it as market manipulation. The salesman made matters quite clear: 'The real issue is have they executed the price in such a way as to maximize the potential profit by trying to ensure that the rate at four o'clock is at a certain level and not another'.[31]

On the basis of this and other evidence, Lord Grabiner concluded that there was no evidence that any Bank of England official was involved in any unlawful or improper behaviour in the FX market. Mallett was singled out for the most serious criticism, since he was aware from May 2008 that banks were having open discussions about their fix positions in chat rooms with a view to matching them off. From at least 28 November 2012, he was concerned about the possibility of collusion and that it could lead to market participants being disadvantaged, but he failed to take any action and did not refer the matter to his line manager or to anyone else. Despite the lack of any formal escalation covering these issues, they were important enough for Mallett to assess the importance of the issues and to exercise judgement.

Lord Grabiner's report was published on 12 November 2014 and was subject to scrutiny by the Treasury Select Committee in March 2015, shortly before the general election in May, which meant that the Committee did not produce its final report at that time. However, even before the report was published, on 11 March 2014, Mark Carney, Governor of the Bank of England, told the Committee:

> [the Bank] was acutely aware of [its] responsibility to complete a thorough, comprehensive investigation of all aspects related to this issue. You rightly said that this is incredibly important for the foreign exchange market and it is fundamentally important to the integrity of the Bank of England. We cannot come out of this at the back end with a shadow of doubt about the integrity of the Bank of England.[32]

The Treasury Select Committee no doubt viewed the Grabiner report in that light and was dissatisfied with the outcome. The Committee's chair suggested the Lord Grabiner's interpretation of Mallett's telephone call with a trader (a crucial part of the report) – namely that the call did not refer to an illegal activity or to what the banks were doing, as opposed to what the brokers were doing – was unsatisfactory. In response, Lord Grabiner wrote to the Committee on 28 January 2015, reiterating his interpretation of the conversation and also providing the text of two long interviews with Mallett.[33] Once again, he concluded that the trader was concerned about the size of the fix orders and that if a broker makes an error, it will be a large one. But with regard to the references to brokers seeking to fix trades to create fees and the reference to banks trying to 'build a book', Mallet thought the reference was to brokers until near the end of the conversation. It was only then that he seemed to grasp the possibility that the reference was to banks as opposed to brokers, but the trader also rejected the inference that the banks were trying to manipulate the market.

The Treasury Select Committee was only able to provide a 'wash-up' of the evidence on this matter and among the questions it raised for the next parliament were: whether or not the terms of reference were appropriate; whether or not Lord Grabiner was wholly independent and able to investigate whatever he thought fit; and what conclusions should be drawn about the quality and completeness of his report. I do not think either the terms of reference or access to data and bank officials limited Lord Grabiner's work, which was to consider the points set out at the start of this section, relating specifically to the involvement of the Bank or its officials within a specific period. The terms of reference also included determining whether or not any official was aware of the sharing of confidential client information, or was aware of the sharing of such information between market participants in order to transact business in the FX market, or was involved in or aware of any other unlawful or improper behaviour or practices in the market.[34] The terms of reference were wide enough and access to data and individuals of all kinds was entirely open to Lord Grabiner and his team for him to provide a thorough report. The problem in my view is that the report was too narrowly focused on one individual (and to a lesser extent on his two deputies) and in showing that the chief dealer, Mallett, who was subsequently dismissed, failed to escalate his concerns. The records of the conversations he had suggest that he did not ask enough questions or pursue them sufficiently to find out what was going on. Telephone calls and discussions took place but they were not followed up and those who were willing to impart their concerns were just allowed to drift away as far as he was concerned.

The Governor of the Bank of England, Mark Carney, when questioned by the Committee, stated that Mallett had made at least 20 'misjudgements' which could have brought the Bank's reputation into disrepute. Carney first of all described the Bank's review of gathering market intelligence as a result of the Grabiner report. This has led to the introduction of a market intelligence charter, so that staff now know how to handle market intelligence; also, a team of 15 staff now work under the direction of a committee of executive directors, whose role it is to set the priorities for market intelligence. As a result of these reforms, Carney revealed that the Bank's market intelligence staff had passed on 50 instances of potential market abuse to their superiors, of which 42 had gone to the FCA.[35]

The Bank of England's Oversight Committee's response was to adopt the recommendations of the Grabiner report, especially in relation to the gathering of market intelligence and record-keeping. An examination of the minutes of the CDSG, which are now publicly available, reveals little about the state of the FX market, and were apparently recorded some time after the event and were not widely distributed. The Committee notes that the Bank currently participates in 15 market-orientated multilateral meeting groups, but that some require clearer terms of reference and better record-keeping, and that the purposes of the meetings and attendees need to be consistently recorded. The Bank in an immediate response to the recommendations contained in the report has produced a formal escalation policy. Staff are actively encouraged to raise any concerns they may have about market misconduct, even if they come to nothing. All staff who have contact with market participants now have to attest to their compliance with the Bank's escalation and record-keeping policies.

These are certainly important recommendations. They should have arisen from the kind of analysis which the FSA instigated in its internal audit in relation to LIBOR manipulation, discussed in Chapter 5. The recommendations are important, but in terms of becoming aware of market abuse and cheating of all kinds, they will not succeed by themselves. It requires a commitment on the part of senior managers in receipt of such reports and suspicions to investigate further, with one person taking the responsibility for coordinating the market intelligence received and ensuring that action is taken. It is clear that, in the case of both the FSA and the Bank of England, even though such information did reach those in a position to take action, none followed. Such rumours and 'information' may be ill-founded but without a look that cannot be known, and persistent rumours can be an important guide. The informal and, increasingly, formal meetings with market participants will continue to be valuable in terms of understanding changes in the market, such as the increasing use of algorithms in FX market, but they are unlikely to reveal much about wrongdoing in the market.

Notes

1 The G10 currencies are as follows: US dollar; euro; Japanese yen; Swiss franc; Australian dollar; New Zealand dollar; Canadian dollar; Norwegian krone; Swedish krona; and British pound (sterling).

2 A one-touch stop loss order is executed if the market trades at the order level. It is only necessary for the market to trade once at that level for the stop loss to be executed.

3 Although Barclays executed the stop loss order by selling £77 million at a rate of 965, it still lost on its trading position at that time. This was because the average price at which it bought sterling in attempting to trigger the stop loss order was higher than the average price at which it sold sterling (including both to the client at a rate of 96.5 and in the market at lower rates, for example, between 11.00 and 11.10 when it reduced some of its London position).

4 Financial Conduct Authority, 'Final notice, Barclays Bank plc', 20 May 2015, pp. 26–8, available at https://www.fca.org.uk/publication/final-notices/barclays-bank-plc-may-15.pdf (accessed 4 May 2018).

5 Commodity Futures Trading Commission, 'Foreign exchange benchmark case: *In re Barclays Bank PLC*', 20 May 2015, available at https://www.

cftc.gov/sites/default/files/idc/groups/public/@newsroom/documents/file/
fxbarclaysmisconduct052015.pdf (accessed 4 May 2018).

6 Financial Conduct Authority, 'Final notice, UBS AG', 11 November 2014, available at https://www.fca.org.uk/publication/final-notices/final-notice-ubs.pdf (accessed 4 May 2018)

7 Commodity Futures Trading Commission, 'In the matter of the Royal Bank of Scotland plc', CFTC Docket No. 15–05, 11 November 2014, 'Order instituting proceedings pursuant to sections 6(c)(4)(A) and 6(d) of the Commodity Exchange Act, making findings, and imposing remedial sanctions', available at https://www.cftc.gov/sites/default/files/groups/public/@ lrenforcementactions/documents/legalpleading/enfroyalbankorder111114. pdf (accessed 4 May 2018).

8 Commodity Futures Trading Commission, 'In the matter of HSBC Bank plc', CFTC Docket No. 15–07, 11 November 2014, 'Order instituting proceedings pursuant to sections 6(c)(4)(A) and 6(d) of the Commodity Exchange Act, making findings, and imposing remedial sanctions', pp. 6–9, available at https://www.cftc.gov/sites/default/files/idc/groups/public/@lr enforcementactions/documents/legalpleading/enfhsbcorder111114.pdf (accessed 4 May 2018).

9 The sterling–dollar currency pairing is routinely described as 'cable' by traders. When an FX trader has orders to sell sterling, it is often referred to as being on the left-hand side (lhs), since sterling is listed on the left-hand side of the sterling–dollar currency pair. If an FX trader references the right-hand side (rhs), it means that the FX trader is a buyer of sterling (and a seller of dollars), as the dollar is listed on the right-hand side of the currency pair.

10 Commodity Futures Trading Commission, 'In the matter of JP Morgan Chase Bank', CFTC Docket No. 15–04, 11 November 2014, 'Order instituting proceedings pursuant to sections 6(c)(4)(A) and 6(d) of the Commodity Exchange Act, making findings, and imposing remedial sanctions', pp. 6–9, available at https://cftc.gov/sites/default/files/groups/public/@lr enforcementactions/documents/legalpleading/enfjpmorganorder111114. pdf (accessed 4 May 2018).

11 Commodity Futures Trading Commission, 'In the matter of Citibank', CFTC Docket No. 15–03, 11 November 2014, 'Order instituting proceedings pursuant to sections 6(c)(4)(A) and 6(d) of the Commodity Exchange Act, making findings, and imposing remedial sanctions', p. 8, available at https://cftc.gov/sites/default/files/groups/public/@lrenforcementactions/ documents/legalpleading/enfcitibankorder111114.pdf (accessed 4 May 2018).

12 New York State Department of Financial Services, 'NYDFS announces Barclays to pay $2.4 billion, terminate employees for conspiring to manipulate spot FX trading market', press release, 20 May 2015, available at https:// www.dfs.ny.gov/about/press/pr1505201.htm (accessed 4 May 2018).

13 US Department of Justice, 'Five major banks agree to parent-level guilty pleas', press release, 20 May 2015, available at https://www.justice.gov/ opa/pr/five-major-banks-agree-parent-level-guilty-pleas (accessed October 2018).

14 United States of America v. UBS AG, Plea agreement, pp. 5–7, available at https://www.justice.gov/file/440521/download (accessed 4 May 2018).

15 New York Department of Financial Services, 'NYDFS announces Barclays to pay additional $150 million penalty, terminate employee for automated, electronic foreign exchange trading misconduct', press release, 18 November 2015, available at https://www.dfs.ny.gov/about/press/pr1511181.htm (accessed October 2018).

16 Ibid.

17 Ibid.; New York State Department of Financial Services, 'Consent order under New York Banking Law §44 in the matter of Barclays Bank plc', 17 November 2015, available at https://www.dfs.ny.gov/about/ea/ea151117.pdf (accessed 4 May 2018).

18 New York State Department of Financial Services, 'Consent order', paras 24–6.

19 New York State Department of Financial Services, 'NYDFS announces Barclays to pay additional $150 million penalty', p. 2.

20 Ibid., p. 2.

21 See Gina Chon and Martin Arnold, 'NY regulator probing Barclays and Deutsche Bank over forex algorithms', *Financial Times,* 11 December 2014, available at https://www.ft.com/content/863a7b3c-813e-11e4-896c-00144feabdc0 (accessed 4 May 2018).

22 Patrick Rucker and Karen Freifeld, 'Fed fines Deutsche Bank for $156.6 million for forex violations', Reuters, 20 April 2017, available at https://www.reuters.com/article/us-deutsche-bank-fed-forex-idUSKBN17M2MK (accessed 4 May 2018).

23 Its terms of reference are 'to provide a senior-level forum for market participants, infrastructure providers and the relevant UK public authorities to meet regularly to discuss conjunctural and structural issues concerning the wholesale foreign exchange market in the UK (the "FX Market") and the associated supporting infrastructure'. See https://www.bankofengland.co.uk/-/media/boe/files/markets/foreign-exchange-joint-standing-committee/terms-of-reference.pdf?la=en&hash=2EBF301BD297B4F1AA259DE7E10371F407A5EDC4 (accessed 4 May 2018).

24 See, for example, Marion Dakers, 'How the forex trading scandal came to light', *Daily Telegraph*, 13 November 2014, available at https://www.telegraph.co.uk/finance/newsbysector/banksandfinance/11227006/How-the-forex-trading-scandal-came-to-light.html (accessed 4 May 2018).

25 Lord Grabiner, 'Bank of England foreign exchange market investigation', 12 March 2014, pp. 19–20, available at https://www.bankofengland.co.uk/-/media/boe/files/report/2014/foreign-exchange-market-investigation-report-by-lord-grabiner (accessed 4 May 2018).

26 Ibid., pp. 20–1.

27 Ibid., p. 21.

28 Bank of England, 'Foreign exchange market review', press release, 5 March 2014, available at https://www.bankofengland.co.uk/-/media/boe/files/news/2014/march/foreign-exchange-market-review.pdf (accessed 4 May 2018).

29 Grabiner, 'Bank of England foreign exchange market investigation', p. 17.

30 Ibid., p. 22.
31 Ibid., p. 32.
32 Mark Carney, before the Treasury Select Committee, quoted in full on the Lexology newsfeed, 25 March 2015.
33 Letter from Lord Grabiner to the Treasury Select Committee, 28 January 2015, available at https://www.parliament.uk/documents/commons-committees/treasury/150128_Lord_Grabiner.pdf (accessed 4 May 2018).
34 The terms of reference and the access to data and officials is set out in detail in appendix 1 of Lord Grabiner's report.
35 'Oral evidence, Bank of England foreign exchange market', Treasury Select Committee, 3 March 2015, pp. 13–17.

Part III: Was the precious metal market rigged?

Chapter 8

Gold and silver fixing

A little history

How and why did London become the centre of the gold and silver markets? The story begins with Moses Mocatta, then in a partnership with the East India Company, who began shipping gold to London in the late seventeenth century. He founded the first bullion brokerage in 1671, which became Mocatta & Goldsmid in 1783, when Asher Goldsmid joined the company. In 1697 the firm established a bullion vault for the first of the gold rushes in Brazil. Abraham Mocatta took over the business from his father in 1693 and became a broker with offices in the Bank of England. The following nine generations presided over the firm until 1976, when family participation in the firm ended. Their position as sole bullion brokers to the Bank of England came to an end in 1840, when the Bank of England finally opened its doors to 'any sworn broker in the purchase and sale of gold bars'.[1] The Mocatta & Goldsmid company was joined by Sharp Wilkins (later Sharps Pixley), Johnson Matthey, Samuel Montagu, bankers and bullion brokers, which opened in 1853, and N. M. Rothschilds. The Rothschilds had a long association with the government and the Bank of England, having supplied gold to the Duke of Wellington when it was desperately needed to pay the troops and pay for supplies during the Napoleonic wars, and having rescued the Bank of England in 1825 when it required large supplies of gold for coinage. The bullion brokers (and indeed the City of London as a whole) benefited from the gold rushes in California, Australia, South Africa and the Yukon between 1850 and 1890, followed by the Klondike gold rush in Canada between 1897 and 1899. These five companies, which would later become the London Gold Market Fixing Company, dominated the gold market in London for over 100 years.

The part played by these brokerages, with long years of knowledge and experience behind them, is not the only and not the most important reason for London becoming the centre of the precious metals market. Significant decisions were taken at an early stage. These include Sir Isaac Newton's introduction of the gold standard and a system of weights and measures, which meant that the gold coins of the realm became the most reliable forms of payment, when he was Master of the Royal Mint from 1696 to 1727. In 1732, the Bank of England opened a bullion vault in London at a time when almost two-thirds of the world's gold production passed through the city.

In 1750, the Good Delivery List was established to provide a list of 'acceptable melters and assayers' so that those who purchased gold in London could be sure that they were buying gold of a standard quality. The five companies comprising the London gold market were also responsible for the custody, maintenance and regulation of gold. The standard now is that the gold bar must 'assay', that is, at least 995 parts in a 1,000 must be pure gold and must contain between 350 and 430 troy ounces of fine gold. The bar must have been melted and stamped by one of the approved refiners on the London market list. The point here is that London early recognised the need for trust. Buyers knew that the gold would be safely stored and that it was of the required standard. That is one of the explanations for the growth of the market.

The London silver market has an equally long history, given that silver was widely used for coinage. London long had the largest share of trade with Asia and India, where silver was all-important, as it was used both as a commodity and a means of exchange. Branches of all the Indian and Far Eastern banks were located in London, and 'these were the principal intermediaries for the mercantile trade with the Far East'.[2] London was also convenient for supplying the coinage require-ments of continental European nations. There were also regular weekly shipments from American and Mexican producers in London, which were dispatched to smelters and refiners before being sold back to India through the London brokers.

During the 1850s the composition of the London silver market changed as Sharps & Wilkins, Pixley & Haggard and Samuel Montague & Co. joined Mocatta & Goldsmid as approved silver brokers to the Bank of England, a position which that company had held as sole silver brokers to the Bank of England between 1721 and 1840, and Johnson Matthey, Rothschild's Royal Mint Refinery and H. L. Raphael's Refinery joined Browne & Wilgrove as the Bank of England's approved refiners.

After 1850, the price of silver declined sharply, with the increased production of gold and the gradual replacement of silver by paper money
(which was eventually linked to the gold standard). Nonetheless, the
Silver Fix was introduced in 1897, when London was the centre of the
silver market, as it handled almost all the silver produced globally. This
followed the collapse of the silver price in 1896 and increased volatility,
which made a daily fixing necessary.[3]

The Gold Fix

In an effort to kick-start the London gold market after World War I, the
five leading bullion dealers met to establish a centralised price of gold
that all five dealers could agree. Before the Fix, the gold price fluctuated
wildly due to the lack of any standardised marketing mechanism. Some
of the five wished to buy gold and others to sell, so it was agreed that
a chairman would recommend a price at which the buyers and sellers
would transact business.

The first meeting was held at Nathan M. Rothschild's office on
12 September 1919 at 11 a.m. to determine the best price for gold.
Rothschild was not involved in market-making before 1914 but was the
main agent for South African mining companies. He was invited by
the Bank of England to act as chairman for the market. The other four
bullion brokers, Mocatta & Goldsmid, Samuel Montagu & Co., Sharps
Wilkins and (later) Johnson Matthey, would then declare whether they
were a buyer or seller or had no interest. If there were only sellers, the
price would be lowered, and vice versa. This process would continue
until the difference between buyers and sellers in terms of volume of
sales was less than 50 bars of gold on either side, and then the price
was fixed. Initially, no outside communication was allowed during the
proceedings and Johnson Matthey was not involved, but was later
allowed to join the proceedings. Over time, telephones were installed,
allowing brokers to maintain communication with their own offices.
The term 'flag up' was adopted at some point to signal a desire to
halt the proceedings for a time. Later, small Union Jacks were used,
apparently a gift from George Matthey. The Bank of England insisted
that the gold should continue to arrive in London, but it should be sold
there through brokers, and the practice of establishing a single price
should be continued. The Governor of the Bank of England, Sir Brien
Cokayne, in communications with Anthony G. de Rothschild in August

1919, commended 'an open market for gold in which not only every seller would know that he would receive the highest price the world could pay but also every buyer would know that he could get his gold as cheaply as the world could supply it'.[4] The Gold Fix was suspended during World War II and was reinstated in 1953.

The Bank of England describes the re-establishment of the London gold market:

> In the English way, the London gold market has no formal or written constitution. Like so many other institutions which are now a normal part of London's daily life, it has developed in response to changing needs and demands over the years and has adapted and modified its rules and procedures as it went along.[5]

The Gold Fix was much the same: Rothschild in the chair and the meetings held at Rothschild's offices with the same four attendees, the representatives of three merchant banks, Sharps, Pixley & Co. (Sharps & Wilkin until 1957) and Mocatta & Goldsmid, and of Johnson Matthey, a metallurgical firm. The fixing then took place at 10.30 a.m. with each present in touch with their trading rooms by telephone or by telex with operators in other countries who might be interested in dealing if the price was right. The chairman suggested a price in terms of pounds, shillings and pence, where he thought the buyers and sellers were likely to be prepared to do business 'down to the last farthing'.[6] When the buyers and sellers agreed, that was the fixing price of the day. Little changed in this post-war arrangement until very recently.

The London silver market

In 1897, the first meeting to arrange the Silver Fix was held at the offices of Sharps & Wilkins in Winchester Street with the other three brokers; thus the four leading precious metals dealers of the day were represented. In 1999, the actual meeting was replaced by a telephone conference and the time was moved to noon each London business day. It was administered by the London Silver Market Fixing Ltd until 14 August 2014, when the company announced that it would cease to provide the Fix, largely as a result of Deutsche Bank's decision to withdraw.

Before then, three banks provided the Fix: Deutsche Bank, which had acquired Sharps Pixley; Scotia Bank, which had acquired Mocatta & Goldsmid; and HSBC, which had acquired Samuel Montagu. The chair was rotated through the membership. All participants, including the members' clients, would put their orders through the three fixing members once the price was fixed. Clients ranged broadly, from silver producers, through miners, refiners, industrialists, jewellers, investors, speculators, private individuals to sovereign states. Clients were not privy to the fixing teleconference but there were no rules preventing them from receiving updates during the fixing, which may have provided them with some insight into the composition of the order book even if only from their own orders, especially if they were bringing a large order.

The process started with an announcement by the chairman to other market makers, then relayed to the dealing rooms, where customers could express their interest as buyers or sellers and also the quantity they wished to trade. The Silver Fix was then set by collating bids and offers until supply and demand were matched. At that point, the price was announced as the 'fixed' price for silver and business was conducted on that basis. The market makers were all members of the London Bullion Markets Association (LBMA), a trade association whose members include refiners, dealers, banks, mining companies and private investors involved in the bullion investment market, especially gold and silver.

It may seem strange that silver is regarded as being so valuable but it is used widely in industrial production, ranging from solar panels, batteries, polyester fibre, especially active wear and underwear, environmental monitoring, healthcare, smart monitoring, surgical tools, catheters, needles, stethoscopes and (because of its antibacterial properties) silver-reinforced bandages. Given this wide range of uses, it is easier to see why the possible manipulation of silver prices matters just as much as the potential for gold price rigging.

Investigations of the manipulation of the gold and silver markets

After the LIBOR and FX scandals detailed in Parts I and II of this book, it was perhaps inevitable that the media and those involved in the gold and silver markets should argue that these markets were rigged. As well as London, the claims also apply to the Chicago Mercantile Exchange, where gold and silver futures contracts are primarily traded. These contracts are for the purchase or sale of 100 troy ounces of 'fine gold' (which is at least 99.5% pure) and a silver futures contract is for the purchase or sale of 5,000 troy ounces 'fine silver' (at least 99.9% pure). As with most futures contracts, the underlying commodity is never actually delivered.

As a background, it is worth setting out the effects of the Gold and Silver Fixes. They not only affect the prices of gold and silver futures and options contracts, but also exchange-traded financial instruments and OTC transactions such as gold and silver swaps and forward agreements, by determining the price per ounce of physical gold and silver. The pricing relationship between a silver futures contract, say (the same will apply to gold), and the underlying physical silver is a product of how futures contracts are structured. Each one represents a bilateral agreement between two parties, a buyer and a seller, the 'long' and the 'short'. As a silver futures contract nears 'expiration', i.e. the last trading day, the long and the short halves of each contract become obligations to exchange physical silver, while the shorts as sellers are required to deliver silver to the buyers, so the value of these contracts is directly tied to the price of physical silver, the 'settlement'. This does not always result in an exchange of actual silver, as market participants can offset or settle their future positions, instead of making or taking delivery of silver. Investors can offset their positions with contracts for an equal but opposite position; for example, the buyer of a silver futures contract who is long can settle the obligation to take delivery of physical silver by settling futures contracts to initiate an equal but opposite short position.

Gold and silver futures markets are extremely active and in a constant state of price discovery. This especially true in the case of gold, which, given its status as a 'safe harbour', is more affected by geopolitical and other events of all kinds, such as wars and rumours of wars, macro-economic developments and fears of recession.

The gold and silver markets have long been plagued with rumours of manipulation, whether by central banks or particular banks, states or wealthy individuals. However, in the context of the financial crisis and the discovery of extensive manipulation of LIBOR and the foreign exchange market, it was essential that regulators conducted thorough investigations, even when, in the case of the UK's FCA, they had no regulatory responsibility for these markets. But, as set out in this chapter, it took much longer for the regulators to find the evidence of manipulation.

CFTC investigations of the silver futures market

The CFTC first reported on this on 13 May 2008, when it pointed out that over the past 20 to 25 years, the Commission had received numerous letters, phone calls and emails from silver investors, alleging that the price of silver futures had been manipulated downwards.[7] Its first response was that long-term manipulation was not plausible and that an analysis of the market did not support that conclusion. However, before further investigation was conducted, silver commentators and a group of investors relying on them claimed once more that the silver market was being manipulated downward by a small group of traders on the short side of the market, so the investigation was reopened. Its conclusions were as follows:

> There is no evidence of manipulation in the silver futures market.
> Silver cash and futures prices have risen dramatically between 2005 and 2007 with silver outperforming the gold, platinum and palladium markets, suggesting that silver prices are not depressed relative to other metals prices.
> NYMEX [New York Mercantile Exchange] silver futures prices tend to track closely the price of physical silver.
> Concentration levels for the top four short futures traders in the silver futures markets are comparable to those observed in the gold and copper futures markets, and are generally lower than the levels seen in the platinum and palladium futures markets.
> The composition of the traders comprising the top four short futures traders, in terms of net positions, changes over time. These traders represent a diverse group, and their futures positions are driven by an even more diverse group of customers.
> There is no observable relationship between short-futures-trader concentration levels and silver prices.
> There is a slightly positive relationship between the total net position of the large short futures traders and silver prices; this suggests that larger short positions are associated with higher, not lower prices.[8]

The CFTC's first investigation found no evidence of manipulation. However, it was not long before the Commission was obliged to undertake a further investigation, beginning in September 2008. Because, unusually, this investigation had been announced, the CFTC decided that there was 'no viable basis to bring an enforcement action' against any of the firms it regulated.[9] The complaints it investigated[10] involved silver futures contracts traded on COMEX.[11] The complainants pointed to the differences between prices in those silver futures contracts and prices in other silver products, including retail silver products. Because prices of coins and bullion had increased, the price of a silver futures contract should also have increased, but the complainants alleged that large shorts in the silver market had been responsible for lower futures prices.

The CFTC's Division of Enforcement conducted a thorough investigation designed to discover whether there was any trading activity taking place which broke regulations, including anti-manipulation provisions. The investigation took over 17,000 staff-hours, spent on reviewing and analysing position and transaction data, including physical, swaps, options, and futures trading data, other information and interviewing witnesses. It included an evaluation of the silver market fundamentals and trading within and between cash, futures and over-the-counter markets, using outside experts as well. In September 2013, the CFTC announced that it had found no evidence of manipulation of the silver futures market.[12]

However, in June 2017, the CFTC did issue an order against David Liew, having found that he had, from at least December 2009 until February 2012, acting individually and in coordination with other traders, engaged in a scheme to manipulate the market price of gold and silver futures contracts. Liew frequently placed orders to buy or sell gold and silver futures contracts that he did not intend to execute ('spoof orders') in an attempt, sometimes successful, to manipulate the price of these contracts. He worked on the precious metals desk at a large financial institution, placing orders and entering into gold and silver futures contracts, but often placed spoof orders, sometimes coordinating with trader A at another financial institution, usually just after another offer or bid had been placed on the other side of the market. In a chat with trader A at the other financial institution, he explained his strategy: 'basically i sold out … by just having fake bids … [in] the futures … i just jam bids below … to clear my offer'.[13] The point was to make it appear that the market interest in buying and selling was greater than it actually was in order to induce other market participants to fill his 'resting' orders on the opposite side of the market from his spoof orders.

On occasion, Liew and trader A succeeded in manipulating the prices of gold and silver futures contracts. For example, on 7 January 2011, Liew asked trader A about the level at which customer stop loss orders were resting, and then told the trader, 'I can hunt with you'. A few minutes later, trader A asked Liew, 'yo can help me push silver down?' Liew agreed to execute trades to push the price of COMEX silver futures down, to trigger the resting stop loss orders, and did so by entering orders to sell with the intent to manipulate prices. When the market reached the stop level they wanted, Liew told trader A, 'there u go'. Liew then bought back the silver contracts, eliminating his exposure to risk from further price movements in the silver futures market and generating a profit. He used similar procedures together with trader A for gold futures contracts.

Press reports in 2015 indicated that both the CFTC and the US Department of Justice were investigating at least 10 banks over their trading in precious metals. HSBC in its annual report and accounts published on 23 February 2015 stated that the CFTC had issued a subpoena to the bank seeking documents relating to its precious metal trading operations. The Department of Justice also issued a request to HSBC Holdings, in November 2014, requesting documents related to a criminal anti-trust investigation which the Department was conducting concerning precious metals. HSBC stated that it was 'co-operating with the US authorities in their respective investigations'.[14] The Department of Justice declined to comment at that time, but the CFTC continued its investigations and eventually took action against HSBC in 2018. Other banks were also said to be under investigation, including the Bank of Nova Scotia, Barclays, Credit Suisse, Deutsche Bank, Goldman Sachs, Societe Generale, Standard Bank and UBS.

Swiss investigation of UBS

The precious metals spot desk at UBS was, from the end of 2008, an organisational unit of its foreign exchange spot desk and was therefore subject to similar control and monitoring processes. These desks were located in Singapore, Stamford and Zurich. It was an over-the-counter business with transactions from principal to principal. Conduct and techniques inadmissible from a regulatory perspective were applied at least in part to spot trading in precious metals. Against the interests of its own clients, the bank shared information on its order books with third parties (for example, stop loss orders). The traders also: shared so-called flow information with third parties on large current or imminent orders; shared client names with third parties; and engaged in front-running and triggering stop loss orders (front-running involves using advance knowledge of large transactions to influence prices to generate illegitimate profits). The traders engaged in repeated front-running (especially in the back book) of the Silver Fix orders of one client. Eventually, the desk supervisors did prohibit front-running, but they did not sanction the traders who had engaged in it. The Director, Mark Branson, said in a conference call with Bloomberg that 'The behaviour patterns in precious metals were somewhat similar to the behaviour patterns in

FX', which was not surprising, since they sat close to each other.[15] UBS manipulated the London Silver Fix and conspired to fix spreads in the silver market, coordinating and manipulating silver transactions and sharing proprietary information with co-conspirator banks.

The Swiss Financial Market Supervisory Authority, FINMA, imposed a fine of CHF134 million and initiated enforcement proceedings against 11 people. Examples of the traders' activities are lacking for the precious metals market, although the ways in which UBS failed to conduct its business according to regulations are clearly set out, as are the required remedial actions. FINMA also reported after the settlement that 'this conduct was partly coordinated with other banks' and that 'electronic communications played a key role'.[16]

The FCA investigation of Daniel James Plunkett

Daniel Plunkett was a director on the precious metals desk at Barclays. He held the customer function and was responsible for pricing products linked to the price of precious metals, including an exotic options contract that referenced the price of gold, fixed above a certain barrier price agreed in the contract. This concerned a single customer of Barclays Bank, who entered into a digital options contract, paying a premium payment of US$4.4 million to Barclays, part of which was attributed as a profit to Plunkett's book. It was also the main risk exposure he had to handle on that day. He had already emailed members of the precious metals desk, saying that he was hoping for a 'mini-puke' – that is, a drop in the price of gold ahead of the fixing on 27 June 2012 – and repeated this on the morning of 28 June, saying 'hopefully we fix at 1558 or 1558.75 ideal'.[17]

The contract referenced the 3 p.m. Gold Fix on 28 June 2012. If the price was fixed above US$1,558.96, then Barclays would have to make a payment to the customer of 9% of the notional value (US$43 million), or US$3.9 million, and part of the payment would be attributed to Plunkett's book. If the price of gold fixed below the barrier, then Barclays would not have to make a payment to the customer and a percentage of this additional profit would go to Plunkett. At that time, Barclays was one of the Gold Fix members.

Plunkett sought to influence the Gold Fix by placing a large sell order of between 100 and 150 bars with the Barclays representative, which was then incorporated into Barclays net seller position of 130 bars at 3.06 p.m., but he then withdrew his entire sell order at 3.07 p.m., reducing the imbalance from 190 bars to 60 bars (155 buying and 215 selling). At 3.09 he again placed a large sell order (150 bars) with the Barclays representative, who, after taking into account customers' orders, declared Barclays' net position as selling 100 bars. Barclays' sell order, of which Plunkett's order was a significant component, had the net effect of bringing the level of buying and selling on the 28 June Gold Fix to a point where the imbalance was 10 bars and the price could be fixed. So at 3.10 p.m. the chairman of the Gold Fix declared the price to be US$1,558.50 – below the barrier.

Plunkett's moves were not as clever as all that. Shortly after the fixing, he repurchased 150 gold bars through an internal trade with Barclays gold spot book to unwind the 150-bar position he had taken during the fixing, but he had to pay a higher price. As a result, his trading book suffered an immediate loss of US$114,000. Then the customer sought an explanation, as recorded by the FCA:

> Customer A became aware that the price had fixed just below the Barrier and sought an explanation from Barclays as to what happened in the Gold Fixing. When Barclays relayed Customer A's concerns to Mr Plunkett on 28 and 29 June 2012, he failed to disclose that he had placed orders and traded during the Gold Fixing. He also failed to provide this information to Barclays' Compliance department when contacted by them on 29 June 2012. Further, during Barclays' subsequent internal investigation and the Authority's own investigation, Mr Plunkett misled both Barclays and the Authority by providing an account of events that was untruthful.[18]

Plunkett was fined £95,000 and had his authorisation withdrawn as from 23 May 2014.

Treasury Select Committee hearings

On 2 July 2014, the Treasury Select Committee took evidence from David Bailey, Head of Markets Infrastructure and Policy at the FCA. He was asked by the chair of the Committee if it was possible that there could have been collusion between members of the Gold Fix panel. Bailey replied, 'It is possible, but I have no clear evidence that that has happened'.[19] He also stressed that the Gold Fix is not a regulated process, and that (at that time) the FCA recommended that any processes which were put in place should follow the 'robust standards we put in place via IOSCO [International Organization of Securities Commissions]'.[20]

Rhona O'Connell, Head of Metals Research and Forecasts at Thomson Reuters, explained the fixing process to the Committee. The risk a bank takes in the fixing process is that when the bank takes an order it goes straight to the fixing process, but the bank is essentially at risk over the period from when the order is received to when the price itself is fixed, because the bank is contractually bound to fill the client's order at that fix. The fixing members are 'facilitators'. 'Where there is a problem is if they have positions of their own'.

In his evidence to the Select Committee, Alberto Thomas, a senior partner in Fideres LLP (a company he founded in 2009 that provides financial analysis to regulators and others) stated that, in his view, the Gold Fix was one of the worst:

> [I]t does not have good governance; there is no way to audit what is happening on that call. There is no data transparency, so no one can question whether the fix is correct or not. It is a tiered market. You have four or five people on a call and you have another market that keeps trading in parallel during that period of time. The evidence we have found is that there is a so-called leakage of information. What happens in the first moment of the call is a very, very good indicator of where the fix is going to be. In other words, no one should really know what has happened on the call, but the whole market ends up knowing, because … you have five banks on the call. Each of those five banks has behind it brokers and other banks which are not members of the panel, and then each of them has clients, and all of them are on the telephone and all of them are being fed information of where the orders are. This information feeds through the market, to the futures market, so effectively you have a massive potential for insider trading in the market and market manipulation. It does not mean it happens every day, but the opportunity is there.

Thomas further pointed out:

> it is very, very hard to identify whether manipulation occurred, but the means is there, the opportunity is there, and if there is a conflict of interest in certain situations, or if on a certain day the dealers who submit the quotations or make submissions to the panels have an economic interest, then the possibility is there. It does not mean that they do it all the time.[21]

He did, however, see the IOSCO principles as an important step forward. These and other reforms will be discussed in the next chapter.

German investigation of possible manipulation of gold and silver prices

It was reported that the German Federal Financial Supervisory Authority, BaFin, began its investigation into gold and silver price manipulation in 2013, as part of its examination into LIBOR, EURIBOR and other benchmarking processes. Although BaFin would not comment on an on-going investigation, it was also reported that staff at Deutsche Bank were interrogated during several on-site visits. The investigation ended on 27 January 2015, when BaFin's Head of Banking Supervision, Raimund Röseler, stated, 'We found no signs of manipulation. If we do not find any additional evidence that manipulation occurred, we will consider the matter settled.'[22]

Further Swiss investigation of banks

On 28 September 2015 the Swiss Competition Authority, WEKO, announced that it would commence an investigation, after a preliminary probe, into whether UBS, Julius Baer, Deutsche Bank, HSBC, Barclays, Morgan Stanley and Mitsui had conspired to set bid–ask spreads. WEKO had indications of possible prohibited agreements in the trading of precious metals. The banks were suspected of violating Swiss corporate laws. At the time of writing, this is an ongoing investigation. WEKO has already given such information as it can legally release: the object of the investigation, its scope and the parties involved. WEKO hoped to complete its investigation in 2017, but it still has done not so, and it is anyway unlikely to provide much insight as section 25 of the Swiss Cartel Act obliges WEKO to safeguard business confidentiality.

The CFTC's further investigations of banks

Almost 10 years after the CFTC first stated that it could not find any evidence of manipulation of the price of silver, on 29 January 2018 it ordered UBS to pay $15 million for attempted manipulation and spoofing in the precious metals futures market between 2009 and 2012. In its 'order' issued on that day, the CFTC stated that from January 2008 to at least December 2013, some of UBS's traders on the spot desk sought to 'manipulate the price of precious metals futures by utilizing a variety of manual spoofing techniques'.[23] They engaged in 'spoofing' aimed at inducing other market participants into buying and selling precious metals futures contracts. The aim was to induce other market participants to fill the resting orders placed by the traders at UBS on the opposite side of the market from the orders that they placed, with the intention of cancelling them before execution. On other occasions, another trader placed orders and executed trades in an attempt to manipulate the price of precious metals futures contracts with the aim of triggering customers' stop loss orders. He coordinated his trades with a trader at another large financial institution. Their actions were designed to allow the UBS trader to buy precious metals futures contracts at artificially high prices, for the benefit of his proprietary trading.

The CFTC provides examples of both activities:

- On 27 November 2009, trader A and trader E, who was employed by another large financial institution, discussed trading activity. Trader A stated in a chat, 'btw the silver I bought the other day was a bit of a spoof, too … we are all big boys here aren't we'. Trader E responded: 'you mean the … "cheapies" you got from me? … bastard'. Trader A wrote further, 'hahahaha … the spoof wasn't designed just for [you]'. Trader E wrote: 'and you hit a bid'. Trader A responded: 'that is nasty … no no just pushed a bit then called out … can't be too obvious'.

- In another example, on 2 August 2010, trader F discussed trading activity with another UBS trader. Trader F wrote: 'u know when u were gone I did the regular bid/offer thing to spoof…. I got lifted twice haha … think that trick is slowly starting to catch up'. Trader F wrote further: 'sometimes … but when I see stuff like that in the futures I have been smacking it … last time me and [financial institution I] were doing that, worked in our favour'.

- Trader F and trader H at financial institution I regularly discussed their attempts to manipulate through the stop loss manipulation strategies.

- On 11 August 2011, trader F and trader H were discussing coordination of stop loss manipulation and trader H wrote: 'the lot I offer … is so powerful … I love it'. Trader F responded, 'it depends what kinda mkt … sometimes u use muscle … sometimes u use blade … this blade … but then two guys doing it like this together is small muscle and blade'. Trader H responded, 'yeah … dude … I like it … double dragon'.

On 29 January 2018, the CFTC ordered Deutsche Bank to pay $30 million for repeated attempts to manipulate the price of precious metals futures contracts through spoofing and triggering customers' stop loss orders. It provides examples of both activities:[24]

- On 16 December 2008, trader A was discussing activity in gold futures with trader B. Trader B indicated: 'I am bidding futur[e]s at 854 in size'. Trader A asked, 'For anyone, Or a spoof?' Trader B responded 'spoof'. In response, trader A stated, 'Don't leave i[t] out too long … U don't. want people leaning on it'.
- In a 29 March 2011 chat, trader G explained his spoofing strategy to a precious metals trader employed by financial institution 1. Trader H said 'basically I sold out … by just having fake bids … [in] the futures … I just spam bids below … to clear my offer'. The 'fake bids' and 'spam bids' trader G referred to were spoof orders. On that day, trader G placed an order to sell silver futures contracts. While that order was pending, he placed and quickly cancelled a series of buy orders, with the intention to cancel before execution.

On other occasions from December 2009 to February 2012, Deutsche Bank through the behaviour of trader G manipulated and intended to manipulate the price of precious metals futures contracts to trigger customer stop loss orders in the market to obtain a profit through proprietary trading. Trader G coordinated this trading with trader H at financial institution I. They often discussed their stop loss strategies. The CFTC provides several examples of these strategies, of which two have been selected:[25]

- On 18 November 2010, trader G told trader H: '[I] have a chunky stop at 27.35 … keep to urself'. Trader H told trader G: 'Go get that chunky monkey', to which trader H responded, 'I am' and asked trader H: 'u wanna come on boar[d]?' Trader H agreed and wrote: 'I'll get a 40 print for you'. Trader G responded by calling them 'the hunt brothers'. In response, trader H wrote: 'chill man, they went to jail'.
- On 29 March 2011, trader H asked trader G for assistance in the gold futures market, asking him to 'push it up' because trader H 'need[ed] a print'. Trader G bought gold futures contracts with the intent to push the prices up as requested. Immediately after trader G's manipulative trading, trader H told him that he 'got it'. A few minutes later, trader H offered to sell trader G gold

futures contracts at an advantageous price 'cause u helped me for the print'.

With regard to HSBC, the CFTC stated that from at least 16 July 2011 through to August 2014, HSBC, through one of its traders, trader A, engaged in spoofing with respect to certain futures products in gold and other precious metals. HSBC was fined $1.6 million on the grounds that it was responsible for the activities of its agent. In this CFTC order, no specific examples of trader misconduct are given.[26]

Academic analyses of the London Gold and Silver Fixes

Some academic articles seek to show either that unusual price activity around 3 p.m. in London suggests illegal behaviour by the banks involved in the fixing or that information from the fixing is leaking to the markets before the results have been published.

Andrew Caminschi and Richard Heaney in 2013[27] investigated the impact of the London Gold Fix on two exchange-traded gold instruments, a gold futures contract and a gold exchange-traded fund (the two most heavily traded instruments). The study analysed two time periods: 1 January 2007 to 31 December 2012, and 18 August 2011 to 31 December 2012. The first allowed for the analysis of the gold derivatives market around the start of the gold price fixing period, while the smaller data set had additional information from the publication time of these fixings, which provides insight into the market's reaction to approaching publication times. This allowed for a direct comparison of market reactions to the fixing start and the fixing end. This study found that the markets in both gold futures contracts and gold exchange-traded funds are sensitive to the fixing, with large statistically significant spikes in trade volume (an increase of over 50%) and price volatility (an increase of over 40%) following the start of the fixing period.[28] The elevation in market activity was marginally higher and persisted for longer for the gold futures contracts than for the gold exchange-traded funds. There was nothing similar for the end of the fixing.

The authors concluded that there were statistically significant differences in the returns that could be earned by informed versus uninformed participants, clustered just after the start and just before the end of the fixings. The informed trader has an advantage of about 10 basis points in the first four minutes following the beginning of the fixing and in the two minutes before the end. These returns exceed trading costs and are economic. There was no evidence of significant returns or increased activity after the fixings. Public market trades just after the fixing began were highly predictive of the fixing price direction, especially with larger price movements.

The authors provided two interpretations of this phenomenon. The first is that fixing participants are leaking price fix information by dealing in exchange-traded instruments ahead of the publication of the fixing price. The second is 'market push', which means that the fixing results are being driven by price changes in the public markets. This means that participants in the public markets are 'pushing' (i.e. manipulating) the short-term prices of exchange-traded instruments to influence the fixing results.

This article shows the limitations of an analysis of trading patterns and movements in prices alone. That is, such an analysis cannot identify what traders were actually doing and there may be some important misunderstandings about what is actually happening in the gold market generally.

Rosa Abrantes-Metz and Albert Metz produced a research paper on the London Fix but it has never been published, although it was discussed by Bloomberg and in interviews given by Abrantes-Metz in 2014. Bloomberg reported in November 2013 that the London Fix had drawn scrutiny. It quotes Abrantes-Metz: 'There's a huge incentive for these banks to try to influence where the benchmark is set, depending on their trading positions'.[29]

In the unpublished research, the authors state that 'the structure of the benchmark is certainly conducive to collusion and manipulation, and the empirical date are consistent with price artificiality', having screened intra-day trading in the spot gold market from 2001 to 2013 for sudden unexplained moves that may indicate illegal behaviour.[30] From 2004, they observed frequent spikes in spot gold prices during the afternoon call, which had not happened before 2004. These large price moves during the afternoon call were overwhelmingly in the same direction – down. Specifically, on days when the authors identified large price moves during the Fix, they were in a downward direction at least two-thirds of the time in six different years between 2004 and 2013. In 2010, large moves during the Fix were negative 92% of the time. Abrantes-Metz stated in an interview with the *Sydney Morning Herald* that there was no obvious explanation for why this began in 2004, why they were prevalent in the afternoon fixing and why price movements tended to be downwards.[31]

To an extent, it is fair to say that some of these concerns are met by a fuller understanding of the role of the morning and afternoon fixes. In his article, Peter Fertig quotes an explanation given by Ross Norman, the Chief Executive of Sharps Pixley, as to why the price changes occur in the afternoon fixing: the fact that it covers trading in both London and New York.[32] This provides commercial participants with higher liquidity and the chance to get a better price, since many producers are located in North America. The COMEX division of the Chicago Mercantile Exchange (CME) trades electronically during the morning but liquidity is higher at the futures exchange in the afternoon.

If a larger order has to be executed, the price impact will be greater in a less liquid market. Thus, a buyer or a seller would still get a better price if it is executed in the afternoon fixing in spite of moving the price considerably before 3 p.m. in London. Secondly, the weekly or monthly price development is well explained by the S&P 500 Index, the US dollar index and crude oil prices: GARCH-X models show that these factors have an impact on the daily return and volatility of gold, so it is not surprising that intra-day spikes in the gold price occur during the afternoon gold fixing.

Often the US gold market reverses direction at around this time, as the institutional investors enter the stock market at about 10 a.m. A popular strategy among intra-day traders is to trade 'break-outs' of the trading range during the first 30 minutes of the trading day. Break-out trading is an attempt to enter the market once the price moves outside a defined price range (called support, above the expected level, or resistance, if the price falls). It is only a genuine break-out if there is an increased volume of trading. So, stock market volatility could also have an effect on the price of gold at that time.

During the period under investigation, many central banks were sellers of gold, and the fixing was one way of selling larger quantities and being able to obtain an 'official price' for audits.

Mining companies also sell their gold in larger quantities at the fixing as hedging and financing operations are often tied to the Fix price. Fertig comments that there are many misunderstandings about the nature of the Fix.[33] The London gold fixing was not a Walrasian market, that is, a type of simultaneous auction where each agent calculates the demand for a good at every possible price and submits this to the auctioneer, and the price is then set so that the total demand across all agents equals the total amount of the good. It was not that. It was a process of price discovery.

The chair called a price close to the actual spot quotations when the fixing started. The five member banks submitted the quantities they would buy or sell based on the orders of their clients or for their own accounts. For the Gold Fix the differences between supply and demand had to be less than 50 bars – about 620 kg. This usually did not happen. If there was excess demand, a higher price was called; a lower price was called if supply exceeded demand. The five banks then contacted their clients with the new price called and collected new bids and offers, then submitted these to the chair. The process of finding the fixing price took about 10 minutes but could be longer.

Markets did not stand still during this process. Trading in gold futures was continuous and prices were known within milliseconds. This information was also available to the clients of the five banks. Clients active in gold spot trading could see indicative bid and ask prices, so when a new price was called these clients were well informed about the current market situation and could adjust the quantities they wanted to buy or sell. But the banks did not know the exact quantities they wanted to buy or sell in total when a new price was called.

If one defines market manipulation as an attempt to move the price, the five banks would have had to agree on this price before the fixing started. In order to push prices artificially lower, for instance, the banks would have had to be willing to sell an unknown quantity of gold, which would have exposed them to significant price risk. At best they might have known the total quantity supplied and demand at the first price called. That gold was not fixed at the first price and that prices moved and more new prices were called is not an indication of price manipulation but quite the reverse. Of course, this applied only to the way in which the Fix operated before 2014. Fertig sought to explain that the method applying at the time was not as open to manipulation as many thought.[34]

The content of Fertig's article has been set out here because it underlines the fact that it is impossible to identify what is going on in complex markets such as those for gold and silver without understanding how the use of a benchmark is linked to, and is influenced by, a derivatives market with more than one financial instrument. It is also important not only to recognise that market prices are set in the context of external trends and events of all kinds but also to understand how the benchmark works. This is not to suggest that the Fix was always operated as an independent benchmark, but to see its structure and the context in which it operated.

All change for the fixings

The Gold Fix

The extensive investigations into gold and silver price rigging led to the end of the telephone auction for the Gold Fix, no doubt expedited by Deutsche Bank's decision to withdraw from it on 29 April 2014, to take effect on 13 May 2014. Deutsche Bank was unable to sell its seat. That left only four banks for the gold benchmark – Barclays, HSBC, Bank of Nova Scotia and Societe Generale – insufficient to continue with the then form of the telephone auction.

The London Bullion Market Association (LMBA) sets and monitors refining standards, creates trading documentation and encourages the development of good trading practices. The Association launched the LBMA Silver Price and the LBMA Platinum and Palladium Prices in 2014, and then the new LBMA Gold Price on 20 March 2015 so that all four precious metal prices were transferred on electronic auction platforms. The LBMA appointed ICE Benchmark Administration to operate a physically settled, electronic and tradeable auction process. The auctions continue to take place at 10.30 a.m. and 3.00 p.m. (London time) with a wider range of banks, including the Bank of Nova Scotia-Mocatta, Barclays, Goldman Sachs, HSBC, Societe Generale, UBS and JP Morgan Chase as the initial participants, now much increased with the addition of the Bank of China, Industrial and Commercial Bank of China, Morgan Stanley and Standard Chartered, among others. Indirect participants are also encouraged; indirect participants do not meet London IBA's criteria to become direct participants but they can access the front-end trading platform if they are clients of direct participants, who must offer that service to them.[35] Any imbalance, that is, up to a 10,000-ounce difference between the entered buying and selling interest, is shared out among the direct participants equally, to ensure continuity and certainty for direct participants.

The auction takes place in rounds of 45 seconds. At the start of each round, the IBA publishes the price for that round and participants enter their buying or selling volume at that price. If the difference between the buying and selling volume is within the imbalance threshold (20,000 troy ounces), the price is set. If not, the IBA announces another price and begins a new auction round. Direct participants' orders carry on from round to round, although participants can cancel or adjust their orders at any time between rounds, or place as many orders as their business requires. When the auction is finished, WebICE (ICE Benchmark's operating system) automatically nets direct participants' orders to produce the minimum number of trades and notifies the counterparties. The Fix is then published in various major currencies. The auction was originally chaired by four independent persons (unnamed) in rotation. In 2017, the chair was replaced by an algorithm to determine the price of each auction round. The IBA claims that the algorithm is designed to be robust across many situations, including data releases and reversals of the direction of the imbalance between prices published and the number of active participants in each round. The algorithm will continue to be overseen by two IBA analysts. In April 2017, the IBA introduced central clearing for direct participants, removing the need for firms to have large bilateral credit lines in place with each other to become a direct participant. It worked after some initial hitches and has helped to increase the volume of trade.

Two further moves were made to help to reduce the risks of the Fix being manipulated: the Oversight Committee and a Code of Conduct. The Committee consists of benchmark users, market input structure providers, direct participants, clients, representatives from the IBA, and two independent directors from outside the gold market. The Committee is responsible for overseeing the rules and methodology of the Gold Fix and for reviewing all aspects of the Gold Fix, including surveillance. It is also responsible for overseeing the Code of Conduct, which applies to all submitters and direct participants. The Code is discussed in more detail in the following chapter. It is clear that much effort has been put into making the Gold Fix free from manipulation, but to ensure that remains the case requires constant surveillance.

The Silver Fix

In March 2017, the LBMA announced that the CME Group and Thomson Reuters had decided to step down from administering the Silver Fix, less than three years after they had successfully bid for it. In August 2014, the LBMA replaced the telephone-based London Silver Fix, which had lasted for over a century, with an electronic-based auction alternative. On 14 July 2017, it announced that the IBA would be responsible for the Silver Fix from September that year. Changes have been made, including removing the seller's premium, hosting the auction on WebICE, setting the auction parameters specifically for the LMBA silver price, increasing the number of silver price currencies and introducing central clearing. Those involved in various capacities are subject to a code of conduct.

Notes

1　See the website of Sharps Pixley (bullion broker): https://shop.sharpspixley. com/history-of-sharps-pixley (accessed October 2018).
2　Michele Blagg, '1897–1939, a new era for the London silver price', *Alchemist*, 75 (October 2014), p. 19.
3　Ibid., p. 20.
4　See Rachel Harvey, 'The early development of the London Gold Fixing', *Alchemist*, 65 (January 2012), p. 4.
5　'The London gold market', *Bank of England Quarterly Bulletin*, March 1964, p. 16, available at https://www.bankofengland.co.uk/quarterly-bulletin/1964/q1/the-london-gold-market (accessed May 2018).
6　Ibid., p. 17.
7　Department of Market Oversight, CFTC, *Report on Large Short Trader Activity in the Silver Futures Market* (CFTC, 13 May 2008).
8　Ibid., p. 1.
9　Commodity Futures Trading Commission, 'CFTC closes investigation concerning the silver markets', press release 6709-13, 25 September 2013, available at https://www.cftc.gov/PressRoom/PressReleases/pr6709-13 (accessed October 2018).
10　Commodity Futures Trading Commission, 'CFTC's 2008 fiscal year enforcement roundup: agency files 40 actions, obtains record amount in penalties and fines, discloses crude oil investigation, forms forex task force', press release 5562–08, 2 October 2008, available at https://www.cftc.gov/PressRoom/PressReleases/pr5562-08 (accessed 9 May 2018).
11　COMEX is the name for the primary market for trading metals such as gold, silver, copper and aluminium. Formerly known as Commodity Exchange Inc., COMEX was formed through a merger with the New York Mercantile Exchange in 1994.
12　Commodity Futures Trading Commission, 'CFTC closes investigation concerning the silver markets'.
13　Commodity Futures Trading Commission, 'In the matter of David Liew', CFTC Docket No. 17–14, 2 June 2017, 'Order instituting proceedings pursuant to sections 6(c) and 6(d) of the Commodity Exchange Act, making findings, and imposing remedial sanctions', available at https://www.cftc.gov/sites/default/files/idc/groups/public/@lrenforcementactions/documents/legalpleading/enfdavidlieworder060217.pdf (accessed 4 May 2018).
14　Henry Sanderson and Gina Chon, 'US investigates banks' precious metals

trading', *Financial Times,* 23 February 2015, available at https://www.ft.com/content/01bdc380-bb79–11e4-b95c-00144feab7de (accessed 9 May 2018).

15 Bloomberg Business News, 'UBS precious metals misconduct found by Finma in FX probe', 12 November 2014.

16 FINMA, 'FINMA sanctions foreign exchange manipulation at UBS', press release, 12 November 2014, available at https://www.finma.ch/en/news/2014/11/mm-ubs-devisenhandel-20141112/ (accessed October 2018).

17 Financial Conduct Authority, 'Final notice, Daniel James Plunkett', 23 May 2014, available at https://www.fca.org.uk/publication/final-notices/daniel-james-plunkett.pdf (accessed 4 May 2018).

18 Ibid., p. 3.

19 Treasury Committee, 'Oral evidence: manipulation of benchmarks', HC 491, 2 July 2014, available at http://data.parliament.uk/writtenevidence/committeeevidence.svc/evidencedocument/treasury-committee/manipulation-of-benchmarks/oral/11200.html (accessed 9 May 2018).

20 Ibid.

21 Ibid.

22 Peter Köhler, Daniel Schäfer and Yasmin Osman, 'Traffic light is flashing yellow', *Handelsblatt Global,* 27 January 2015, available at https://global.handelsblatt.com/finance/traffic-light-for-banks-is-blinking-yellow-132357 (accessed 9 May 2018).

23 Commodity Futures Trading Commission, 'In the matter of UBS AG', CFTC Docket No. 18–07, 29 January 2018, 'Order instituting proceedings pursuant to sections 6(c) and 6(d) of the Commodity Exchange Act, making findings, and imposing remedial sanctions', available at https://www.cftc.gov/sites/default/files/idc/groups/public/@lrenforcementactions/documents/legalpleading/enfusbagorder012918.pdf (accessed October 2018).

24 Commodity Futures Trading Commission, 'In the matter of Deutsche Bank AG and Deutsche Bank Securities Inc.', CFTC Docket No. 18–06, 29 January 2018, 'Order instituting proceedings pursuant to sections 6(c) and 6(d) of the Commodity Exchange Act, making findings, and imposing remedial sanctions', available at https://www.cftc.gov/sites/default/files/idc/groups/public/@lrenforcementactions/documents/legalpleading/enfdeutschebankagorder012918.pdf (accessed October 2018).

25 Ibid.

26 Commodity Futures Trading Commission, 'In the matter of HSBC Securities (USA) Inc.', CFTC Docket No. 18–08, 29 January 2018, 'Order instituting proceedings pursuant to sections 6(c) and 6(d) of the Commodity Exchange Act, making findings, and imposing remedial sanctions', available at https://www.cftc.gov/sites/default/files/idc/groups/public/@lrenforcementactions/documents/legalpleading/enfhsbcsecuritiesorder012918.pdf (accessed October 2018).

27 Andrew Caminschi and Richard Heaney, 'Fixing a leaky fixing: short-term market reaction to the London pm gold price fixing', *Journal of Futures Markets,* 34:11 (September 2013), pp. 1–37.

28 The gold futures contracts market is in a standard gold futures contract

representative of 100 troy ounces of gold, and the gold exchange-traded fund market refers to shares in exchange-traded funds, which can be traded throughout the day at prevailing market prices.

29 Liam Vaughan, Nicholas Larkin and Suzi Ring, 'London Gold Fix calls draw scrutiny amid heavy trading', Bloomberg, 26 November 2013, available at https://www.bloomberg.com/news/articles/2013-11-26/gold-fix-drawing-scrutiny-amid-knowledge-tied-to-eruption (accessed 9 May 2018).

30 As reported in 'The fix is in: are gold prices a gigantic bank scam?', *Sydney Morning Herald*, 3 March 2014, available at https://www.smh.com.au/business/investments/the-fix-is-in-are-gold-prices-a-gigantic-bank-scam-20140303-3402k.html (accessed 9 May 2018).

31 Ibid.

32 Peter Fertig, 'Has there been a decade of London pm gold fixing manipulation?', *Alchemist*, 73 (March 2014), pp. 14–15, available at https://www.lbma.org.uk/assets/blog/alchemist_articles/Alch73.pdf (accessed 9 May 2018).

33 Ibid.

34 Ibid.

35 The criteria for direct participants are set out on ICE Benchmark Administration website, under the LMBA Gold and Silver price.

Part IV: Regulatory reform

Chapter 9

Reforming benchmarks

In a communiqué of February 2013, the G20 stated that it expected 'more progress on measures to improve the oversight and governance frameworks for financial benchmarks coordinated under the current FSB [Financial Stability Board] agenda this year, including the promotion of widespread adoption of principles and good practices'.[1] It appears that this is the first time the G20 raised the issue but it can perhaps be assumed that it falls under the rubric of the requests for the FSB, an international body, to press for a wide range of regulatory reforms following the financial crisis. After the discovery of the manipulation of benchmarks, in particular the LIBOR and the FX benchmarks, the G20 asked the FSB to undertake a 'fundamental review of major interest rate benchmarks and plans for reform to ensure that those plans are consistent and coordinated and that interest rate benchmarks are robust and appropriately used by market participants'.[2] The first step was taken in July 2013 with the establishment of an Official Sector Steering Group, consisting of senior officials from central banks and regulatory authorities. The aim was to find a benchmark that could fulfil the same functions as LIBOR and to design it in such a way that it would be much harder to manipulate. This also involved an 'analysis of the FX market structure and incentives that may promote particular types of trading activity around the benchmark fixings'.[3]

In 2014, after considering a wide range of other potential benchmarks, the FSB recommended improving the existing benchmarks for key interbank offered rates (IBORs) in the unsecured lending markets and to continue to develop the nearly risk-free benchmark rates. The IBORS were: LIBOR, EURIBOR and TIBOR. Given the wide range of uses of the IBORs, the view has often been taken that a wider choice of reference rates might be more appropriate for all the different uses of the rates by market participants. However, market participants have generally not taken that view but have preferred the familiar IBORS.

A nearly risk-free rate is more appropriate for many derivative products, which do not need a reference rate that includes credit risk, as stated by the FSB:

> With respect to derivatives contracts, in terms of the economic exposures to which the counterparties would ideally be exposed, many transactions do not need a reference rate which includes bank credit risk.[4]

This risk-free rate is generally taken to be the return on government bonds (in some currencies), since this is an asset which is generally regarded as indeed being virtually risk free. Other possibilities include overnight index swap rates, often considered to be a good indicator of the interbank credit markets, policy rates and secured funding rates but so far none of these has been sufficiently developed to corner the market for derivatives. Market participants also noted the continued need for a reference rate *with* bank credit risk. This is seen as more appropriate for products where there is a need to hedge general bank credit risk such as bank-provided credit products. It was noted that the use of LIBOR as a 'loan-pricing benchmark ... allowed banks in London to hedge their cost of funds with their floating rate loan revenues'.[5]

The FSB's final report made two major recommendations:[6]

- to strengthen existing IBORs and other potential reference rates based on unsecured bank funding costs by underpinning them to the greatest extent possible with transactions data;
- to develop alternative, nearly risk-free reference rates, to meet the principle of encouraging market choice.

The benchmarks had to be developed in accordance with the IOSCO principles, which were published in July 2013.[7]

IOSCO principles for financial benchmarks

First of all, the principles are designed for the benchmark administrators, not for the users of benchmarks (traders). The principles are not enforceable, nor do they replace national law or regulations; instead, they provide a set of standards for assessments of the administration of EURIBOR, LIBOR and TIBOR undertaken by a review team consisting of staff drawn from IOSCO members. The results of the first two reviews to have been carried out have been published.[8] This is likely to be an effective enforcement tool for benchmark administrators, who have both a reputation and a role to maintain. Secondly, the principles provide much more detail about the way in which they should be implemented, signifying a development in the style of such principles. They were often expressed in such general terms in the past that it was unclear how they applied to the conduct of financial services business, with too many assumptions about the financial markets to which they were expected to apply. That is no longer the case. A brief summary of the principles is set out here. They are divided by IOSCO into four sections: governance, quality of the benchmark, quality of the methodology and accountability.

Governance

The administrator of the benchmark is responsible for every aspect of the development and the actual benchmark each day, as well as credible and transparent oversight and governance, including the establishment of an oversight body responsible for the integrity of the benchmark. There should be clear written arrangements for each person's roles and obligations in setting the benchmark, especially for any third parties involved. There should also be procedures in place for the documentation, implementation and procedures for identifying, disclosing, managing and avoiding conflicts of interest.

There should be a control framework at the administrator of the process for determining and distributing the benchmark, and all of the procedures should be documented and available to regulatory authorities and stakeholders. This should include arrangements for whistleblowing, so that any potential misconduct can be identified quickly. Governance should include an oversight committee to review and challenge all aspects of benchmark determination.

Quality of the benchmark

The design should take into account all the features which can ensure that it really does represent the economic realities of the interest rate that the benchmark is seeking to measure, and exclude any features that might distort the price, rate, index or value of the benchmark. The data on which it is based should be based on prices, rates, indices or values in an active market and on observable *transactions* between buyers and sellers. The reference to 'transactions' here is in italics since this is the major and most significant change in the construction of LIBOR.

This principle is not intended to exclude the use of other data, but may use data such as executable bids or offers as a means to construct benchmarks from time to time, if there are insufficient transactions on some days. But there must be clear guidelines regarding the hierarchy of data inputs and the exercise of expert judgement. When the benchmark is published, there should be an explanation which is sufficient to enable a subscriber or a regulatory authority to understand the basis of the judgement and why it was used.

The quality of the methodology

The administrator should periodically review the conditions in the underlying interest rate that the benchmark measures to consider whether or not structural changes have taken place which might require a change in the methodology and that should be made publicly available. The principles also require the publication of the minimum information about the methodology used to make benchmark determinations so that stakeholders can understand how the benchmark is derived and assess its relevance to their needs. The rationale for any change in the methodology and the procedures for making any changes, or even for the cessation of the benchmark, should be public as well. There should be guidelines for the submitters' code of conduct and relevant internal controls over the administrator's data collection and transmission processes. This should cover the process for selecting the source, collecting the data and protecting the integrity and confidentiality of the data.

Accountability

This refers to external auditors and written complaints procedures.

ICE LIBOR

ICE Benchmarks Ltd became the administrator of LIBOR on 1 February 2014. Since ICE took over LIBOR, it has published two position papers and associated feedback statements on the evolution of LIBOR, after conducting extensive consultation over 18 months. Roundtable meetings were hosted by the Bank of England, the Bank of Japan, the Banque de France, the Swiss National Bank, the Federal Reserve Bank of New York and the Board of Governors of the US Federal Reserve. Based on the feedback that ICE Benchmark Administration Limited (IBA) received from all the consultations, the benchmark administrator has developed and strengthened the reliability of LIBOR as the benchmark.

ICE LIBOR is the benchmark published under that name or as 'LIBOR' and calculated by the IBA on London business days. ICE LIBOR has decided to use the LIBOR 'output statement' as the new definition of LIBOR:[9]

> A wholesale funding rate anchored in LIBOR panel banks' unsecured wholesale transactions to the greatest extent possible, with a waterfall to enable a rate to be published in all market circumstances.

In order to produce LIBOR for each currency tenor pair, and panel banks are asked to base their submissions on the following LIBOR submission question:

> At what rate could you borrow funds, were you to do so, by asking for and then accepting interbank offers in a reasonable market, just prior to 11 am?

LIBOR panel banks are required to base their submissions on eligible wholesale unsecured funding transactions to the greatest extent available. The rule is that LIBOR submissions in response to the above question are:

> determined based on data from a range of relevant transaction types. These may also utilise qualitative criteria such as the expert judgement of the submitter. Each LIBOR panel bank must ensure that its submissions are determined using an effective methodology based on objectively based and relevant market information.

The so-called 'waterfall' consists of three levels:

- *Level 1 (transactions)*. Where a panel bank has sufficient eligible transactions, it gives a volume-rated average price of such eligible transactions with a higher weighting for transactions booked closer to 11 a.m. London time. The transactions need not be with other commercial banks, but can be with central banks, government entities, multilateral development banks, non-bank financial institutions (such as pension funds), sovereign wealth funds, supranational organisations and corporations, but only for maturities of more than 35 days.
- *Level 2 (transaction-derived data)*. If a LIBOR panel bank does not have enough eligible transactions, it will seek to make a submission based on transaction-derived data, subject to specific rules laid down by the IBA. Using historical transactions involves a bank taking its

transactions from previous day(s) and adjusting them by a change of correlated rates such as futures, short-dated government bonds, repos and central bank rates. The LIBOR Oversight Committee has set a matrix of the maximum number of LIBOR submission days for which historical transactions can be used. They are also subject to weighting according to currency, tenor and proximity to the time of submission. Where suitable submissions are not available, linear interpolation may be used to fill the gaps in the curve.

- *Level 3 (expert judgement).* Where a panel bank has insufficient transaction data to provide a level 1 or 2 submission then the submission must be based on the panel bank's internally approved procedures, which have been agreed with the IBA, and formulated using the inputs agreed by the IBA. It must be accompanied by full documentation of the rationale for the submission and with supporting evidence provided to the IBA. The range of allowable inputs is quite wide but is limited by the parameters set out by the IBA. These include related market instruments, such as interest rate futures, broker quotes, policy rate changes and a published and verified change in the credit standing of the banks.

The 'waterfall' methodology is designed to base LIBOR to the greatest extent possible on transactions, as well as to reflect the changes in bank funding models – less borrowing from other banks and more from other financial institutions. It is calculated every London business day for five currencies with seven maturities, producing 35 rates. LIBOR is normally published by the IBA at 11.55 a.m. London time. It is a trimmed arithmetic mean that excludes the highest and lowest quartiles of submissions. All panel banks' submissions carry equal weight, subject to the trimming.

The IBA has added other restrictions on submissions, including the size of the trade, which must be more than 10 million in all the currencies, except the Japanese yen, which must be 1,000 million or more. The length of time of the loan (its tenor) has to fit in with IBA rules for consistency. The requirement for banks to exercise judgement was removed. Submission data are now published after the three months of embargo on a non-attributed basis. These and other technical details (all available on ICE Benchmark Administration's website) are designed to make it as difficult as possible, if not impossible, to manipulate LIBOR.

The last safeguard against manipulation is establishing the rules for the algorithms which banks apply to their own transaction data used to generate their level-2 submissions. The rules also allow for the occasions when the bank does not have enough transactions on that particular day and has to use some judgement on 'market colour' (level 3). ICE also has a 'surveillance' team to assess the submissions after the publication of the rates. The ICE processes some 4.5 million data points and comparisons, using robust algorithms and a team composed of academics, mathematicians and former traders to look at the results in terms of what they might consider to be anomalies. Determining the daily rate is now far ahead of the Reuters calculations. LIBOR panel banks' submissions for each tenor and currency pair are ranked by the IBA and the upper and lower quartiles are excluded to remove outliers. The relevant rate is then calculated as the trimmed arithmetical mean of the remaining submissions, rounded to five decimal places. Each LIBOR panel bank's submission carries equal weight, subject to the trimming. The panel banks may use their own algorithms in determining their submission, especially if it depends on the bank's own expert judgement. The IBA has its own experts who retrospectively check the algorithms used by each panel bank.

The IBA is authorised and regulated by the FCA. It now meets all the IOSCO principles, and has established a board and an Oversight Committee with observers from the Bank of England, the Swiss National Bank and the Chicago Mercantile Exchange in attendance.

The FSB's report on progress, published in October 2017, concluded that the IBOR administrators have taken important steps to implement the FSB's recommendations. However, the report finds that:

> in the case of some IBORS, such as LIBOR and EURIBOR, underlying reference transactions … are scarce and submissions therefore necessarily remain based on a mixture of factors, including judgment by submitters. Regulators have taken a number of steps to address these issues, including developing powers to require mandatory contributions to benchmarks, but it remains challenging to ensure the integrity and robustness of benchmarks and it is uncertain whether submitting banks will continue to make submissions over the medium to long term.[10]

Despite all these efforts to reinstate LIBOR and to re-establish trust in the benchmark, a rash of headlines appeared in the press announcing the 'death of LIBOR'.[11] These appeared as a result of a speech given on 27 July 2017 by Andrew Bailey, Chief Executive of the FCA, in which he raised the question of the future of LIBOR, because the 'underlying market which LIBOR seeks to measure – the market for unsecured wholesale term lending to banks – is no longer sufficiently active'.[12] In a review of data gathering, the FCA had concluded that there were relatively few eligible term borrowing transactions by any large banks and Bailey stated in his speech that this raised a serious question about the sustainability of LIBOR benchmarks.

Bailey noted that LIBOR will have to be sustained until such times as alternatives are available and the transition arrangements are well advanced. Indeed, that is essential. Bailey points out that current UK and EU legislation gives the FCA the power to compel banks to contribute to LIBOR where necessary, though it prefers not to do so. But that changed when EU Regulation 2016/1011 came into force on 1 January 2018.[13] The nature of those powers will change once LIBOR is designated as a critical benchmark under that EU Regulation: the UK may not be able to use those powers indefinitely. (It is not, however, clear whether or not this Regulation will apply after Brexit.) Other alternatives have been proposed, such as a broad treasuries rate in the USA, overnight rates such as the European EONIA, the Swiss SARON and Japan's TONAR, where the data are produced by central banks. The Bank of England had been working for some time to reform the SONIA benchmark, having taken over the production of SONIA, including the calculation and publication from the Wholesale Market Brokers Association. SONIA refers to the Sterling Overnight Index Average, which is a widely used interest rate benchmark and the reference rate for sterling overnight indexed swaps (OISs). The reforms involved broadening the inputs so that unsecured transactions negotiated bilaterally were included, as well as those arranged through brokers. The calculation of SONIA was changed to a volume-weighted trimmed mean, and the rate is published at 9 a.m. the following London business day, to allow time for processing the larger volume of transactions it captures.

The Bank of England has taken a number of steps to ensure the quality of the benchmark. It is based entirely on transactions reported to the Bank, thus providing a representative coverage of the market which the benchmark is designed to measure and a statutory footing for data reporting. Arrangements are in place for data validation and plausibility checking. The Oversight Committee is chaired by the Chief Operating Officer and the SONIA Stakeholder Advisory Group provides advice and technical input to the Bank and Oversight Committee. It became operational on 24 April 2018.

The problem with overnight rates is that they cannot fill the place of LIBOR, as term rates are needed for hedging or pricing purposes because of the market risk of interest rate changes (both absolutely and along the yield curve). SONIA and other overnight rates would have to develop a yield curve if they are to be an alternative to LIBOR, and that has not yet been achieved. Although not theoretically risk free, LIBOR is considered to a good proxy against which to measure the risk–return trade-off for short-term floating-rate instruments. The LIBOR curve can be predictive of longer-term interest rates. Bailey recognised that the transition would take a long time, perhaps up to 2021, given the trillions of dollars of financial instruments of all kinds referencing LIBOR.[14] It is for this reason that such a transition may take much longer than had been thought. Work continues on SONIA although it is recognised that it is only an alternative, not a replacement. However, on 3 April 2018 the New York Federal Reserve launched the secured overnight financing rate (SOFR), based on the overnight Treasury repurchase agreement market, which trades about $800 billion daily. It is part of a plan to move derivatives away from LIBOR. SOFR, though, is limited to dollars – it does not include sterling or euros; moreover, it, too, is an an overnight measure, and does not have a yield curve. The pressure for change comes from central banks, which regard overnight rates as risk-free rates, but realise that such rates do not meet market participants' need for a wide range of contracts.

Although it is certainly possible to have more than one rate, and for the user to decide which one is the most appropriate for pricing a debt instrument or revaluing a portfolio, the use of a particular rate would have to be fully explained to those who are depending on it. They need to be sure that the rate provides some kind of objective measure, for asset managers, pension funds and other long-term investments.

But LIBOR's administrator will still be able to publish the dollar rate after 2021 (when LIBOR is due to be replaced), and five years may not be long enough for the banks to overhaul the $350 trillion of outstanding derivatives, loans and mortgages tied to LIBOR. Banks, companies, insurers and pension funds are among many participants with swaps and debts that are likely to be affected by changes in short-term interest rate in the money market.[15] The one- or three-month maturities are necessary for the floating-rate market. At least some market partici-pants and analysts see that LIBOR and certainly dollar IBOR will have to continue for longer, to allow for all contracts based on LIBOR to expire. All that can be said with certainty at present is that LIBOR is not yet dead, but when and whether we can expect its obituary in the next few years remains uncertain.

Fixes for foreign exchange rates

This work focuses on the two most important benchmarks: the 4 p.m. London fix provided by WM Reuters (WMR), the dominant benchmark;[16] and the European Central Bank's benchmark at 2.15 p.m. Central European Time, used by a wide range of participants but especially the non-financial corporate and the non-deliverable forwards market. The former are based on actual transactions, even for the less well traded currencies, where active bids and offers are used.

The FSB sets out a number of recommendations, of which the ones concerning WMR's methodology for the benchmark calculation are the main concern here.[17]

- The fixing window should be widened from one minute to five minutes. This strikes a balance between reducing incentives for manipulation, while at the same time ensuring the fix is fit for purpose, by generating a replicable market price. For less liquid (less traded) currencies, the window could be wider, but the appropriate width of the window should be decided by WMR in consultation with market participants.
- WMR should incorporate price feeds and transactions data from a broader range of sources to increase its coverage of the FX market during the fixing window, provided it is sure that the additional sources are of sufficient quality and are representative of the market. WMR should regularly assess its coverage as the market structure continues to develop. However, it does receive data feeds from three different currency platforms, in some cases using others as back-up when the primary source is insufficient. The core electronic platforms of Thomson Reuters Marching and EBS are especially important because they are where the dealers typically manage their risk. The more data sources are used, the more resilient the fix will be. This should also reduce the scope, at the margin, for fixing rates to be manipulated. The FSB also recommended that in deciding which platforms should be incorporated, consideration should be given as to how representative different platforms are of the market as a whole, especially at the time of the 4 p.m. London fix, and check whether the platform and its trading rules are of a suitable standard.
- WMR should expand its consultation to a named user group to consider any changes in the methodology and to ensure that it remains appropriate in the future.

With regard to trading volumes and volatility, the FSB analysed the general daily trading patterns of seven currencies against the US dollar, using high-frequency transactional data from the EBS platform and Thomson Reuters between April and September 2013, with the aim of understanding the average behaviour of exchange rates and of trading activity on these two trading platforms around the WMR 4 p.m. fix. All currencies exhibit sharp spikes in trading volumes at certain times of day, some of which are common to all and some of which relate to a particular currency. The WMR 4 p.m. London fix generates the highest average volume spike in the day, generally at least 10 times greater than the one-minute mean trading volume for that currency. The other usual significant peaks in volume occur at the North American data releases at 8.30 a.m. and 10 a.m. Eastern Time North American option expiration times. However, trading volume rises during London daytime hours and is highest when London and New York are actively trading. The volume spikes associated with the WMR 4 p.m. fix tend to be highest at month ends and quarter ends, probably reflecting larger portfolio rebalancing needs at those times.

As far as volatility is concerned, the increase in trading volume around the WMR London fix is not associated with a large spike in volatility around that time; indeed, the highest average volatility during the day in a one-minute trading window is associated with the 8.30 a.m. North American data release, when important macroeconomic information is incorporated into asset prices. Average volatility rises relative to the minutes before and after the 4 p.m. fix, but this is nothing special given the high volume of trades and large order imbalance, positive or negative, although this varies from day to day.

With regard to the one-minute fixing window at 4 p.m., this is very concentrated for all seven currencies, because traders do not begin to exercise their fixing-related trades until they are very close to the start of the one-minute calculation, very likely because (according to the FSB) 'dealers are trying to minimise their tracking or pricing error relative to the fixing price they guarantee their customers'.[18] Studying second-by-second data shows that trading volumes rise substantially as the fixing window opens and then decline gradually as the fixing proceeds. At the time of the WMR 4 p.m. London fix, the EBS euro–dollar data break down trading volume into three groups: dealers trading manually, dealers trading algorithmically and prime-brokered customers trading algorithmically. HFT accounts for the majority of the third group's trading volume. The share of overall trading by the HFT group declines rapidly, while the share of trading by the manual group rises sharply.[19]

Two comments should be made about the FSB's analysis: first, there is little criticism of the WMR methodology, apart from lengthening the time of the fix to five minutes; and second, the analysis provided by the FSB explains spikes, volatility and concentration of trades not as anomalies which require explanation in terms of possible manipulation. The explanations offered are reasonable enough, but the FSB may not have considered whether altering the time frame for the fix would be sufficient to make manipulation more difficult.

The second IOSCO report on the WMR spot rate, published in February 2017, noted the change of ownership and that the closing spot rate is now regulated by the FCA and that most of the IOSCO principles had been applied.[20] This is especially important in terms of the changes to the methodology, taking account of two reviews the administrator conducted for calculating the benchmark. The extension of the calculation window to five minutes for trade currencies and two to five minutes for non-trade currencies was carried out on 2 February 2015. Thomson Reuters Matching data were included in calculations for additional currencies and the methodology was updated to blend data sources together for currencies, where considered appropriate. A further review is still in progress to decide whether it would be appropriate to expand the use of EBS transaction data for an additional six currencies.

The IOSCO report stated that further work should be carried out to ensure that the data on which it relies from various platforms have adequate controls, surveillance and governance in place by setting out clear due diligence policies. The administrator should also consider what further steps should be taken to make sure that the transactions on which it relies for setting the closing spot rate are 'bona fide', by perhaps seeking undertakings from the providers. WMR has already taken steps, by holding meetings with data providers, to sort out data quality standards, trading activity, monitoring and surveillance, service review and updates. The review, however, suggests that greater transparency is needed in some areas, such as more information about the determination of the rate and the hierarchy of data input, without compromising other competing aims. An examination of the WMR website (https://financial.thomsonreuters.com) reveals quite comprehensive information, so much progress has been made.

The FX Global Code

The FX Global Code is a code of conduct, first published on 27 May 2017, by the Global Foreign Exchange Committee, as a result of a partnership between central banks and market participants from 16 jurisdictions throughout the world. It is designed to promote 'a robust, fair, liquid, open and appropriately transparent market',[21] instead of the vast, largely unregulated, market, too easily open to manipulation hitherto. It cannot impose legal or regulatory obligations on market participants, but is instead a code of good practice. It is extremely comprehensive. Not only does it provide an exhaustive set of principles, but it also seeks to illustrate what those principles mean in practice, by providing examples of how they would apply in specific practical situations. By so doing, it constitutes a step forward in providing more than just a set of principles, but also a better explanation of the way in which they should apply. The Code applies to *all* market participants, whereas the IOSCO Code applies only to benchmark administrators. That is understandable, in that the first step in attempting to restore trust was to make the benchmarks themselves 'manipulation proof' as far as possible.

It is impossible to cover every aspect of the Code, with its 55 principles grouped around six major themes: ethics; governance; execution; information sharing; risk management; and compliance, confirmation and settlement processes. These apply to all market participants. I shall take just a few examples from the Code, all of which relate to the types of manipulation and collusion which took place for over the years before the regulatory and other authorities (such as the US Department of Justice and the UK's Serious Fraud Office and the courts) investigated and fined the financial institutions and individuals involved.

Principle 10

Here the general principle is that 'Market Participants should handle orders fairly, with transparency, and in a manner consistent with the specific considerations relevant to different order types'.

An example of what that might mean in practice in relation to the handling of a client's stop loss order is given in the Code.[22] Market participants handling a client's stop loss order should agree the terms of the order such as the reference price, order amount, time period and trigger. Some of the unacceptable practices which traders engaged in include trading in such a way as to move the market to the stop loss level.

Examples include buying or selling a larger amount than is in the client's interest within seconds of the fixing calculation window with the intent of inflating or deflating the price against the client or showing a large interest in the market during the fixing window in order to manipulate the price against the client.

Principle 12

Here the Code states that 'Market Participants should not request transactions, create orders, or provide prices with the intent of disrupting market functioning or hindering the price discovery process'. The Code refers to a whole range of practices, including those which could cause 'latency or artificial price movements' which result in 'a false impression of market price, depth or liquidity'. Examples include a trader entering into a bid or offer with the intent to cancel before execution ('spoofing', 'flashing' or 'layering') to create a false sense of market price, depth or liquidity. The Code provides worked examples of manipulative behaviour:

> A Market Participant wishes to sell a large amount of USD/MXN [Mexican peso]. It repeatedly places small offers to sell on a widely viewed E-Trading Platform. The Market Participant chooses to use another dealing code of the same institution on the same E-Trading Platform in order to lift these successive higher offers with the intention of misleading the market.[23]

This strategy would breach principle 12 as the false impression is given that multiple counterparties are participating in a rally when they are actually from the same institution.

Principle 17

This refers to the controversial 'last look', which some commentators considered might be ruled out by the Code. It was not. Instead, principle 17 seeks to protect the client. Last look is used in electronic trading activities, whereby a market participant receiving a trading request has a final opportunity to accept or reject the request against its quoted price. Market participants employing last look should be transparent regarding its use and provide appropriate disclosures to clients. The market participant should at the very least disclose whether (and if so how) changes to price in either direction may impact the decision to accept or reject the trade. The participant should also set out the expected or usual time period for making that decision and what the point of the 'last look' is. In other words, the use of the 'last look' should be hedged about with all kinds of disclosures to protect the client.[24]

Principles 19 and 22

Market participants should clearly and effectively identify and appropriately limit access to confidential information, which includes information relating to past, present or future trading activity or positions of the market participants themselves or their clients. These could be details of a market participant's order book or orders for benchmark fixes. For prime brokers in particular, there should be a clear separation of their prime brokerage business and their other sales and trading business. This is linked to principle 22, which states that 'market colour' should be communicated without compromising confidential information (any specific information about client names, or code names which would give that away, or any information about individual trading positions, and flows should only be disclosed by price range, not by exact rates referring to a specific client). Market participants should not seek confidential information when providing or receiving information about market colour.

These two principles are important, since traders colluded in the manipulation of the price by sharing confidential information and they frequently used the provision of 'market colour' as a cover for collusion. Principle 22 sets out exactly what can and cannot count as 'market colour'. This can only refer to quite general information about what is happening in the market and what the trends might be. Two examples are provided:

> A hedge fund manager attends a portfolio review with a large Client. At the review, the manager learns that the Client will soon be shifting part of its currency allocation into another currency pair. The manager is asked for advice, but not awarded the allocation mandate. Upon leaving the meeting, the manager makes a call to his own trading desk to inform them of the impending trade.[25]

In this example, the planned currency allocation is confidential information which has been disclosed to the hedge fund manager for advice only. It should not be disclosed to the trading desk. The reference here is to principles 19 and 20.

An example of a breach of principle 22 involves an asset manager talking to a bank market-maker: 'I hear that you've been a big buyer of GBP/USD. Is it for the same UK corporate(s) again?' Market participants should not solicit confidential information, including the trading activity of a specific client. Trading should not be related to a specific client as the asset manager has done in this example.

Conclusion

What is valuable about the Code is not that it will change behaviour in and of itself but that it provides a clear and comprehensive picture of what counts as good behaviour. A statement of commitment to the Code may help, since a financial institution signing it is making a public declaration of its intent to align its activities with the principles of the Code. It is recognised that market participants will need some time to review and adjust their practices to conform to the principles of the Code, but they were given 12 months for this work to be carried out. In addition, a public register was created where market participants can publicly demonstrate their use of the Code, although that is still work in progress. That would certainly make it difficult, in terms of its public face, to allow breaches of the Code to continue unchecked. The BIS stresses the importance of the role of central banks both in following the Code themselves and in being committed to owning and maintaining the Code.[26] But the Code itself cannot be enforced, except to the extent that regulations reflect the principles set out in it.

In August 2018, the Global Foreign Exchange Committee published a review, *The FX Global Code at One Year: A Look Back and a Look Ahead*, which noted achievements across three core areas: awareness and commitment to the Code; embedding the Code and integrating it into the FX market; and the evolution of the Code. The Committee noted that Statements of Commitment are being widely used to demonstrate adoption of the Code; 12 public registers and a Global Index have been launched. It reported that an increasing number of market participants are reviewing their practices to make sure that they align with the Code, developing and using training programmes encapsulating the Code and revising and updating disclosures, taking into account the principles set out. The Code remains the centre of attention in public discussions of FX market developments and some changes have been made to principle 17, which retained the much criticised 'last look' provision.

The Gold and Silver Fixes

On 20 March 2015, the IBA became the administrator for the LBMA Gold Fix, which replaced the London Gold Fix as the principal global benchmark for daily gold prices. The new arrangements are set out at the end of the previous chapter.

In accordance with the IOSCO principles, an LBMA Oversight Committee has been established, which, apart from governance issues, is the means by which the market provides ongoing advice and guidance to ensure the credibility of the benchmark. One immediate decision was to remove the 'seller's premium', a market convention of adding $0.15 for settlement purposes. The IBA has researched the history of this premium but found little information about it, apart from the possibility that it was put in place a long time ago to encourage miners to bring their metal through London.

The IBA set up its platform in such a way as to minimise conflicts of interest. A key potential conflict of interest can arise when market participants manage both client and house orders in IBA auctions and have information about their client order flow. The website can be configured separately for each firm so that the firm can either route all client orders through the house desk or can segregate house and client orders to different desks. This provides indirect participation for clients; they can participate in the auction process with the same information and order management capability as the direct participants. This segregation also simplifies the process, and the separation of the house and client orders provides a full audit trail for all the changes during the auction. The IBA runs daily surveillance of the auction activity on ICE's trading platform, which provides straight-through processing for many firms and a full audit trail for compliance departments. The auction was originally run by rotating chairmen, all ex-bankers, but in March 2017 they were replaced by a price-fixing algorithm. Now there is no human input. A further change, which took place in April 2017, was the introduction of central clearing to the gold price auction, enabling a wider range of participants to join it. By July 2017, over 4 million troy ounces of gold had cleared the market through ICE, the equivalent of nearly $5 billion. The volume that is cleared increased from 30% at the launch of central clearing to 67% for the week ending 28 July 2017.

In July 2017, the LBMA announced that the IBA would take over from the CME Group and Thomson Reuters as administrator of the London Silver Fix with effect from autumn 2017. The CME Group and

Reuters stepped down from providing the silver auction less than three years after they had won the contract. It was also announced that ICE Futures US would begin trading the silver daily futures contract from 5 September 2017. ICE Futures US began trading a new gold daily futures contract on 30 January 2017. Eligible contract dates are all London business days on which commercial banks are open for business in New York. This is a physically settled contract traded in increments of US$0.01 per ounce, involving a transfer of ownership of gold held in a London precious metals vault on an unallocated basis. The same approach to the contract applies to the silver futures contract. These contracts are traded in New York but physically settled in London, an arrangement which reflects the greater regulatory certainty surrounding capital and reporting requirements, as well as the uncertainty surrounding Brexit. It also enables traders to avoid European regulatory requirements, such as the Markets in Financial Instruments Regulation.

There is a Code of Conduct for the IBA gold auction and the LBMA gold price benchmark. This Code, dated January 2016, is intended to 'work together with the IBA Gold Auction Rule Book to set out the framework which Participants in the IBA Gold Auction should observe to ensure consistency, reliability and high standards of conduct'.[27] The Code can be amended only after prior consultation with the participants and other stakeholders identified by the Oversight Committee. The latter may make such amendments to the Code which it considers necessary.

The Code covers internal systems and controls around activity on the gold price auction; staff training and experience; order management and recording; handling conflicts of interest, including having a policy and being aware of any changes in the structure of the company or changes in an individual's responsibilities which could give rise to new conflicts of interest; whistle-blowing; and record-keeping. Record-keeping (all for five years) includes written records of activity, key details of representatives participating in the gold auction, including the representatives' names and job titles and the underlying client and house orders relayed by representatives during the IBA gold auction. Companies must also keep written findings of any client reviews and any internal or external orders of processes and procedures associated with participation in the auction. If this seems unduly bureaucratic, then it should be remembered that the regulators had to spend many long hours trawling through endless emails and chat rooms to find out what went on in the attempts to manipulate the earlier Gold and Silver Fixes.

The LBMA launched the Global Precious Metals Code on 27 May 2017, the same day as the FX Code was launched. This Code sets out the standards and best practice expected from participants in the global over-the-counter wholesale market for precious metals.[28] It follows a similar pattern as the other codes: ethics, governance, compliance, risk management and business conduct. It applies to a very wide range of market participants, ranging from LBMA members, refiners and mining companies, financial institutions and banks to jewellery companies and benchmark platform operators.

With reference to past behaviours, the strictures on the sharing of information are extremely detailed, leaving little room for doubt as to what kind of information must be treated as strictly confidential, such as:

- details of a market participant's order book;
- other market participants' axes (that is, an interest that a market participant might have to transact in a given product at a price that may be better than the prevailing market rate);
- spread matrices provided by market participants to their clients;
- orders for and during the benchmark process;
- details of an individual client's vault holding;
- designated confidential information.

Further, market participants should clearly identify confidential information, which may be part of a written non-disclosure agreement.

EU and UK regulation

These various codes are in addition to changes in rules and regulations introduced by various regulatory authorities after the extent of manipulation came to light. The FCA now regulates the administrators of all benchmarks, notably LIBOR, SONIA, the WMR 4 p.m. closing spot rate, the ICE swap rate and the LBMA Gold and Silver Fix. LIBOR was regulated from April 2013 and the other major benchmarks from April 2015. That followed the Chancellor's Fair and Effective Markets Review, published in June 2015.[29] The FCA also worked with the Treasury on the development of the EU's Market Abuse Regulation (596/2014/EU) (MAR), which came into force on 3 July 2016. The summary of the Regulation defines market manipulation as follows:

Market manipulation: entering into a transaction or behaviour that:

- gives or is likely to give false or misleading signals as to the supply/demand of a financial instrument;
- secures or is likely to secure the price of a financial instrument at an abnormal level.

It may also consist of:

- a transaction or behaviour by using a fictitious device or other form of deception;
- disseminating misleading information;
- transmitting false or misleading information;
- providing false or misleading inputs; or
- any action which manipulates the calculation of a benchmark.[30]

The MAR creates for the EU (but not the UK) minimum rules for criminal sanctions for market abuse. For the UK, the criminal regime for market abuse established by the Criminal Justice Act 1993 and the Financial Service Act 2012 remains unchanged. The MAR includes two new offences: attempted market manipulation and the manipulation of benchmarks. The first is defined as any attempt to engage in any of the activities amounting to market manipulation and also applies to any situation that is started but not completed, for example an instruction to trade that is not acted upon. The MAR market manipulation offence includes the manipulation of benchmarks but the UK legislation already goes beyond that, as it is a criminal offence under the Financial Services Act 2012 (section 91) to make false or misleading statements relating to benchmarks or to engage in a course of conduct that creates a false or misleading impression that may affect the setting of a benchmark. The MAR does, though, allow for 'market soundings'.

The objectives of the MAR are to reinforce the capacity of regulators to detect and sanction abuse and to enhance cooperation between regulators. It lays an obligation on trading venues to have arrangements, procedures and systems in place aimed at preventing and detecting market abuse. The same obligation (to have arrangements to detect and record suspicious orders and transactions) applies to any professional arranging or executing transactions in financial instruments.

The MAR greatly extends the scope of the new market abuse regime beyond regulated markets to financial instruments traded on multilateral trading facilities or other organised trading facilities and OTC financial products such as derivatives and credit default swaps, both within and outside the EU in relation to instruments admitted to trade on an EU trading venue. This territorial reach could have sweeping consequences, so it will be interesting to see how the USA views this.

The codes, the UK legislation, the FCA rules and the Market Abuse Regulation are comprehensive. This plethora of attempts to regulate every possible area of potential manipulation will not succeed on their own. For that, much more is needed and these are the issues to be discussed in the next chapter. The FSA and later the FCA were able to hold banks to account for their failure to abide by long-standing principles, even without detailed rules. In the next chapter, I explore the banks' failures to abide by the principles, and how senior management responsibility could change that, with special reference to the Foreign Exchange Working Group's description of the process of 'embedding'.[31] The chapter will also discuss who should be held to account for what, in the light of the manipulation of all the benchmarks considered here.

Notes

1 Communiqué of meeting of G20 finance ministers and central bank governors, 16 February 2013, available at http://www.g20.utoronto.ca/2013/2013-0216-finance.html (accessed October 2018).
2 See Financial Stability Board, *Progress Report on the Oversight and Governance Framework for Financial Benchmark Reform: Report to G20 Finance Ministers and Central Bank Governors* (FSB, 29 August 2013), p. 1, available at http://www.fsb.org/wp-content/uploads/r_130829f.pdf (accessed October 2018).
3 Financial Stability Board, *Foreign Exchange Benchmarks: Final Report* (FSB, 30 September 2014), p. 1, available at http://www.fsb.org/wp-content/uploads/r_140930.pdf (accessed October 2018).
4 Financial Stability Board, *Reforming Major Interest Rate Benchmarks* (FSB, 22 July 2014), p. 11, available at https://www.fsb.org/wp-content/uploads/r_140722.pdf (accessed 4 May 2018).
5 Ibid., p. 11.
6 Ibid., pp. 57–8.
7 International Organization of Securities Commissions, *Principles for Financial Benchmarks: Final Report*, FR07/13 (IOSCO, July 2013), available at https://www.iosco.org/library/pubdocs/pdf/IOSCOPD415.pdf (accessed October 2018).
8 International Organization of Securities Commissions, *Review of the Implementation of IOSCO's Principles for Financial Benchmarks* (IOSCO, 2015) and *Second Review of the Implementation of IOSCO's Principles for Financial Benchmarks by Administrators of EURIBOR, LIBOR and TIBOR* (IOSCO, 2016), both available at https://www.iosco.org.
9 The information and quotes here and below are taken from the ICE LIBOR web page of the Intercontinental Exchange, at https://www.theice.com/iba/libor (accessed October 2018).

10 Financial Stability Board, *Reforming Major Interest Rate Benchmarks Progress Report on Implementation of July 2014 FSB Recommendations* (FSB, 10 October 2017), p. 8, available at https://www.fsb.org/wp-content/uploads/P101017.pdf (accessed 9 May 2018).

11 Just one example of such a headline is Suzi Ring, 'Libor funeral set for 2021 as FCA abandons scandal-tarred rate', Bloomberg, 27 July 2017.

12 Andrew Bailey, 'The future of LIBOR', speech at Bloomberg, London, 27 July 2017, available at https://www.fca.org.uk/news/speeches/the-future-of-libor (accessed 9 May 2018).

13 Regulation (EU) 2016/1011 of the European Parliament and of the Council of 8 June 2016 on indices used as benchmarks in financial instruments and financial contracts or to measure the performance of investment funds and amending Directives 2008/48/EC and 2014/17/EU and Regulation (EU) No 596/2014, available at https://publications.europa.eu/en/publication-detail/-/publication/5f55dd2e-3dbb-11e6-a825-01aa75ed71a1/language-en (accessed May 2018).

14 Bailey, 'The future of LIBOR'.

15 Alexandra Scaggs, 'The demise of Libor is not a done deal for markets', *Financial Times,* 2 August 2017, available at https://www.ft.com/content/43e1dcbc-7754--11e7--90c0--90a9d1bc9691 (accessed 9 May 2018).

16 In April 2016, Thomson Reuters acquired the World Markets Company's FX benchmark from the State Street Corporation. It is still known as WM/Reuters Fix, run by Thomson Reuters.

17 Financial Stability Board, *Foreign Exchange Benchmarks: Final Report* (FSB, 30 September 2014), pp. 24–6, available at https://www.fsb.org/wp-content/uploads/r_140930.pdf (accessed 9 May 2018). The report of a working group, chaired by Guy Debelle of the Reserve Bank of Australia and Paul Fisher of the Bank of England, was incorporated in this FSB report.

18 Ibid., p. 19.

19 Ibid., pp. 16–19.

20 International Organization of Securities Commissions, *Second Review of the Implementation of IOSCO's Principles for Financial Benchmarks in Respect of the WM/Reuters Closing Spot Rate* (IOSCO, February 2017).

21 Global Foreign Exchange Committee, *FX Global Code: A Set of Global Principles of Good Practice in the Foreign Exchange Market* (GFEC, 27 May 2017), p. 1, available at https://www.globalfxc.org/docs/fx_global.pdf (accessed May 2018).

22 There are a number of variants on a stop loss order, so it is important to provide the client with a clear definition, including the reference price, order amount, time period and trigger.

23 Global Foreign Exchange Committee, *FX Global Code*, p. 56.

24 'Last look' originated in the early years of electronic trading in the FX market, where it was intended to ensure that the market-maker's price was not based on stale market data for the purposes of price information and that the market-maker had credit available to trade with the client. Some argue that it is not a risk management tool but is used to generate profits. Buy-side customers may be uncertain why their FX trades are being rejected.

25 Ibid., p. 62.

26 Foreign Exchange Working Group, *Report on Adherence to the FX Global Code* (Bank for International Settlements, May 2017), available at https://www.bis.org/mktc/fxwg/adherence_report.pdf (accessed 9 May 2018).

27 *Code of Conduct for the IBA Precious Metals Auctions and the LBMA Gold and Silver Price Benchmarks* (issue 3) (ICE, 25 September 2017), p. 1, available at https://www.theice.com/publicdocs/LBMA_Gold_Price_Code_of_Conduct.pdf (accessed May 2018).

28 The Code is available on the LBMA website, http://www.lbma.org.uk (accessed May 2018).

29 Bank of England, *Fair and Effective Markets Review – Final Report* (BoE, 10 June 2015), available at https://www.bankofengland.co.uk/report/2015/fair-and-effective-markets-review---final-report (accessed 4 May 2018).

30 'Preventing market abuse in financial markets. Summary of Regulation (EU) No 596/2014 on market abuse', available at https://eur-lex.europa.eu/legal-content/EN/LSU/?uri=CELEX:32014R0596 (accessed October 2018).

31 Foreign Exchange Working Group, *Report on Adherence to the FX Global Code*.

Chapter 10

Holding senior bankers to account

As the fines imposed on banks for their part in the manipulation of LIBOR, the foreign exchange market and the Gold and Silver Fixes have mounted up, the question posed by the public both in the UK and in the USA is: why have so few senior bankers gone to jail? The public saw a handful of traders tried and jailed (and sometimes set free on appeal) and a few senior bankers resigned or were asked to resign, while retaining comfortable pensions and even bonuses. The UK and EU regulators considered that reforming the methods of provision of the benchmarks and reforming their governance were vital but insufficient on their own. The behaviour of banks and their senior management is crucial for the operation of the benchmarks and for the restoration of trust.

Parliament, the government and the regulatory authorities sought ways of ensuring that senior bankers are accountable. The Financial Services and Markets Act 2000 was amended by the Financial Services (Banking Reform) Act 2013 and the Bank of England and Financial Services Act 2016. Both Bills were introduced by government after extensive discussions between Treasury civil servants, staff of the FSA and then the FCA, and the Bank of England. These Acts, like their predecessors, provide the legislative framework for financial regulation, granting powers to the regulatory authorities to make all the necessary rules and regulations within the scope of the legislation. This chapter explores the reasons for the new powers and for introducing the Senior Managers Regime (SMR). The conclusion is that the SMR will not only provide a means of holding senior bankers to account but may well also promote higher standards of diligence and responsible management.[1]

Under the regulations available at the time, the FSA/FCA's fines on the banks were made on the basis of the banks breaking its 'Principles for Business' and for the CFTC on the basis of the US Commodities Exchange Act (CEA). The CEA specifically makes it unlawful to deliver false or misleading information, and to manipulate or attempt to manipulate the price of any commodity in interstate commerce. Sections 6(c), 6(d) and 9(a) of the CEA clearly prohibit acts of attempted manipulation. Two elements are required to prove an attempted manipulation: an intent to affect the market price and an overt act in furtherance of that intent. The CFTC was able to fine Barclays for collusion in the attempted manipulation. Barclays was guilty of collusion under the CEA section 13(a). Liability as aider and abettor requires proof that the CEA was broken, that the aider and abettor knew about the wrongdoing underlying the breach of the law, and that the aider and abettor intentionally assisted the primary wrongdoer. The CFTC had at its disposal not only the frequently amended Act but also considerable case law. The CFTC made Barclays pay a fine of $200 million based on detailed legal considerations. The CFTC was also in a position to hold Barclays responsible for the activities of its agents under section 2(a) of the Act, and the Commission's own rules imposes strict liability on principals for the actions of their agents. Lacking the legislation and regulations now in force in the UK and the EU, neither the FSA nor its successor the FCA had such grounds, but was able to rely on the 'Principles for Businesses', which provide the framework and the overarching principles from which detailed rules may be derived. There may be advantages in the latter approach, since the detailed and extensive laws and regulations which apply to financial institutions may not cover an actual situation and provide considerable scope for legal challenges. As the FCA Handbook notes:

> since the Principles are also designed as a general statement of regulatory requirements applicable to new or unforeseen situations and in situations where there is no need for guidance, the FCA's other rules and guidance or EU regulations should not be viewed as exhausting the Principles themselves.[2]

In this chapter, it will be argued that the huge fines imposed on banks failed both in terms of justice and in terms of bringing about changes in culture and behaviour. Moreover, those fines did not punish the individuals responsible for the offences. The practice was roundly condemned by Judge Jed Rakoff in the USA after the financial crisis, who described the whole process in the following terms:

> Just going after the company is also technically and morally suspect because, under the law, you should not indict or threaten to indict a company unless you can prove beyond reasonable doubt that some managerial agent of the company committed the alleged crime; and if

you can prove that, why not indict the manager? And from the moral standpoint, punishing a company and its many innocent employees and shareholders for the crimes committed by some unprosecuted individuals seems contrary to elementary notions of moral responsibility.[3]

It should be noted that 'shareholders' does not refer to a few wealthy individuals, but pension funds and mutual funds, investing on behalf of many small savers. The size of the fines and the reputational damage affect not only the share price with the knock-on effects on people's investments, but threatens the viability of the bank itself, especially when a bank is faced with separate fines from multiple agencies.[4]

With regard to the boards of banks, according to UK regulations the role of the chairman is separate from that of the chief executive officer (CEO). The chairman is subject to the 'fit and proper' requirements, as are all other members of the board. The non-executive chairman's responsibilities are set out in detail in the supervisory statement, but they include both chairing and overseeing the development of the board and leading the development of the firm's culture by the board. In addition, the board has four committees – audit, risk, remuneration and nomination – each headed by a non-executive member of the board. The chair of the audit committee is responsible for ensuring and overseeing the integrity and independence of the internal audit function, including the head of internal audit. The chair of the risk committee is responsible for overseeing the independence of the firm's risk function, including the independence of the chief risk officer. A bank's finance, internal audit and compliance departments can discuss matters of concern with the chair of the audit committee, and the head of the risk management department can bring any such issues to the chair of the risk committee. The chair of the bank is in contact with all four committees of the board and, through the chairs of these committees, together with any informal discussions with heads of departments, has the means to be fully informed about every aspect of the bank's operations. The role is a demanding one, taking up to three days a week, and is designed to enable the board to oversee the bank's strategy on the basis of full information and agree the bank's strategy, within its risk appetite and with a sustainable business model, to meet its regulatory objectives. Such a structure may have enabled senior managers to identify the risks involved in the behaviour of their traders and their managers, but it would not have been enough on its own.[5]

This chapter begins by describing the changes to the Senior Managers Regime in the UK, following not only the financial crisis but the widespread manipulation of benchmarks. The new regime will help to ensure that senior management carelessness, negligence, or worse, is prevented by the implementation of a clear managerial structure and proper systems and controls. This is much more than setting 'the tone at the top', which involves statements of management's leadership, commitment to openness, honesty, integrity and ethical behaviour. The trouble is that public statements by CEOs, articulating the standards they want others to work by, are not regularly measured or evaluated and are often undermined by their own leadership teams' behaviour. CEOs are not necessarily seen as role models. Setting the 'tone at the top' is not by any means enough on its own and may well be viewed with a certain degree of cynicism by staff. Much more than that is required to ensure proper standards of behaviour throughout the firm, and the advantage of the new structure for senior management is that it provides a managerial framework for that to be carried out.

The new structure does provide a means of holding senior managers accountable, since they have to set out exactly what their responsibilities are in the bank. That will be discussed in more detail later in the chapter. The extent of the managerial failures is revealed in the final notices issued to various banks by the FCA. Of course, they show the evidence for manipulation of benchmarks, but the final notices have the advantage of revealing the underlying causes of the manipulation and the full extent of mismanagement, or indeed the failure to impose any kind of managerial structure at all. Taking Deutsche Bank as an example (although the final notices issued to other banks reveal similar issues), the FCA commented:

> Although between January 2005 and June 2011, Deutsche Bank had in place general policies and procedures concerning compliance standards which required, amongst other things, staff to act with integrity, *it had no IBOR-specific systems and controls in place*.[6]

No records were kept of which individuals made IBOR submissions and nor were records kept of the rationale behind the rates submitted. No formal training on the LIBOR or EURIBOR submissions processes took place. The conflict of interest between the same group of traders making the submissions and trading derivatives directly influenced by those rates was not even recognised. Money market traders and derivatives traders were encouraged to share information on a daily basis without regard to any actual or possible conflict of interest; in some instances the trader and the submitter were the same person.

The inadequate systems and controls around trading came to light when investigations took place. The trader audit system worked by allocating each trader a random recording device, so the system recorded the telephone calls of a single trader on many different audio-tapes, making it very difficult to scrutinise the behaviour of any particular trader over a period of time. There was no system for identifying which traders were responsible for which trading books and which trades. In February 2011, Deutsche Bank was asked by the FCA for an attestation as to the adequacy of the systems and controls in place, a task which was delegated to a compliance officer, who, in the course of his investigations, was advised that there were no specific systems and controls designed to ensure the integrity of the bank's LIBOR submissions. Nevertheless, the attestation was signed to the effect that Deutsche Bank 'currently has adequate systems and controls in place for the determination and submission of [its] LIBOR fixings'.[7] It even claimed that 'spot checks' had taken place when they had not. Although the task had been delegated to a single compliance officer, two *senior managers* signed it off without any further checks.

The regulatory changes and new management structure described below may be regarded by many as an onerous external burden. I would suggest, instead, that its key elements are those which should be in place in *any* well-managed bank. The proposed management information systems would support senior management in carrying out their responsibilities by identifying potential weaknesses in the performance of certain units or of key individuals at an early stage. It would also save the banks the huge costs in time, legal fees and reputation they have had to face. It is now clear that, for some major banks, recovering from the large fines imposed by many regulators and law suits against them is proving to be more of a struggle than they may have expected at an earlier stage in the whole saga. The changes introduced make it clear that managing the bank is the responsibility of the bank, not the regulators.

The Senior Managers Regime (SMR): its origins

The demise in 1995 of Barings, Britain's oldest merchant bank and then still under Barings' family control, was brought about by hubris of the part of trader Nick Leeson, weak oversight and a lack of checks and balances (Leeson ran both the front and back office for trading in

10-year Japanese bonds and futures). The leading regulator at the time was the Securities and Investment Board (SIB), which found that both company law and financial services legislation did not give the SIB the powers to hold senior managers to account. An early form of the SMR was introduced in the UK when Sir Andrew Large was chairman of the SIB which made it possible for the regulators to declare an individual unfit to work in the financial services industry at any particular level.[8]

Although it could have been a useful tool, the decision to withdraw 'approval' from a senior manager was not often used. When the attempt was made to apply it after the financial crisis, it was found to be insufficiently effective, for example in the case of Fred Goodwin, the chief executive of RBS (a bank that required a government bail-out). The FSA admitted it had not identified any breaches of its own rules. The reasons for the failure to take action are detailed in the FSA's report.[9]

In his foreword, the FSA's chair, Adair Turner, explained:

> There is neither in the relevant law nor the FSA rules a concept of 'strict liability': the fact that a bank failed does not make its management or Board automatically liable to sanctions. A successful case needs clear evidence of actions by particular people that were incompetent, dishonest or demonstrated a lack of integrity.
>
> Errors of commercial judgement are not in themselves sanctionable unless either the processes or controls which governed how the judgements were clearly deficient, or the judgements were clearly outside the bounds of what might be considered reasonable. The reasonableness of judgements, moreover, has to be assessed within the context of the information available at the time, and not with the benefit of hindsight.
>
> The implication of these points is that an investigation can identify evidence of numerous poor decisions and imperfect processes, without that establishing a case for enforcement action which has reasonable prospects of success in Tribunal or court proceedings.[10]

The FCA's Enforcement Division agreed that disciplinary action against individuals responsible for any misconduct would serve as a greater deterrent than a sanction against a bank that had already failed. Such actions require 'strong evidence of an individual's personal culpability',[11] but, looking at all the instances of poor judgement (such as the purchase of ABN-AMRO), the FCA indicated that they were 'not outside the bounds of reasonableness given all the circumstances of the time'.[12] Further:

> For legal sanction to be appropriate, it has to be clear that there was strong evidence that individuals broke specific rules, and/or that decisions were

made which were not only mistaken in retrospect but were outside the
bounds of reasonableness at the time they were taken.[13]

There was a separate issue in this case of whether disqualification
proceedings could be brought against any former directors of RBS,
under the Company Directors Disqualification Act 1986, but that was
a matter for the government's Department for Business, Innovation and
Skills (BIS).

Development of the Senior Managers Regime after the financial crisis

Following the financial crisis and criticism from Parliament and the
public over the inability to take action against individuals, the regulatory authorities in the UK now specify a senior management regime,
known as 'the Senior Managers Regime' or SMR. This took effect on
7 March 2016. Both the PRA and the FCA set out a new regulatory
framework to 'strengthen accountability in banking', and to strengthen
'individual accountability' in particular, to make it possible for both
banks and regulators to hold individuals to account.[14]

First of all, it is necessary to identify senior managers and then to
set out their responsibilities. The regime creates direct accountability
to the regulators for individuals taking (or participating in) important
decisions about a firm's affairs and also running significant areas of
the business. They are subject to approval by the FCA and/or the PRA,
which may be subject to conditions and/or time limits. The assessment
of the individual's 'fitness and properness' will have regard to the
person's honesty, integrity and reputation, competence, capability and
financial soundness. The assessment, according to the guidelines of the
European Banking Authority, will include an interview process in which
the proposed candidate's knowledge, experience, application of skills in
previous occupations, as well as other qualities, such as 'decisiveness,
strategic vision, judgment on risks, leadership, independence of mind,
persuasive power and the ability and willingness to engage in continuous
learning and development' will be assessed.[15] Criminal checks must be
included as part of this. Senior managers are those who hold one or more
key senior management functions (SMFs) within a firm, and include: the
chief executive officer; chief finance officer; executive director; chief
risk officer; heads of key business areas; group entity senior manager;
chair of the company; and the chairs of various committees, such as

the risk, audit, remuneration and nominations committees, as well as compliance, oversight and money-laundering reporting. The SMR has undergone some changes since its post-crisis reintroduction. The Senior Managers and Certification Regime replaced the Approved Persons Regime. One of the most important features is the introduction of the Statement of Responsibility and its role in enforcement. Details of the Statement have been altered since its introduction and these will be discussed below. But first, the Certification Regime.

The Certification Regime

Banks have to take on a new responsibility: the certification regime. This applies to all employees who are not senior managers but whose role means that it is possible for them to cause significant harm to the bank or its customers. The FCA Handbook provides a long list of roles of these employees together with complicated definitions, so some examples relevant to recent history will be sufficient.[16] These include: benchmark submission and administration; proprietary traders; material risk takers; client-dealing; algorithmic trading; and heads of units, such as retail banking, personal lending and corporate lending.[17] A bank has to certify, on an annual basis, that both senior managers and certified employees are fit and proper to carry out their roles. The requirement to certify employees is a sea change from the hiring of FX staff as described by Kevin Rodgers, a manager at Deutsche Bank:

> The e-trading team was expanding and so was my derivatives (options) team, especially the section of it called 'complex risk.' Interviews for these posts were often conducted in an impenetrable, blended patois of English and maths and the whiteboards in the interview rooms were inevitably covered in a dense thicket of equations afterwards; the geekiness of the FX trading team was increasing rapidly.[18]

This description of hiring FX traders shows how difficult it could be for senior managers without expertise in the FX market to assess whether or not a trader would meet the requirements of the Certification Regime. A senior manager may not have sufficient technical skills to ensure that traders were still competent, had updated their skills and were aware of the regulations governing their role. That could lead to the introduction of annual tests. But it could well be more difficult to be sure that the trader continued to act 'with integrity'.

The conduct rules

Both the FCA and the PRA have set out conduct rules. Tier 1 are general high-level rules applying to all staff. They are: 'You must act with integrity'; 'You must act with due skill, care and diligence'; and 'You must be open and cooperative with the FCA, the PRA and other regulators'. To these the FCA adds 'You must pay due regard to the interests of customers and treat them fairly' and 'You must observe proper standards of market conduct'. The tier 2 rules apply to senior managers, who must take reasonable steps:

- to 'ensure that the business of the firm for which you are responsible is controlled effectively';
- to 'ensure that the business of the firm for which you are responsible complies with the relevant requirements and standards of the regulatory system';
- and to 'ensure that any delegation of your responsibilities is to an appropriate person and that you over see it effectively'.

In addition, the senior manager must disclose appropriately any information of which the FCA or the PRA would reasonably expect notice.[19]

Senior management conduct rules

These are called tier 2 rules. Senior managers must take reasonable steps to ensure that the business of the firm for which they are responsible is controlled effectively; that it complies with the relevant requirements and standards of the regulatory system; and that any delegation of their responsibilities is to an appropriate person and that they oversee the discharge of the delegated responsibility effectively. They must also disclose any information of which the FCA or PRA would reasonably expect notice.

Banks must report to the FCA or to the PRA breaches of conduct rules by senior managers within seven business days of becoming aware of the breach; breaches by certified staff can be reported annually; but *significant* breaches by senior managers *or* certified staff must be reported immediately after the bank becomes aware of them.

Mapping responsibilities

Once a bank has allocated responsibilities amongst its senior managers, the SMR requires the bank to record the allocation and that the FCA and the PRA are duly notified. The selection of senior managers to carry out various roles is the responsibility of the bank. Nevertheless, the SMR requires the bank to ensure that certain senior management functions are filled, but the bank selects the individuals to fulfil those roles. The functions are obvious – for example, chief executive; group entity senior management function; chief finance function; and chairman function.

Each individual senior manager must complete a 'Statement of. Responsibilities' clearly setting out the role they are undertaking and describing those areas of the bank for which they are responsible. The statutory duty of responsibility applies to all senior managers and requires them to take reasonable steps to prevent regulatory breaches in the areas of the banks for which they are responsible.

Banks will be required to write and maintain a comprehensive 'management responsibilities map' which describes the bank's management and governance in a single document. This should include key reporting lines, committee structures and details about key managers and their responsibilities. For large, complex organisations, the preparation of this map will be time-consuming and complicated. But, apart from the list of new responsibilities set out below, any such organisation should and generally does have at least an organisational chart, which could be used as the basis. It is surely important for the running of its business that there are clearly designated roles for senior managers of major areas of business. The required management functions are defined, since the responsibility is inherent, inseparable from and intrinsically built into the specific role; for example, the head of internal audit is defined as 'having responsibility for the management of the internal audit function of the firm and for reporting directly to the governing body of the firm on the internal audit function'.

Both the PRA and the FCA have produced a prescribed list of responsibilities which must be assigned to a specific senior manager. For the PRA, among the obvious responsibilities, such as the treasury management functions, six out of the 20 are related to maintaining the map, the performance of the bank of its obligations under SMR and the certification rules, but, more important, to staff at all levels. These include: induction, training and professional development of senior managers; leading the development of the firm's culture and standards in relation to the conduct of business and the behaviour of staff; and embedding those standards and the bank's culture in relation to the conduct of business and day-to-day management of the firm. The FCA prescribes similar responsibilities to senior managers but, given that the

FCA regulates a wide range of retail firms, the FCA Handbook adds a list of the main business activities and functions of a relevant authorised person, including payment services, investment management, trading for clients, mortgage and investment advice.

The mapping itself can easily be seen as a bureaucratic exercise, but determining who is responsible for what is the first step towards ensuring that the appropriate action is taken at the right time. If the task is not assigned to anyone, then nobody takes it on and nothing gets done. Although the FSA was not a commercial organisation, its internal audit showed that checking information or rumours about LIBOR were not anyone's responsibility, so no questions were raised with the BBA or with banks.

Both the FCA and the PRA set out highly general principles, such as all staff, including senior managers, acting with integrity. However, the PRA's decision to separate the responsibilities for ensuring proper standards of behaviour from the responsibilities of the senior managers involved in LIBOR or the foreign exchange market may not be the right decision. It would be better if individual senior managers are responsible for ensuring that the appropriate standards of behaviour are being applied in their particular areas of responsibility, since they know and understand how standards apply; other senior managers should have responsibility for seeing that senior managers in fact carry out their duties in this regard.

Because the benchmark codes, described in the last chapter, are voluntary, a crucial element of them is 'embedding'. For instance, the Foreign Exchange Working Group of the BIS, in its *Report on Adherence to the FX Global Code*, states:

> It is important for market participants to embed the Code's guidance in their day-to-day operations and help create a strong culture, both within their organisation but also in the market as a whole, where good practices are promoted and fostered.[20]

That is where worked examples come in – different examples (often changed) can be used as a way of embedding the required behaviour. The examples set out in the *FX Global Code* itself (annex 1) illustrate both the right and the wrong way to conduct FX operations and provide much more detail to show FX traders exactly what the more general rules mean in practice.

They have their uses but codes will not change behaviour in the market on their own. Moreover, embedding principles and practices will require considerable resources for staff training. Such training will have to cover explanations of the rules, what constitutes good practice and why, and what counts as ethical behaviour. Sponsorship and endorsement by the senior manager responsible for that part of the business are critical. Not only should leaders take part in the training themselves, but they must also support the investment upfront and reinforce the significance of the training through their actions as well as in their communications. That will include monitoring and disciplining those who fail to take part.

Many banks use e-training and e-testing to support training in regulations, good practice and ethical behaviour. That is where worked examples come in for the codes for market participants. These show that the approach to testing comprehension of what constitutes good practice can be accomplished by asking certified staff to respond to illustrative scenarios. Annual refresher training is essential and, again, all staff must undertake such training, especially if there are changes in the structure of the market or new regulations. In addition, there must be an environment in which employees feel confident enough to make decisions that align with the principles and rules of the business, but they also need to have a point of contact where they can ask questions if they are uncertain and need further explanations without fearing a black mark against them and also where they can report possible examples of improper behaviour.

The statement of responsibility

The concept of the statement is straightforward enough. Individual senior managers must complete a 'statement of responsibility' which clearly sets out the role they are undertaking and describes those areas of the bank's business for which they are responsible. The statement should also show how the individual senior manager's responsibilities fit in with the bank's overall governance and management arrangements, and must also be consistent with the management responsibilities map. The statement must give clear descriptions of each responsibility in no more than 300 words of free text. There is a list of prescribed responsibilities, which is simply a list of the obvious functions which a senior manager must carry out, ranging from the chief executive and chief finance officer, heads of key business areas to the responsibility for compliance oversight and the allocation and maintenance of capital funding. A bank obviously has to have senior managers in key roles.

In a supervisory statement, the PRA provides further details about the statement of responsibility, which shows that it is more than just a bureaucratic burden.[21] The PRA points out that these statements encapsulate what a bank should be doing for the benefit of its own business:

> [they] provide for a more targeted assessment of the fitness and propriety of prospective and incumbent Senior Managers by allowing their competence, knowledge, experience, qualifications, training and, where relevant, proposed time commitment to be measured against the responsibilities they have been allocated.[22]

It is obviously important to have the right person for the right job and to ensure that they are still appropriate for the role. Both these statements and the maps should be used to assist banks in their internal corporate governance, succession planning and the continuing professional development of senior managers (always a difficult and sensitive task). They may also assist in developing certified employees, who have shown they have the capacity and commitment to progress through, for example, their readiness to take on new tasks and to gain professional qualifications.

The statements should indicate whether or not a senior manager has overall responsibilities for any business areas, activities or management functions not listed in the prescribed responsibilities. This should also apply to the responsibility of overseeing a short-term project of some kind. Just listing these may reveal that one manager is being asked to do too much and that the additions may prevent the manager from carrying out any duties efficiently. Any short-term project should be removed once it has been completed. These projects may be very time-consuming; examples would be a major acquisition, a flotation or the creation of a ring-fenced bank, or a regulatory demand for an internal review of the firm or an enforcement action.

For the free text, the statement should break down certain responsibilities into key component tasks. For example, 'developing and maintaining the firm's recovery plan and resolution pack', which is a prescribed responsibility, should include in the free text 'presenting the recovery plan to the board before submitting it to the PRA' and 'ensuring that the PRA is notified of any material changes made to the resolution pack promptly and, in any event, one month before the change'.

Finally, if there is a significant change in a senior manager's responsibilities, then the PRA must be notified. The PRA's assessment of whether or not it is 'significant' will depend on: the importance to the firm of the responsibilities being taken on or given up; whether it alters the seniority of the individual in the firm; any change in the identity, number or seniority of the individuals reporting to the senior manager; and whether there are any changes to the skills, knowledge or experience required by the manager. In other words, these requirements ensure that the bank considers the appointment or changes in the senior team and their specific roles – who is responsible for what – very carefully, and so can be a very useful managerial tool.

Why is there a 'statement of responsibility' as opposed to a 'rebuttable presumption of responsibility'?

The statement of responsibility was originally a 'duty of responsibility' and signed by the senior managers concerned. The application form has now changed and, although it clearly identifies the individual, it is not quite the same as the original idea. The 'rebuttable presumption of responsibility' was discussed only with reference to failed banks, since the manipulation of benchmarks had not then emerged into the full light of day. The original proposal, which had the support of regulators, the Treasury and the Parliamentary Commission, has changed. The FCA has issued 'guidance' in the framework of its *Decision Procedure and Penalties Manual* on how it enforces the 'duty of responsibility'. The duty came into force on 10 May 2016, but the guidance took effect only from 3 May 2017. According to this guidance:

> Under the duty of responsibility, we [the FCA] and the PRA can take action against Senior Managers if they are responsible for the management of any activities in their firm in relation to which their firm contravenes a regulatory requirement, and they do not take such steps as a person in their position could reasonably be expected to take to avoid the contravention occurring (or continuing).[23]

It is to be hoped that the present framework meets an expectation set out by the Parliamentary Commission on Banking Standards:

> senior managers of banks will no longer be able to hide behind an accountability firewall, where they are too distant from the consequences of their responsibilities to be held clearly accountable when things go wrong. A future investigation into a scandal such as Libor manipulation should not result in the trail going cold half-way up the organisation, but should be capable of leading directly to the senior executive whose lack of oversight permitted it to happen.[24]

Part of the rationale for holding senior bankers to account was provided by Lord Turner in his Foreword to the FSA report *The Failure of the Royal Bank of Scotland*:

> Banks are different because excessive risk-taking by banks (for instance through an aggressive acquisition) can result in bank failure, taxpayer losses, and wide economic harm. Their failure is of public concern, not just a concern for shareholders. There is therefore a strong public interest in ensuring that bank executives and Boards strike a different balance between risk and return than is acceptable in non-bank companies. This argues for ensuring that bank executives face different personal risk return trade-offs than those which apply in non-banks.[25]

Andy Haldane, Executive Director, Financial Stability, Bank of England, as a witness for the Parliamentary Commission on Banking Standards, also emphasised the importance of sanctions in encouraging those at the most senior levels to assume greater responsibility:

> Not knowing cannot be a legitimate excuse. If it was made clear that, whatever the product or asset, if it is not doing what it was meant to be doing, the sanction will be meted out at the highest level of the firm, and that those incentives would run down the core of the firm from the top, that would help. I think that if the CEO or the chief risk officer or the chief operating officer, knew that their job was on the line, their behaviours would then rub off all the way down the organisation.[26]

Banks occupy a special place in the economy as a whole. The economic system simply will not work unless banks can be trusted to take care of the monies belonging to individuals, corporations, government bodies, charities and institutions of all kinds, in investments, deposits, transfers, loans and all the other services they provide to enable the functioning of a modern economy. That puts bankers in a special position of trust as well.

The Parliamentary Commission agreed that loss of livelihood (by withdrawal of authorisation) would indeed be a powerful sanction but noted that many of those who served at senior levels in banks that failed (citing RBS in particular) have gone on to work elsewhere in the financial services sector. Even where some senior directors have resigned from their positions at a particular bank, they have sufficient resources to re-establish themselves in other enterprises, in start-ups even in the financial services industry, or in another country.

Lord Turner, chair of the FSA until March 2013, came out in favour of rules which would automatically ban senior executives and directors of failing banks from future positions of responsibility in financial services unless they could demonstrate that they were active in identifying, arguing against and seeking to rectify the causes of failure. For the Parliamentary Commission he added:

> I honestly feel, having looked very carefully at how these processes of legal proof work, that it always be difficult in courts of law to have people proved directly responsible for prudential problems going wrong.[27]

Proving responsibility may be much more difficult in the case of the failure of a bank but less so in the cases of manipulation which have been considered here.

In July 2012, the Treasury published proposals to introduce such a mechanism by creating a 'rebuttable assumption, that a director of a failed bank is not suitable to be approved by the regulator as someone who could hold a position as a senior executive in a bank'.[28] Until 2015, SMR included the 'presumption of responsibility' together with the 'reasonable steps defence' under section 66 of the Financial Services and Markets Act, which allows the PRA to take action if it appears that the person is guilty of misconduct and that it is appropriate to take action against him or her. Whether or not the senior executive was responsible for managing the activities involved will be a question of fact to which the statements of responsibilities and management responsibilities maps will provide the evidence, as long as these are clear and accurate. The senior manager would not be guilty of misconduct provided that he or she 'had taken such steps as a person in that position could reasonably be expected to take to avoid the contravention or occurring or continuing'.[29] The PRA would then expect the individual to submit evidence and make representations.

The change was quite sudden. Media reports began to appear in the early hours of 15 October 2015 that the government had decided to abandon the 'presumption of responsibility' and shortly after that the government published the Bank of England and Financial Services Bill, which became law on 4 May 2016. It was part of the Financial Services (Banking Reform) Act 2013. What reasons did the government have for changing its mind so late in the day?

Some of the reasons were voiced during the deliberations of the Parliamentary Commission. For example, the Financial Services Consumer Panel (an independent statutory body that represents the interests of consumers in the regulation of financial services), in its written evidence to the Commission, stated that it did not support the introduction of

a 'rebuttable presumption', as it could well have 'a perverse effect, dis-
couraging the far-sighted and diligent from accepting key management
positions'.[30] The Panel did, however, want to see an ethical code for
all banking directors, which would also address reckless misconduct,
breaches of which could lead to criminal sanctions; it also believed
that regulators should exercise more vigorously the sanctions already
available in order to keep out of the industry those who cannot meet
the standards of fitness and propriety. There were also concerns among
lawyers, in particular, that the rebuttable presumption was contrary to
the presumption of innocence, offending notions of natural justice and
due process. With regard to a failed bank and a director who had left the
bank, access to documents and other relevant material would simply be
unavailable. These are the key objections to the rebuttable presumption,
which may explain why it was eventually dropped, albeit suddenly, after
considerable public debate.

Interestingly enough, other objections to the rebuttable presumption
are still made but apply to SMR and the statement of responsibilities.
These include claims made by the banks that they will find it difficult
to attract people to fill senior management roles. There is a risk that
suitable candidates will prefer to work overseas or in other industries
where they are not so regulated. These concerns continue to be voiced
to the regulators and to the Treasury. However, given the status and
potential earnings, there will still be applications for these roles – at
least the executive roles. Banks may well find it useful to recruit from
their own ranks following careful training and preparation of staff,
especially in understanding the extent of the responsibilities and how
these are handled within the bank.

Enforcement

The statement of responsibility

Senior managers and the industry more widely are still concerned about
the statement of responsibility and the duty of responsibility, and their
enforcement, despite the removal of the presumption of responsibility.
Some would say that this is not surprising. Senior managers have certainly been spending time considering their potential liability under
the new scheme, especially with the presumption of liability. Banks
were putting in place very extensive arrangements around their senior
managers to ensure that all their key discussions and decisions were

documented in detail, which is presumably what any well run bank should do. The process could help to ensure that the consequences of key decisions have been carefully considered.

The duty of responsibility

A 'supervisory statement' issued by the PRA in May 2017 sets out when disciplinary action will be taken against a senior manager under section 66 of the Financial Services and Markets Act (FSMA). There are four criteria:

- the person is or was a senior manager as the relevant author-ised person;
- there has been or continues to be a 'contravention' of a relevant requirement;
- the senior manager was at the relevant time responsible for the management of any of the firm's activities in relation to which the contravention occurred;
- the senior manager did not take such steps as a person in the senior manager's position could reasonably be expected to take to avoid the contravention occurring or continuing.

The senior manager will not be guilty of misconduct if the PRA finds that they have taken all the steps that a person in that position could reasonably be expected to take to avoid the contravention occurring or continuing. As with any disciplinary action under the FSMA, section 66(2) (3) or (5), the PRA must consider each of these conditions separately. The PRA must first confirm that a person is guilty of misconduct if:

- the person is or was a senior manager or relevant authorised person;
- there has been or continues to be a contravention of the relevant requirement;
- the senior manager at the relevant time was responsible for the management of the firm's activities in relation to which the con-travention occurred.[31]

Each of the above points is considered separately. The burden of proof is on the PRA. Thus the PRA has to confirm that the person was a senior manager at the time and that they were responsible for the activities of the bank when the offence occurred; it is only then that the issue of reasonable steps is relevant. The matter will be discussed with the individual before an initial 'decision notice' is issued. The PRA outlines the ways in which it assesses what steps the senior manager could have taken as against the steps they actually took.[32] They include considerations such as what the senior manager ought to have known as opposed to what they actually did know; what expertise they had or should have had; what steps they could have taken; the actual responsibilities of the senior manager and the relationship between those responsibilities and the responsibilities of other senior managers at the firm; any delegation of responsibilities; and the environment in which the firm was operating at the time. The evidence which the PRA would take into account includes board and board committee minutes; minutes of other internal meetings; statements of responsibilities and maps; organisational charts and information reporting lines; emails and telephone recordings; and regulatory correspondence and interviews.[33]

Andrew Bailey, Deputy Governor, Prudential Regulation, Bank of England, and chief executive of the PRA, sought to reassure managers that the aim of the regime was primarily to encourage a sense of responsibility on the part of bankers:

> The key principle of that regime is to establish clearly appropriate responsibility for the governance of firms. Put like that, it is not meant to be radical or life-changing, despite what you might hear or read. Clarity of responsibility is I hope unobjectionable. But this is not clarity in the sense of witch hunts.[34]

How can senior managers know what is going on throughout their area of activity in a bank?

The supervisory statement does provide a useful summary of what counts as 'reasonable steps', but senior managers are understandably concerned as to whether what they offer as 'reasonable steps' is sufficient or will be regarded as such by the regulators. The simple answer to the above question is: they can't. The PRA has made it plain that the SMR applies only to the most senior executive managers in a bank, not to mid-level management. The most senior executives in a large national bank or a global bank will ultimately be responsible for several thousand employees, scattered throughout the globe. Barclays' former chief executive, Bob Diamond, during his appearance before the Treasury Select Committee, stated that only 14 traders were at fault, out of 'a couple of thousand traders'. He also pointed out that 'none of this information, until the investigation, came above desk supervisor level'.[35] That gives some idea of the scale of such banks and illustrates that it is impossible for the most senior executive to know each one and to assess that individual. That is true, but, with SMR, mapping, clear reporting lines and certification provide part of the answer.

The regulators make it clear that a bank should have proper systems and controls in place, so that reporting lines are clear and consistent. If middle and line managers report to more than one senior manager, then it should be clear what exactly is reported to whom. Reporting lines will be the critical element, which means that dotted, dual or complex reporting lines should be avoided or explained so that there is clarity in the chain of command, all the way up and down from the senior managers. The structure of the organisation requires careful planning, and may need revising if new businesses are introduced and after an acquisition or merger takes place.

Much can be learnt about what to do from the failures as described in the final notices served by the FCA on various banks. For example, in the case of RBS, the front office had primary responsibility for identifying, assessing and managing the risks associated with its G10 FX trading business, but no one checked what the front office was doing, or even whether staff at the front office knew what they were doing. Moreover,

> [RBS] failed to take adequate steps to ensure that general policies concerning confidentiality, conflicts of interest and trading conduct were effectively implemented in its G10 spot trading business. *There was insufficient training and guidance on how these policies should be applied specifically to that business. They contained few practical examples about their application and inadequate guidance on what amounted to unacceptable behaviour by G10 spot FX traders.*[36]

The importance of worked examples is recognised in the *FX Global Code*. The FCA does not claim that such training will eliminate the risk but it should reduce it. In the case of UBS, no attempt was made to determine the right structure: for example, between January 2005 and September 2009, UBS 'combined the roles of determining its LIBOR and EURIBOR submissions and proprietary trading in derivative products referenced to LIBOR and EURIBOR',[37] showing that senior managers did not understand the principles. Its systems and controls were also defective in that they could not identify 'wash trades' either. In neither of these examples would a senior manager be able to claim that they 'took all reasonable steps' to prevent serious breaches of regulations and, indeed, criminal activities.

Clearly, senior managers have to rely on the information provided to them by those who report to them. That assurance will depend to a large extent on the certification process, which should identify those with the relevant skills, knowledge, competence and reliability, and then at least the senior manager can rely on such reports initially. But that will not be enough. The system should incorporate 'red flags': for example, as far as traders are concerned, and counterintuitively, a trader who is consistently outperforming his colleagues deserves a 'second look'. That will not necessarily be to congratulate the trader, but rather the reverse. With the small margins legitimately available, it is difficult to continually outperform other traders. This is not to say that the very successful trader is automatically engaged in manipulation but it is a 'red flag', that is, something requiring further investigation.

It is, of course, possible to identify such a trader, since bonuses are awarded on the basis on individual performance, that is, how much profit the individual has made for the bank. That makes Jerry del reply as former chief operating officer for Barclays to questions at the Treasury Select Committee hearing disingenuous:

> Q1024 Andrea Leadsom: Could you tell us, for our own information, how you would benefit your own bonus by asking submitters to falsify the LIBOR submissions?
>
> Jerry del Missier: It is very complex, and it is not entirely obvious that you are benefiting your own profitability, but the theory would be that if you got a certain rate submitted, the book that you were trading would benefit from that submission. It is important to understand that it is not even the whole bank – it is one particular book. On any given day, the bank does not know whether it benefits from high rates or low rates but, again, because of the complexity of the averaging process, it is extremely difficult to see how one rate would have an impact, and then how that would necessarily flow through to compensation is very convoluted.[38]

A bank both needs to know and does know which business units are profitable: that would be a matter of interest and a failing unit would be subject to scrutiny, but one that was successful may be subject to much less scrutiny. Units are identifiable, as is the performance of individuals in those units. Not all of that information will appear in annual financial reports but it does underpin them.

Senior managers should also recognise and respect the independent duties of the risk management, compliance and internal audit functions and should not interfere with the exercise of such duties. Nevertheless, a senior manager would be wise to take note of their reports, and consider further investigations if there are warning signs in any of them. With regard to LIBOR and FX manipulation, however, the FCA criticised the quality of compliance and noted outright compliance failures. Making sure that compliance is up to the demands of the role is obviously important. It is possible to have an excellent risk management function in place, but it must also influence the decisions of senior managers. Dick Fuld, a former chief executive of Lehman Brothers, had what certainly seemed to be a risk management team in place, not afraid to advise him. He sacked the manager of the risk management team, having ignored all her warnings, and presided over the collapse of the company.

If all of this sounds as though it is expensive and time-consuming, it is worth banks remembering the billions of dollars spent in fines, legal costs, time taken and reputational damage. Banks are rightly willing to restore trust, but, once destroyed, it takes time, patience and hard work to restore it.

Notes

1 The 2013 Act amends the Financial Services and Markets Act, sections 59 and 60, to include 'senior management functions' and the 'statement of responsibilities'. The 2016 Act is primarily concerned with the establishment of the PRA, but Part 2, 25, 2f establishes the assignment of responsibility to the senior manager if the 'senior manager did not take such steps as a person in a senior manager's position could reasonably be expected to take to avoid the contravention occurring or continuing'.

2 The FCA Handbook of rules and guidance is available on the FCA's website at https://www.handbook.fca.org.uk (accessed October 2018), which 'contains the complete record of FCA Legal Instruments and presents changes made in a single, consolidated view'.

3 Jed S. Rakoff, 'The financial crisis: why have no high level executives been prosecuted?', *New York Review of Books*, 9 January 2014, available at https://www.nybooks.com/articles/2014/01/09/financial-crisis-why-no-executive-prosecutions (accessed 9 May 2018).

4 Details of the myriad fines are presented in Appendix (pp. 262–7).

5 The role of the board is set out by the Prudential Regulation Authority (PRA) in 'Strengthening individual accountability in banking', supervisory statement 28/15, July 2015, p. 7, available at https://www.bankofengland.co.uk/prudential-regulation/publication/2015/strengthening-individual-accountability-in-banking-ss (accessed October 2018).

6 Financial Conduct Authority, 'Final notice, Deutsche Bank AG', 23 April 2015, p. 20, emphasis added, available at https://www.fca.org.uk/publication/final-notices/deutsche-bank-ag-2015.pdf (accessed 4 May 2018).

7 Ibid., p. 30.

8 When I was on the board of the SIB, I put in a proposal in a formal letter (with the knowledge of the chair of the SIB) that senior managers should be

held responsible for any contraventions of the rules and regulations to the team drafting the Financial Services and Markets Bill (composed of Treasury officials and staff of the regulatory authorities). The proposal was rejected.

9 Financial Services Authority, *The Failure of the Royal Bank of Scotland: Financial Services Authority Board Report* (FSA, December 2011), p. 31, available at https://www.fca.org.uk/publication/corporate/fsa-rbs.pdf (accessed 9 May 2018).

10 Ibid., p. 7.

11 Ibid., p. 31.

12 Ibid., p. 35.

13 Ibid., p. 17.

14 Financial Conduct Authority, *Strengthening Accountability in Banking: UK Branches of Foreign Banks (Final Rules)*, PS15/30 (FCA, December 2015), available at https://www.fca.org.uk/publication/policy/ps15-30.pdf (accessed 9 May 2018); Financial Conduct Authority, *Strengthening Accountability in Banking: Final Rules Including Feedback on CP14/31 and CP15/5 and Consultation on Extending the Certification Regime to Wholesale Market Activities*, CP15/22 (FCA, July 2015), available at https://www.fca.org.uk/publication/consultation/cp15-22.pdf (accessed 9 May 2018); Prudential Regulation Authority, *Strengthening Accountability in Banking: Responses to CP14/14, CP28/14 and CP7/15*, PS16/15 (PRA, July 2015), available at https://www.bankofengland.co.uk/-/media/boe/files/prudential-regulation/policy-statement/2015/ps1615.pdf?la=en&hash=4F83474FB28C11AD79AB37ED2CAC391B4E13F3CE (accessed 9 May 2018).

15 European Banking Authority, *Guidelines on the Assessment of the Suitability of Members of the Management Body and Key Function Holders*, EBA/GL/2012/06 (EBA, 27 November 2012), p. 15, available at https://www.eba.europa.eu/documents/10180/106695/EBA-GL-2012-06--Guidelines-on-the-assessment-of-the-suitability-of-persons-.pdf (accessed 9 May 2018).

16 Financial Conduct Authority, Handbook, 'Certification Regime', 5.2.

17 Ibid.

18 Kevin Rodgers, *Why Aren't They Shouting? A Banker's Tale of Change, Computers and Perpetual Crisis* (Random House Business Books, 2016), p. 67.

19 Unusually, the PRA provided explanations of the applications of these very general principles, first of all in *Strengthening Individual Accountability in Banking*, supervisory statement 28/15 (Bank of England, May 2017), pp. 20–3, available at https://www.bankofengland.co.uk/prudential-regulation/publication/2015/strengthening-individual-accountability-in-banking-ss (accessed 9 May 2018). See also the document as updated in May 2017, pp. 35–9, although there are no significant changes from the earlier text – available at https://www.bankofengland.co.uk/-/media/boe/files/prudential-regulation/supervisory-statement/2017/ss2815update (accessed October 2018).

20 Foreign Exchange Working Group, *Report on Adherence to the FX Global Code* (BIS, May 2017), p. 2, available at https://www.bis.org/mktc/fxwg/adherence_report.pdf (accessed 9 May 2018).

21 Prudential Regulation Authority, *Strengthening Individual Accountability in Banking*.

22 *Ibid.*, p. 20.

23 Financial Conduct Authority, *Guidance on the Duty of Responsibility: Final Amendments (Including Feedback on CP16/26) to the Decision Procedure and Penalties Manual*, PS17/9 (FCA, May 2017), available at https://www.fca.org.uk/publication/policy/ps17-09.pdf (accessed 9 May 2018).

24 Parliamentary Commission on Banking Standards, *Fifth Report: Changing Banking for Good* (Stationery Office, 12 June 2013), para. 1116, available at https://publications.parliament.uk/pa/jt201314/jtselect/jtpcbs/27/27ii02.htm (accessed 9 May 2018).

25 Financial Services Authority, *The Failure of the Royal Bank of Scotland: Financial Services Authority Board Report* (FSA, December 2011), p. 9, available at https://www.fca.org.uk/publication/corporate/fsa-rbs.pdf (accessed 9 May 2018).

26 Parliamentary Commission on Banking Standards, *Fifth Report*, p. 498.

27 *Ibid.*, p. 504.

28 HM Treasury, *Sanctions for the Directors of Failed Banks* (Treasury, 3 July 2012), para. 3.11, p. 10, available at https://assets.publishing.service.gov.uk/government/uploads/system/uploads/attachment_data/file/81565/consult_sanctions_directors_banks.pdf (accessed 10 May 2018).

29 Prudential Regulation Authority, *Strengthening Individual Accountability in Banking*, para. 2.59, p. 13.

30 Parliamentary Commission on Banking Standards, *Fifth Report*, 'Written evidence from the Financial Services Consumer Panel'.

31 Prudential Regulation Authority, *Strengthening Individual Accountability in Banking*, para 2.58, p. 13.

32 The PRA procedure is set out ibid., paras 2.70ff, pp. 14–15.

33 Ibid., pp. 26–9.

34 Quoted by Huw Jones, 'Bank of England's Bailey says new banker rules not a "witch hunt"', Reuters, 21 May 2015 (accessed October 2018).

35 House of Commons Treasury Committee, *Fixing LIBOR: Some Preliminary Findings, Second Report of Session 2012–13* (Stationery Office, August 2012), Q128 and Q137, vol. 2, available at https://publications.parliament.uk/pa/cm201213/cmselect/cmtreasy/481/481.pdf (accessed 4 May 2018).

36 Financial Conduct Authority, 'Final notice, The Royal Bank of Scotland', 11 November 2014, para. 4.26, p. 13, emphasis added, available at https://www.fca.org.uk/publication/final-notices/final-notice-rbs.pdf (accessed 10 May 2018).

37 Financial Services Authority, 'Final notice, UBS AG', 19 December 2012, para 27, p. 5, available at https://www.fca.org.uk/publication/final-notices/ubs.pdf (accessed 10 May 2018).

38 House of Commons Treasury Committee, *Fixing LIBOR*, vol. 2, p. 88.

Appendix: fines imposed on banks by regulatory authorities

This appendix provides a list of fines imposed on all banks for manipulating LIBOR, global foreign exchange benchmarks and gold and silver prices, as of March 2018.

Fines for manipulation of LIBOR

Financial Conduct Authority, UK, final notices

Barclays Bank	£59.5 million	24 June 2012
UBS	£160 million	12 December 2012
RBS	£87.5 million	6 February 2013
ICAP Europe	£14 million	25 September 2013
Rabobank	£105 million	29 October 2013
HBOS and Lloyds	£104 million	28 July 2014
Deutsche Bank	£277 million	23 June 2015

Commodities Futures Trading Commission, USA, orders

Barclays	$200 million	27 June 2012
UBS Securities Japan	$700 million	19 December 2012
RP Martin Holdings and Martin Brokers (UK)	$1.2 million	15 May 2014
Lloyds Bank	$105 million	28 July 2014
Rabobank	$475 million	29 October 2014
RBS Japan	$325 million	6 February 2013
ICAP Europe	$65 million	23 September 2013
Deutsche Bank	$800 million	23 April 2015

Fines for manipulation of the Gold and Silver Fixes (and those for other precious metals)

Commodity Futures Trading Commission, USA, orders

Citibank	$175 million	25 May 2016
Deutsche Bank	$30 million	29 January 2018
UBS	$15m million	29 January 2018

US Department of Justice

Barclays	$160 million	27 June 2012
RBS	$150 million	2 February 2013
Rabobank	$325 million	29 October 2013
UBS Securities Japan	$100 million	19 December 2012
UBS	$400 million	18 September 2013
Deutsche Bank	$775 million	23 April 2015
Deutsche Bank AG	$625 million	28 March 2017
Deutsche Bank Group Services UK	$150 million	28 March 2017

New York Department of Financial Services

Deutsche Bank	$600 million	23 April 2015

European Commission, 'Euro interest rate derivatives', press release, 4 December 2013

UBS received full immunity for revealing the existence of cartels and so avoided a fine of €2.5 billion.

Barclays received full immunity for revealing the existence of the cartel and so avoided a fine of €690 million.

Deutsche Bank	€465,861 million	4 December 2013
RBS	€131,004 million	4 December 2013
Societe Generale	€227,718 million	4 December 2013

Fines imposed for manipulation of the euro interest rate derivatives market

UBS received full immunity for revealing the existence of cartels and thereby avoided a fine of around €2.5 billion for its participation in five of the seven infringements.

Citigroup received full immunity for one of the infringements of in which it participated, thereby avoiding a fine of €55 million.

RBS	€260.05 million
Deutsche Bank	€259.499 million
JPMorgan	€79.897 million
Citigroup	€70.02 million
RP Martin	€247,000

Fines imposed for manipulation of the Swiss franc interest rate derivatives market

European Commission, press release, 21 October 2014

RBS was not fined because it revealed the existence of the cartel and thereby avoided a fine of €5 million.

UBS	€12.65 million
JP Morgan	€10.35 million
Credit Suisse	€9.171 million

European Commission, press release, 7 December 2016

Credit Agricole	€115.6 million
HSBC	€33.6 million
JPMorgan	€337.1 million

Fines for participation in the EURIBOR cartel

Swiss Competition Commission (COMCO), press release, 21 December 2016

Deutsche Bank received full immunity for revealing the existence of the cartel to COMCO.

Barclays	CHF27.77 million	21 December 2016
RBS	CHF12.33 million	21 December 2016
Societe Generale	CHF3.25 million	21 December 2016

Fines for participation in the yen LIBOR and Euro-yen TIBOR cartels

Citigroup	CHF 3.77 million
Deutsche Bank	CHF5.02 million
JPMorgan	CHF 1.70 million

Fines for participation in the Swiss franc spread cartel

UBS received full immunity for revealing the existence of the cartel to COMCO.

Credit Suisse	CHF2.04 million
JPMorgan	CHF2.59 million
RBS	CHF0.56 million

Dutch National Bank
(for LIBOR and foreign exchange benchmark manipulation)

Rabobank	€70 million	29 October 2013

Fines for foreign exchange manipulation

Financial Conduct Authority, UK, final notices

Citibank	£225.5 million	11 November 2014
HSBC	£216.3 million	11 November 2014

JPMorgan Chase	£222.6 million	11 November 2014
RBS	£217.0 million	11 November 2014
UBS	£233.8 million	11 November 2014
Deutsche Bank	£226.8 million	23 April 2014
Barclays	£284.4 million	20 May 2015

Commodity Futures Trading Commission, orders

Citibank	$310 million	12 November 2014
HSBC	$275 million	12 November 2014
JP Morgan Chase	$310 million	12 November 2014
RBS	$290 million	12 November 2014
UBS	$290 million	12 November 2014
Barclays	$400 million	20 May 2015

Federal Reserve, USA, press releases, 20 May 2015, 20 April 2017 and 17 July 2017

Bank of America	$205 million	20 May 2015
Barclays Bank	$342 million	20 May 2015
JP Morgan Chase	$342 million	20 May 2015
RBS	$274 million	20 May 2015
UBS	$342 million	20 May 2015
Deutsche Bank	$136.9 million	20 April 2017
BNP Paribas	$246 million	17 July 2017

Department of Justice, press release, 20 May 2015

Barclays	$650 million	20 May 2015
Citibank	$925 million	20 May 2015
JP Morgan Chase	$550 million	20 May 2015
RBS	$385 million	20 May 2015

New York Department of Financial Services, press release, 24 May 2017

Barclays	$485 million	20 May 2015
Barclays	$150 million	15 November 2015
BNP Paribas	$350 million	24 May 2017
Credit Suisse	$135 million	13 November 2017

Office of the Comptroller of the Currency, 12 November 2014

Bank of America	$250 million	12 November 2014
Citibank	$350 million	12 November 2014
JP Morgan Chase	$350 million	12 November 2014

Select bibliography

Abrantes-Metz, R., Kraten, M., Metz, A. D. and Seow, G., 'LIBOR manipulation?', *Journal of Banking and Finance*, 36:1 (2012), pp. 136–50.

Allen, T. J., 'Developments in the international syndicated loan market in the 1980s', *Bank of England Quarterly Bulletin*, February 1990, pp. 71–7, available at https://www.bankofengland.co.uk/-/media/boe/files/quarterly-bulletin/1990/developments-in-the-international-syndicated-loan-market-in-the-1980s (accessed 4 May 2018).

Bailey, A., 'The future of LIBOR', speech at Bloomberg, London, 27 July 2017, available at https://www.fca.org.uk/news/speeches/the-future-of-libor (accessed 9 May 2018).

Bank for International Settlements, *Triennial Central Bank Survey: Foreign Exchange and Derivatives Market Activity in 2004* (BIS, March 2005), available at https://www.bis.org/publ/rpfx05t.pdf (accessed 4 May 2018).

Bank for International Settlements, *Triennial Central Bank Survey: Report on Global Foreign Exchange Market Activity in 2010* (BIS, Monetary and Economic Department, December 2010), availbale at https://www.bis.org/publ/rpfxf10t.pdf (accessed 4 May 2018).

Bank for International Settlements, *High-Frequency Trading in the Foreign Exchange Market* (BIS, September 2011), available at https://www.bis.org/publ/mktc05.pdf (accessed 4 May 2018).

Bank for International Settlements, *Forex Global Code of Conduct* (BIS, 27 May 2017).

Bank of England, 'The London gold market', *Bank of England Quarterly Bulletin*, March 1964, pp. 16–21.

Bank of England, 'The secondary banking crisis and the Bank of England's support operations', *Bank of England Quarterly Bulletin*, April 1978, pp. 230–9, available at https://www.bankofengland.co.uk/-/media/boe/files/quarterly-bulletin/1978/the-second-banking-crisis-and-the-boes-support-operations.pdf (accessed 17 April 2018).

Bank of England, 'Evidence submitted by the Bank of England to the Committee to Review the Functioning of Financial Institutions, Second Steps, Evidence', cmnd 7937, vol. 4, June 1980.

Bank of England, 'Supervisory statement: strengthening individual accountability', SS28/15, May 2015.

Bank of England, *Fair and Effective Markets Review – Final Report* (BoE, 10 June 2015), available at https://www.bankofengland.co.uk/report/2015/fair-and-effective-markets-review---final-report (accessed 4 May 2018).

Barr, A., 'BBA to start Libor review earlier as rate spikes', MarketWatch, 17 April 2008, available at https://www.marketwatch.com/story/review-of-libor-brought-forward-as-closely-watched-rate-spikes (accessed 4 May 2018).

Blagg, M., '1897–1939, a new era for the London silver price,' *Alchemist*, 75 (October 2014), pp. 18–20.

Borrie, G., 'Legal and administrative regulation in the United Kingdom of competition and consumer policies', *University of New South Wales Law Journal*, 5 (1982), p. 82.

British Bankers' Association, *Understanding the Construction and Operation of BBA LIBOR – Strengthening for the Future* (BBA, June 2008).

Caminschi, A. and Heaney R., 'Fixing a leaky fixing: short-term market reactions to the London pm gold price fixing', *Journal of Futures Markets*, 34:11 (September 2013).

Chester, A. C., 'The international bond market', *Bank of England Quarterly Bulletin*, November 1991, p. 521.

Chon, G. and Arnold, M., 'NY regulator probing Barclays and Deutsche Bank over forex algorithms', *Financial Times,* 11 December 2014, available at https://www.ft.com/content/863a7b3c-813e-11e4–896c-00144feabdc0 (accessed 4 May 2018).

Committee to Review the Functioning of Financial Institutions, *Second Stage Evidence* (HMSO, 1979).

Commodity Futures Trading Commission, 'In the matter of the Royal Bank of Scotland plc and RBS Securities Japan Limited', CFTC Docket No. 13–14, 6 February 2013, 'Order instituting proceedings pursuant to sections 6(c) and 6(d) of the Commodity Exchange Act, making findings and imposing remedial sanctions', available at https://www.cftc.gov/sites/default/files/idc/groups/public/@lrenforcementactions/documents/legalpleading/enfrbsorder020613.pdf (accessed 4 May 2018).

Commodity Futures Trading Commission, 'In the matter of Lloyds Banking Group plc and Lloyds Bank plc', CFTC Docket No. 14–18, 28 July 2014, 'Order instituting proceedings pursuant to sections 6(c) and 6(d) of the Commodity Exchange Act, making findings, and imposing remedial sanctions', available at https://www.cftc.gov/sites/default/files/idc/groups/public/@lrenforcementactions/documents/legalpleading/enflloydsorderdf072814.pdf (accessed 4 May 2018).

Commodity Futures Trading Commission, 'In the matter of Citibank', CFTC Docket No. 15–03, 11 November 2014, 'Order instituting proceedings pursuant to sections 6(c)(4)(A) and 6(d) of the Commodity Exchange Act, making findings, and imposing remedial sanctions', available at https://cftc.gov/sites/default/files/groups/public/@lrenforcementactions/documents/legalpleading/enfcitibankorder111114.pdf (accessed 4 May 2018).

Commodity Futures Trading Commission, 'In the matter of HSBC Bank plc', CFTC Docket No. 15–07, 11 November 2014, 'Order instituting proceedings pursuant to sections 6(c)(4)(A) and 6(d) of the Commodity Exchange Act, making findings, and imposing remedial sanctions', available at https://www.cftc.gov/sites/default/files/idc/groups/public/@lrenforcementactions/documents/legalpleading/enfhsbcorder111114.pdf (accessed 4 May 2018).

Commodity Futures Trading Commission, 'In the matter of JP Morgan Chase Bank', CFTC Docket No. 15–04, 11 November 2014, 'Order instituting proceedings pursuant to sections 6(c)(4)(A) and 6(d) of the Commodity Exchange Act, making findings, and imposing remedial sanctions', available at https://cftc.gov/sites/default/files/groups/public/@lrenforcementactions/documents/legalpleading/enfjpmorganorder111114.pdf (accessed 4 May 2018).

Commodity Futures Trading Commission, 'In the matter of Citibank', CFTC Docket No. 15–03, 11 November 2014, 'Order instituting proceedings pursuant to sections 6(c)(4)(A) and 6(d) of the Commodity Exchange Act, making findings, and imposing remedial sanctions', available at https://cftc.gov/sites/

default/files/groups/public/@lrenforcementactions/documents/legalpleading/enfcitibankorder111114.pdf (accessed 4 May 2018).

Commodity Futures Trading Commission, 'In the matter of HSBC Bank plc', CFTC Docket No. 15–07, 11 November 2014, 'Order instituting proceedings pursuant to sections 6(c)(4)(A) and 6(d) of the Commodity Exchange Act, making findings, and imposing remedial sanctions', available at https://www.cftc.gov/sites/default/files/idc/groups/public/@lrenforcementactions/documents/legalpleading/enfhsbcorder111114.pdf (accessed 4 May 2018).

Commodity Futures Trading Commission, 'In the matter of JP Morgan Chase Bank', CFTC Docket No. 15–04, 11 November 2014, 'Order instituting proceedings pursuant to sections 6(c)(4)(A) and 6(d) of the Commodity Exchange Act, making findings, and imposing remedial sanctions', available at https://cftc.gov/sites/default/files/groups/public/@lrenforcementactions/documents/legalpleading/enfjpmorganorder111114.pdf (accessed 4 May 2018).

Commodity Futures Trading Commission, 'In the matter of the Royal Bank of Scotland plc', CFTC Docket No. 15–05, 11 November 2014, 'Order instituting proceedings pursuant to sections 6(c)(4)(A) and 6(d) of the Commodity Exchange Act, making findings, and imposing remedial sanctions', available at https://www.cftc.gov/sites/default/files/groups/public/@lrenforcementactions/documents/legalpleading/enfroyalbankorder111114.pdf (accessed 4 May 2018).

Commodity Futures Trading Commission, 'Foreign exchange benchmark case: *In re Barclays Bank PLC*', 20 May 2015, available at https://www.cftc.gov/sites/default/files/idc/groups/public/@newsroom/documents/file/fxbarclaysmisconduct052015.pdf (accessed 4 May 2018).

Commodity Futures Trading Commission, 'In the matter of Citibank, N.A.; Citibank Japan Ltd; and Citigroup Global Markets Japan Inc.', CFTC Docket No. 16–17, 25 May 2016, 'Order instituting proceedings pursuant to sections 6(c) and 6(d) of the Commodity Exchange Act, making findings and imposing remedial sanctions', available at https://www.cftc.gov/sites/default/files/idc/groups/public/@lrenforcementactions/documents/legalpleading/enfcitibanklibororder052516.pdf (accessed 4 May 2018).

Commodity Futures Trading Commission, 'In the matter of David Liew', CFTC Docket No. 17–14, 2 June 2017, 'Order instituting proceedings pursuant to sections 6(c) and 6(d) of the Commodity Exchange Act, making findings, and imposing remedial sanctions', available at https://www.cftc.gov/sites/default/files/idc/groups/public/@lrenforcementactions/documents/legalpleading/enfdavidlieworder060217.pdf (accessed 4 May 2018).

Commodity Futures Trading Commission, 'In the matter of Deutsche Bank AG and Deutsche Bank Securities Inc.', CFTC Docket No. 18–06, 29 January 2018, 'Order instituting proceedings pursuant to sections 6(c) and 6(d) of the Commodity Exchange Act, making findings, and imposing remedial sanctions', available at https://www.cftc.gov/sites/default/files/idc/groups/public/@lrenforcementactions/documents/legalpleading/enfdeutschebankagorder012918.pdf (accessed October 2018).

Commodity Futures Trading Commission, 'In the matter of HSBC Securities (USA) Inc.', CFTC Docket No. 18–08, 29 January 2018, 'Order instituting proceedings pursuant to sections 6(c) and 6(d) of the Commodity Exchange Act, making findings, and imposing remedial sanctions', available at https://www.cftc.gov/sites/default/files/idc/groups/public/@lrenforcementactions/documents/legalpleading/enfhsbcsecuritiesorder012918.pdf (accessed October 2018).

Commodity Futures Trading Commission, 'In the matter of UBS AG', CFTC Docket No. 18–07, 29 January 2018, 'Order instituting proceedings pursuant to sections 6(c) and 6(d) of the Commodity Exchange Act, making findings, and imposing remedial sanctions', available at https://www.cftc.gov/sites/default/files/idc/groups/public/@lrenforcementactions/documents/legalpleading/enfusbagorder012918.pdf (accessed October 2018).

Dakers, M., 'How the forex trading scandal came to light', *Daily Telegraph*, 13 November 2014, available at https://www.telegraph.co.uk/finance/newsbysector/banksandfinance/11227006/How-the-forex-trading-scandal-came-to-light.html (accessed 4 May 2018).

Davies, R., Richardson, P., Katinaite, V. and Manning, M., 'Evolution of the UK banking system', *Bank of England Quarterly Bulletin*, December 2010, pp. 321–32, available at https://www.bankofengland.co.uk/-/media/boe/files/quarterly-bulletin/2010/quarterly-bulletin-2010-q4.pdf (accessed 17 April 2018).

Defang, D., Koop, G. and Potter, S. M., *Understanding Liquidity and Credit Risks in the Financial Crisis* (Research & Statistics Group Federal Reserve Bank of New York, May 2011), available at http://citeseerx.ist.psu.edu/viewdoc/download?doi=10.1.1.307.3757&rep=rep1&type=pdf (accessed 4 May 2018).

Department of Market Oversight, CFTC, *Report on Large Short Trader Activity in the Silver Futures Market* (CFTC, 13 May 2008).

EMEA Centre for Regulatory Strategy, *Senior Managers Regime: Individual Accountability and Reasonable Steps* (EMEA, May 2015), available at http://docplayer.net/38952002-Senior-managers-regime-individual-accountability-and-reasonable-steps.html (accessed 10 May 2018).

European Banking Authority, *Guidelines on the Assessment of the Suitability of Members of the Management Body and Key Function Holders*, EBA/GL/2012/06 (EBA, 27 November 2012), p. 15, available at https://www.eba.europa.eu/documents/10180/106695/EBA-GL-2012-06--Guidelines-on-the-assessment-of-the-suitability-of-persons-.pdf (accessed 9 May 2018).

Fertig, P., 'Has there been a decade of London gold price fixing manipulation?', *Alchemist*, 71 (March 2014), available at https://www.lbma.org.uk/assets/blog/alchemist_articles/Alch73.pdf (accessed 9 May 2018).

Fforde, J. S., 'Competition, innovation and regulation in British banking', *Bank of England Quarterly Bulletin*, September 1983, pp. 363–76, available at https://www.bankofengland.co.uk/archive/Documents/historicpubs/qb/1983/qb83q3363376.pdf (accessed 1 May 2018).

Financial Conduct Authority, 'Final notice, UBS AG', 19 December 2012, available at https://www.fca.org.uk/publication/final-notices/ubs.pdf (accessed 4 May 2018).

Financial Conduct Authority, 'Final notice, Rabobank', 29 October 2013, available at https://www.fca.org.uk/publication/final-notices/rabobank.pdf (accessed 4 May 2018).

Financial Conduct Authority, 'Final notice, Daniel James Plunkett', 23 May 2014, available at https://www.fca.org.uk/publication/final-notices/daniel-james-plunkett.pdf (accessed 4 May 2018).

Financial Conduct Authority, 'Final notice, Lloyds Bank plc, Bank of Scotland plc', 28 July 2014, available at https://www.fca.org.uk/publication/final-notices/lloyds-bank-of-scotland.pdf (accessed 4 May 2018).

Financial Conduct Authority, 'Final notice, The Royal Bank of Scotland', 11 November 2014, available at https://www.fca.org.uk/publication/final-notices/final-notice-rbs.pdf (accessed 10 May 2018).

Financial Conduct Authority, 'Final notice, UBS AG', 11 November 2014, available at https://www.fca.org.uk/publication/final-notices/final-notice-ubs.pdf (accessed 4 May 2018).

Financial Conduct Authority, 'Final notice, Deutsche Bank AG', 23 April 2015, available at https://www.fca.org.uk/publication/final-notices/deutsche-bank-ag-2015.pdf (accessed 4 May 2018).

Financial Conduct Authority, 'Final notice, Barclays Bank plc', 20 May 2015, available at https://www.fca.org.uk/publication/final-notices/barclays-bank-plc-may-15.pdf (accessed 4 May 2018).

Financial Conduct Authority, *Strengthening Accountability in Banking: Final Rules Including Feedback on CP14/31 and CP15/5 and Consultation on Extending the Certification Regime to Wholesale Market Activities*, CP15/22 (FCA, July 2015), available at https://www.fca.org.uk/publication/consultation/cp15-22.pdf (accessed 9 May 2018).

Financial Conduct Authority, *Strengthening Accountability in Banking: UK Branches of Foreign Banks (Final Rules)*, PS15/30 (FCA, December 2015), available at https://www.fca.org.uk/publication/policy/ps15-30.pdf (accessed 9 May 2018).

Financial Conduct Authority, *Guidance on the Duty of Responsibility: Final Amendments (Including Feedback on CP16/26) to the Decision Procedure and Penalties Manual*, PS17/9 (FCA, May 2017), available at https://www.fca.org.uk/publication/policy/ps17-09.pdf (accessed 9 May 2018).

Financial Services Authority, *The Failure of the Royal Bank of Scotland: Financial Services Authority Board Report* (FSA, December 2011), available at https://www.fca.org.uk/publication/corporate/fsa-rbs.pdf (accessed 9 May 2018).

Financial Services Authority, 'Final notice, Barclays Bank plc', 27 June 2012, available at https://www.fca.org.uk/publication/final-notices/barclays-jun12.pdf (accessed 3 May 2018).

Financial Services Authority, 'Final notice, UBS AG', 19 December 2012, available at https://www.fca.org.uk/publication/final-notices/ubs.pdf (accessed 10 May 2018).

Financial Services Authority, 'Final notice, The Royal Bank of Scotland plc', 6 February 2013, available at https://www.fca.org.uk/publication/final-notices/rbs.pdf (accessed 4 May 2018).

Financial Services Authority, *Internal Audit Report: A Review of the Extent of Awareness within the FSA of Inappropriate LIBOR Submissions* (FSA, March 2013), available at https://www.fca.org.uk/publication/corporate/fsa-ia-libor.pdf (accessed 3 May 2018).

Financial Stability Board, *Progress Report on the Oversight and Governance Framework for Financial Benchmark Reform: Report to G20 Finance Ministers and Central Bank Governors* (FSB, 29 August 2013), available at http://www.fsb.org/wp-content/uploads/r_130829f.pdf (accessed October 2018).

Financial Stability Board, *Market Participants Group on Reforming Interest Rate Benchmarks: Final Report* (FSB, March 2014), available at https://www.fsb.org/wp-content/uploads/r_140722b.pdf?page_moved=1 (accessed 4 May 2018).

Financial Stability Board, *Reforming Major Interest Rate Benchmarks* (FSB, 22 July 2014), available at https://www.fsb.org/wp-content/uploads/r_140722.pdf (accessed 4 May 2018).

Financial Stability Board, *Foreign Exchange Benchmarks: Final Report* (FSB, 30 September 2014), available at http://www.fsb.org/wp-content/uploads/r_140930.pdf (accessed October 2018).

Financial Stability Board, *Reforming Major Interest Rate Benchmarks Progress Report on Implementation of July 2014 FSB Recommendations* (FSB, 10 October 2017), available at https://www.fsb.org/wp-content/uploads/P101017.pdf (accessed 9 May 2018).

Foreign Exchange Working Group, *Report on Adherence to the FX Global Code* (BIS, May 2017), available at https://www.bis.org/mktc/fxwg/adherence_report.pdf (accessed 9 May 2018).

Furness, Hannah, 'Regulating the banks: what politicians used to say about the City', *Daily Telegraph*, 4 July 2012.

Gadenecz, B., 'The syndicated loan market: structure, development and implications', *BIS Quarterly Review*, December 2004, pp. 75–89, available at https://www.bis.org/publ/qtrpdf/r_qt0412g.htm (accessed 4 May 2018).

Gilbert, M., 'Barclays takes a money market beating', Bloomberg, 3 September 2008.

Global Foreign Exchange Committee, *FX Global Code: A Set of Global Principles of Good Practice in the Foreign Exchange Market* (GFEC, 27 May 2017), available at https://www.globalfxc.org/docs/fx_global.pdf (accessed May 2018).

Gower, L. C. B., *The Gower Report: A Review of Investor Protection,* command no. 9125 (HMSO, 1984).

Gower, L. C. B., '"Big Bang" and City regulation', *Modern Law Review*, 51:1 (1988), pp. 1–22.

Grabiner, A., 'Bank of England foreign exchange market investigation', 12 March 2014, pp. 19–20, available at https://www.bankofengland.co.uk/-/media/boe/files/report/2014/foreign-exchange-market-investigation-report-by-lord-grabiner (accessed 4 May 2018).

Gyntelberg, J. and Wooldridge, P., 'Interbank rate fixings during the recent turmoil', *BIS Quarterly Review*, March 2008, p. 70, available at https://www.bis.org/repofficepubl/arpresearch_dev_200803.02.htm (accessed 3 May 2018).

Hammond, G. M. S., 'Recent developments in the swap market', *Bank of England Quarterly Bulletin*, February 1987, pp. 66–79, available at https://www.bankofengland.co.uk/-/media/boe/files/quarterly-bulletin/1987/recent-developments-in-the-swap-market (accessed 4 May 2018).

Harvey, R., 'The early development of the London Gold Fixing', *Alchemist*, 65 (January 2012), pp. 3–6.

HM Treasury, *The Wheatley Review of LIBOR: Final Report* (Stationery Office, October 2011), available at https://www.gov.uk/government/publications/the-wheatley-review).

HM Treasury, *Sanctions for the Directors of Failed Banks* (Treasury, 3 July 2012), available at https://assets.publishing.service.gov.uk/government/uploads/system/uploads/attachment_data/file/81565/consult_sanctions_directors_banks.pdf (accessed 10 May 2018).

House of Commons Treasury Committee, *Fixing LIBOR: Some Preliminary Findings, Second Report of Session 2012–13* (Stationery Office, August 2012), available at https://publications.parliament.uk/pa/cm201213/cmselect/cmtreasy/481/481.pdf (accessed 4 May 2018).

ICE Benchmark Administration, 'Roadmap for ICE LIBOR', 18 March 2016, available at https://www.theice.com/publicdocs/ICE_LIBOR_Roadmap0316.pdf (accessed 4 May 2018).

ICE Benchmark Administration, 'LIBOR Code of Conduct', 29 June 2016.

ICE Benchmark Administration, 'ICE LIBOR evolution: additional consultation', 24 January 2017.

ICE Benchmark Administration, 'Summary of ICE LIBOR evolution', 24 January 2017.

ICE Benchmark Administration, 'Evolution of ICE LIBOR: feedback statement on additional consultation', 3 March 2017.

ICE Benchmark Administration, 'ICE LIBOR: IOSCO self-assessment report', August 2017.

International Monetary Fund, *Global Financial Stability Report. Financial Stress and Deleveraging: Macro-Financial Implications and Policy* (IMF, 8 October 2008), available at https://www.imf.org/en/Publications/GFSR/Issues/2016/12/31/

Global-Financial-Stability-Report-October-2008-Financial-Stress-and-Deleveraging-Macrofi-22027 (accessed 3 May 2018).

International Organization of Securities Commissions, *Principles for Financial Benchmarks: Final Report*, FR07/13 (IOSCO, July 2013), available at https://www.iosco.org/library/pubdocs/pdf/IOSCOPD415.pdf (accessed October 2018).

International Organization of Securities Commissions, *Review of the Implementation of IOSCO's Principles for Financial Benchmarks* (IOSCO, 2015), available at https://www.iosco.org.

International Organization of Securities Commissions, *Second Review of the Implementation of IOSCO's Principles for Financial Benchmarks by Administrators of EURIBOR, LIBOR and TIBOR* (IOSCO, 2016) available at https://www.iosco.org.

International Organization of Securities Commissions, *Report on Guidance on the IOSCO Principles for Financial Benchmarks: Final Report*, FR13/2016 (IOSCO, December 2016).

Kerr, I. M., *History of the Eurobond Market: The First 21 Years* (Prentice Hall, 1984).

King, M. and Rime, D., 'The $4 trillion question: what explains FX growth in the BIS 2007 survey?' *BIS Quarterly Review*, December 2010, pp. 27–42, available at https://www.bis.org/publ/qtrpdf/r_qt1012.pdf (accessed 4 May 2018).

Köhler, P., Schäfer, D. and Osman, Y., 'Traffic light is flashing yellow', *Handelsblatt Global*, 27 January 2015, available at https://global.handelsblatt.com/finance/traffic-light-for-banks-is-blinking-yellow-132357 (accessed 9 May 2018).

Lamb, A., 'International banking in London, 1975–85', *Bank of England Quarterly Bulletin,* September 1986, pp. 367–78, available at https://www.bankofengland.co.uk/-/media/boe/files/quarterly-bulletin/1986/international-banking-in-london-1975-85 (accessed 4 May 2018).

Lascelles, D., *The Story of Minos Zombanakis: Banking Without Borders* (Economia Publishing, 2011).

Melvin, M. and Taylor, M. P., 'The crisis in the foreign exchange market', working paper no. 2707 (CESifo, March 2009), available at https://papers.ssrn.com/sol3/papers.cfm?abstract_id=1437408 (accessed 4 May 2018).

Michaud, F.-L. and Upper, C., 'What drives interbank rates? Evidence from the Libor panel', *BIS Quarterly Review*, March 2008, pp. 47–58, available at https://www.bis.org/publ/qtrpdf/r_qt0803f.pdf (accessed 4 May 2018).

Mollenkamp, C., 'Bankers cast doubt on key rate amid crisis', *Wall Street Journal*, 16 April 2008, available at https://www.wsj.com/articles/SB120831164167818299 (accessed 4 May 2018).

Mollenkamp, C., Ng, S., Norman, L. and Hagerty, J. R., 'Libor's rise may sock many borrowers', *Wall Street Journal*,19 April 2008.

Mollenkamp, C. and Whitehouse, M., 'Study casts doubt on key rate', *Wall Street Journal,* 29 May 2008, available at https://www.wsj.com/articles/SB121200703762027135 (accessed 4 May 2018).

New York State Department of Financial Services, 'NYDFS announces Barclays to pay $2.4 billion, terminate employees for conspiring to manipulate spot FX trading market', press release, 20 May 2015, available at https://www.dfs.ny.gov/about/press/pr1505201.htm (accessed 4 May 2018).

New York State Department of Financial Services, 'Consent order under New York Banking Law §44 in the matter of Barclays Bank plc', 17 November 2015, available at https://www.dfs.ny.gov/about/ea/ea151117.pdf (accessed 4 May 2018).

New York State Department of Financial Services, 'NYDFS announces Barclays to pay additional $150 million penalty, terminate employee for automated, electronic foreign exchange misconduct', press release, 18 November 2015, available at https://www.dfs.ny.gov/about/press/pr1511181.htm.

Northedge, R., 'The men who lit the fuse for the exchange', Interviews, *The Telegraph*, 8 October 2006.

O'Malley, C., *Bonds Without Borders* (John Wiley & Sons, 2015).

Parliamentary Commission on Banking Standards, *Fifth Report: Changing Banking for Good* (Stationery Office, 12 June 2013), available at https://publications.parliament.uk/pa/jt201314/jtselect/jtpcbs/27/27ii02.htm (accessed 9 May 2018).

Prudential Regulation Authority, *Strengthening Accountability in Banking: Responses to CP14/14, CP28/14 and CP7/15*, policy statement 16/15 (Bank of England, July 2015), available at https://www.bankofengland.co.uk/-/media/boe/files/prudential-regulation/policy-statement/2015/ps1615.pdf?la=en&hash=4F83474FB28C11AD79AB37ED2CAC391B4E13F3CE (accessed 9 May 2018).

Prudential Regulation Authority, *Strengthening Individual Accountability in Banking*, supervisory statement 28/15 (Bank of England, May 2017), available at https://www.bankofengland.co.uk/prudential-regulation/publication/2015/strengthening-individual-accountability-in-banking-ss (accessed 9 May 2018).

Rakoff, J. R., 'The financial crisis: why have no high-level executives been prosecuted?', *New York Review of Books*, 9 January 2014, available at https://www.nybooks.com/articles/2014/01/09/financial-crisis-why-no-executive-prosecutions (accessed 9 May 2018).

Rime, D. and Schrimpf, A., 'The anatomy of the global FX market through the lens of the 2013 Triennial Survey', *BIS Quarterly Review*, December 2013, available at https://www.bis.org/publ/qtrpdf/r_qt1312e.pdf (accessed 4 May 2018).

Rodgers, K., *Why Aren't They Shouting? A Banker's Tale of Change, Computers and Perpetual Crisis* (Random House Business Books, 2016).

Rucker, P. and Freifeld, K., 'Fed fines Deutsche Bank for $156.6 million for forex violations', Reuters, 20 April 2017, available at https://www.reuters.com/article/us-deutsche-bank-fed-forex-idUSKBN17M2MK (accessed 4 May 2018).

Sanderson, H. and Chon, G., 'US investigates banks' precious metals trading', *Financial Times,* 23 February 2015, available at https://www.ft.com/content/01b-dc380-bb79–11e4-b95c-00144feab7de (accessed 9 May 2018).

Scaggs, A., 'The demise of Libor is not a done deal for markets', *Financial Times,* 2 August 2017, available at https://www.ft.com/content/43e1dcbc-7754--11e7--90c0--90a9d1bc9691 (accessed 9 May 2018).

Snider, C. and Youle, T., 'Does LIBOR reflect banks' borrowing costs?', 2 April 2010, available at https://papers.ssrn.com/sol3/papers.cfm?abstract_id=1569603 (accessed 4 May 2018).

Spafford, M. L. and Stanaway, D. F., 'The extraterritoriality reach of the Commodity Exchange Act in the wake of *Morrison* and Dodd-Frank', *Futures and Derivatives Law Report*, 37:7 (July 2017).

Spira, P., *Ladders and Snakes: A Twist in the Spiral Staircase* (privately printed, 1997).

Tett, G., 'Libor's value is called into question', *Financial Times*, 25 September 2007, available at https://www.ft.com/content/8c7dd45e-6b9c-11dc-863b-0000779fd2ac (accessed 4 May 2018).

Tett, G. and Mackenzie, M., 'Doubts over Libor widen', *Financial Times*, 21 April 2008, available at https://www.ft.com/content/d1d9a792-0fbd-11dd-8871-0000779fd2ac (accessed 4 May 2018).

Thomson Reuters, 'Syndicated loans review: full year 2011', available at http://dmi.thomsonreuters.com/content/files/4q11_global_loans_review.pdf (accessed 3 May 2018).

Treasury Select Committee, *Sixth Report: The Regulation of Financial Services in the UK*, 1994–5, HC 322-I.

Vaughan, L. and Finch, G., *The Fix: How Bankers Lied, Cheated and Colluded to Rig the World's Most Important Number* (John Wiley & Sons, 2017).

Vaughan, L., Larkin, N. and Ring, S., 'London gold fix calls draw scrutiny amid heavy trading', Bloomberg, 26 November 2013.

Index